What the Wine-Sellers Buy
Plus Three

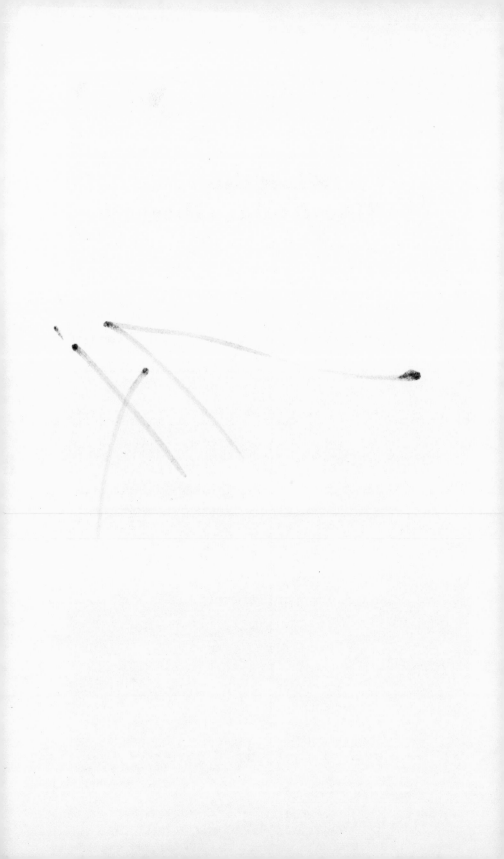

What the Wine-Sellers Buy Plus Three

FOUR PLAYS BY RON MILNER

FOREWORD BY AMIRI BARAKA

INTRODUCTION BY
WOODIE KING, JR.

Wayne State University Press
Detroit

AFRICAN AMERICAN LIFE SERIES

A complete listing of the books in this series can be found at the back of this volume.

Series Editors:

Manufactured in the United States of America.

Library of Congress Cataloging-in-Publication Data

Milner, Ron.
"What the wine-sellers buy" plus three : four plays / by Ron Milner ; foreword by Amiri Baraka ; introduction by Woodie King, Jr.
p. cm.—(African American life series)
Includes index.
ISBN 0-8143-2977-2 (cloth : alk. paper)—ISBN 0-8143-2929-2 (pbk. : alk. paper)
1. African Americans—Drama. I. Title. II. Series.
PS3563.I44 W47 2001
812'.54—dc21 2001001686

Contents

Ron Milner: The Artist as Cultural Worker
Amiri Baraka
7

No Identity Crisis: An Introduction to the Plays of Ron Milner
Woodie King, Jr.
11

Checkmates
(1990)
21

Urban Transition:
Loose Blossoms
(1995)
75

Jazz-Set
(1979)
139

What the Wine-Sellers Buy
(1974)
193

For Woodie King,
who pointed out this road,
and Eloise and Dr. Charles Whitten,
whose applause confirmed
that the journey was worthwhile.
—Ron Milner, 2000

Ron Milner: The Artist as Cultural Worker

Amiri Baraka

Ron Milner is an artist who has also been an activist cultural worker for the last few decades, characterized by consistent creativity, progressive philosophy and the commitment to self-determination which has had him building theaters, drama companies, teaching and speaking and consulting across the country.

During this same period, Milner has written and staged plays that are artistically powerful and socially positive and provoking. And even though he has plays on Broadway (*Checkmates, Don't Get God Started,* and *What the Wine-Sellers Buy*) Ron Milner has remained one of the most prolific, focused and craft-sensitive writers of the Black Arts Movement which emerged in the U.S. during the mid-sixties. Milner has never been accorded the acclaim that the quality and consistency of his work should command. Ironically, these otherwise positive qualities are probably part of the reason the historically reactionary theater "establishment," which included theaters, schools, media, and critics, have stepped obviously around his work, saying little of anything.

Why? Because Milner, like other Black and progressive artists of his generation, has had the unceasing temerity to speak out openly about the necessity of building independent arts institutions, particularly Black theaters and companies, and not merely squall passively as a crypto-collaborator with the notoriously racist and elitist establishment brutes of U.S. arts sponsorship and production.

Milner's work is characterized by its attention to Afro-American social and psychological culture. His focus has been on the struggles and desires of the Black working class and the lower middle class, "the people," and out of these lives Milner has constructed a continuum of social and critical realist works, rooted in the dynamic heartbeat of Black life.

Who's Got His Own, The Warning, What the Wine-Sellers Buy, Jazz-Set are works that are slowly becoming required texts in many of the emerging repertory theaters of the Black and progressive theater communities. Only the narrow racist obloquy of bourgeois theater prevents these works from being in the well-advertised *alabastorium* of so-called "mainstream" U.S. theater.

Who's Got His Own is about the psychology of desire, how it often confuses what it is with what it wants, completely uninformed about what it needs. *Wine-Sellers* reflects on the antagonistic contradictions between the Black working-class community and those who prey upon them. What is so important about this is that in the 1960s too often pimps, dope pushers, prostitutes and various other "colorful and rebellious" lumpen were projected as "Black" heroic prototypes by petty bourgeois artists confusing unreal stereotypes elicited from the bias and misunderstanding of their own alienated idealism with real life.

Jazz-Set uses the jazz orchestra as a form creating the dramatis personae for the play: the family, the community, historical cultural forms. Milner has sought to recreate Afro-American life as the principal text for his works, always digging into the socio-psychological drama that is the actual animating objective of history and future.

Checkmates gives us an "introduction" to that recently emerging sector of the petty bourgeois that we have labeled "Buppies," the Black version of the "Young Upwardly Mobile Professionals." What has changed in the process of living and marrying each other? And here, Milner brings the youthful travail into class, social and personal confrontation and conflict with an older couple as the generational continuum of revelational experience, relationship and teaching.

From the degree of our comprehension of what Milner projects as dimensions of Afro-American life, we can gain an understanding of the historic, factual or mythic wisdom which is extended from elders to youth, parents to children, working class to petty bourgeois, from both men and women to each other, or, as in *Jazz-Set*, from leader to sideman, or vice versa in all cases, as its dialectic. Where are we, what is the nature of our lives, as such, this place that has shaped us so painfully?

Milner is a moralist of the *place* we are actually at, whether we understand it or not. He means always to *teach*, his creative rendering itself concerned with the infinite variety of *form(s)* and their exclamation as real life. Ron Milner is a skilled and passionate craftsman, expertly creating the "well-made play" for our time, place, condition, and concerns, understanding that his own intellectual, sensuous, and aesthetic depth is best expressed as clearly and accessibly as the most common perception of reality, given explanation and rationale as an advanced form of dramatic art, the act of which is, itself, consciousness raising and emotionally penetrating drama.

No Identity Crisis: An Introduction to the Plays of Ron Milner

Woodie King, Jr.

The Black Literature of the 1940s, '50s, and '60s seemed consumed with the search for identity, for example the writings of Richard Wright, Ann Petry, Ralph Ellison, and James Baldwin. The prevalent question seemed to be, are we to define ourselves in relationship to white people? . . . to the white world? Playwright Ron Milner responded to this question by devising another structural and thematic approach to his writing: "A lot of us young writers of the 1960s viewed that question as a continuation of the old 'slave narrative'. . . . We decided to let our music be our form for our way of expressing and being in the world. Our music simply spoke of us and to us—and let the world react as it chose. I decided to approach my plays, the writing of them, that way."

The music. There were all kinds of music around Detroit, and everywhere else in the mid-1960s, early 1970 years: blues, gospel, bop, doo-wop. The sounds, the rhythms that were to become first the Motown, then the Philly, and then the Memphis sound were evident, omnipresent. However, it was not until the emergence of Ron Milner that those sound/rhythms entered into our plays, not only in the language, but also in the form.

In 1962, Milner received a John Hay Whitney Fellowship, and shortly thereafter he was awarded a John Saxton Award to complete a novel. Having read excerpts of the novel, I urged him to write for the theater. *Life Agony* was the first result. I produced, directed and starred in this one-act play at the Unstable Coffeehouse Theater—where aspiring actors like Lily Tomlin often performed at the time. It ran on a bill of plays including Saroyan's *Hello Out There* and Tennessee Williams's *Talk to Me Like the Rain.* Two years later,

Robert Hook's Group Theatre Workshop in New York City produced it in conjunction with Public Theatre's Experimental Negro Theatre.

It was about this time that we saw Lorraine Hansberry's *A Raisin in the Sun,* directed by Lloyd Richards. Like myself, Milner became very excited about this award-winning play. He was deeply moved by the story and the creative approach. He kept repeating, "This is it. Here it is," and I knew what he meant. Here were strong, real black characters we could identify with and embrace totally. There was no apologizing for who they were. There was no supplication for the white world to "understand" and give them some kind of pity break. They knew who they were and what they were up against. They were committed to doing everything they could to better their condition. Meanwhile—to paraphrase Langston Hughes—trying to get a little love in between.

After seeing *A Raisin in the Sun,* Milner abandoned his novel and became a playwright. As Milner explained:

> It wasn't quite that decisive, not that cut and dry. What *Raisin* did was confirm some things for me. One, I could put the kind of people, themes, and dynamics I wanted on stage without worrying about stream of consciousness and other novelistic narrative devices; and two, that the stage was less elitist and therefore more accessible to many of the people I wanted to talk to and about. Many of them would not, maybe could not, sit down and read Ralph Ellison's *Invisible Man,* but they could see/hear/feel it if it was presented in three-dimensional form. I think it was the last point that sowed the seeds in me to leave other genres and to commit totally to the theatre. It was not only a step closer to the oral tradition of our culture, but it was also a move closer to the immediate response and interplay with the audience that musicians enjoy. How could I resist that?

Life Agony evolved into a much larger work, *Who's Got His Own* (1965). Like the title, taken from the Billie Holiday song "God Bless the Child," the form was derived from jazz. Milner explained, "I just used the straight out old basic jazz form: an ensemble work, where someone steps down front and takes a solo; an ensemble, another solo . . . And so on. I saw each of the characters as a particular musical instrument."

I hand-carried the first draft of *Who's Got His Own* from Detroit to New York and to the American Place Theatre where I was beginning an internship. (The lead role, Tim Jr., was an actor's dream come true.) Wynn Handman, the director of the theatre, loved the play. (But unfortunately, not with me in the lead role.) Upon my suggestion, the play was offered to Lloyd Richards, the same ex-Detroiter who had knocked us out with his direction of *A Raisin in the Sun.* We were ecstatic when he agreed to direct the play. In the 1955/56 season, the American Place Theatre produced *Who's Got His Own* under the brilliant direction of Lloyd Richards, and Glynn Thurman played Tim, Jr.

Although imbued with rhythms and black music structures, *Who's Got His Own* is not a play about "street life." It is a play about a black family struggling to find answers, searching for forgiveness and redemption. Milner's characters are crafted out of jazz instruments and vocals:

> On the symbolic level, if the dead father, Tim Sr., is the Negro past, then in the remaining family what you have are three reactions to that history. The son, Tim Jr., is a painful, screaming, hard-blowing anger working its way toward the militant attitudes and definitions of the younger brothers of the 1960s. I saw him as a tenor/scat singer. Then there was the daughter Clara, who wanted to close out all the pain and hard memories to float above them. She wanted to mesh, meld, "integrate" into some abstract new future of race-lessness. I heard her as a pop-singing pianist.

In the play, Clara says: "What was it like looking in his, Wreyford's, eyes? I'll tell you, dear brother. Like being on a hill looking down a sweet green valley. How's that . . . Like sitting beside a clear green pool. They were so green, Mama. I wanted to walk right down to the bottom of them; just take off my shoes and stay there forever. Yes, beneath all that cool clear green . . ."

Milner continued: "The mother, Cora, was conceived as a deep bass organist, intoning understanding, acceptance, and empathy for all God's children. But it is a song her children don't want to hear in the throes of their pain."

After Robert Macbeth chose *Who's Got His Own* for the premiere show for the 1966/67 season for his New Lafayette Theatre, it gained the distinction of being the first black play to be produced downtown in a white theatre and then produced uptown in Harlem. It won critical acclaim in both arenas.

In 1968, Milner's long one-act play *The Warning: A Theme for Linda* was produced off-Broadway as a part of an evening of plays under the title *A Black Quartet.* The three other playwrights included in the Quartet were Amiri Baraka, Ed Bullins, and Ben Caldwell. Baraka (aka Leroi Jones) had won the 1964 off-Broadway Obie Award for *Dutchman.* Ed Bullins was the outspoken award-winning playwright-in-residence at the New Lafayette Theatre in Harlem; and Ben Caldwell, an underground legend, was one of the most-produced playwrights in small theatres across America during the Black Arts Movement.

Whereas the music in the *Theme for Linda* was drawn from the rhythm and blues of Motown for the young female lead, the contrasting, low-down blues was adopted for the voice of her elders. Milner said, "I heard Smokey Robinson for that play. In fact, Smokey's 'More Love' was Linda's theme.

Smokey's song is a young girl's daydream fantasies. . . . Then comes the hard, deep, funky blues of the mother and grandmother telling Linda their histories, their Man-warnings."

The title of *What the Wine-Sellers Buy* is derived from Omar Khayyam's poem, "The Rubayiat." The core of the play revolves around a war for the mind and soul of Steve, a teenager who is torn between the influences of Rico, a Faustian-like hustler/pimp character, and the teachings of his mother. Milner took the Hastings Street of Detroit past, from the 1950s and 1960s, and brought it back to life on the stage. Hastings Street existed in our youth, not as a ghetto slum, but as a home. Milner honors the people in our home.

"With *The Wine-Sellers,* the theatre exploded inside my head," Milner explained.

> I went beyond just words to the full language of the theatre itself: the lights, the visuals, the actors, the spaces, the possibilities with parallel time, and time overlapping. I no longer contained the action in a single kitchen or a living room. I had the whole community on my canvas. New York had happened to me. The minimalism of Caldwell and Baraka, the theatricalness of Joe Papp's Public Shakespeare Theatre affected me. I finally sensed how to use it "all."

Some critics call *What the Wine-Sellers Buy* a morality play. I don't see any problem with that definition. I believe we began as a moral people. Milner created the amoral image of the Rico character because he believed that Rico's value system was derived from the lessons of the larger, white mainstream society, that is, buy and sell anything in the name of profit. Though his statements are couched in black rhythms, Rico's value system is definitely mainstream. Without a doubt, Rico is one of the most fascinating characters in contemporary black theatre. At one point he tells Steve, "Only two kinds of people in this world: Those standin' 'roun' tremblin' waitin' to be told when and how to move—and those wit guts enough to jump in and tell 'em when and how."

By contrast, Jim Aaron, a character who is a deacon in the church where Steve's mother seeks grace and release, gives Steve another frame of reference: "Because when you look back at that first woman of yours—that woman in there now—you see, along with your father, where your life came from. And when you look at whatever woman you choose to be with now, you lookin' at where your next life, your children, might be comin' from. And that ain't nothin' to be tradin' for some "things." The tree of life? The reflection of you an' your life? No. Uh-uh, no tradin' . . ."

But Milner resists the category of moralist:

> I don't think of myself as a moralist as such. Far from it. But I want my work to be useful in some sense, instructive in some sense.

> Have some effect on its time. Langston Hughes said I was more psychologist than playwright. I shirked it off as one of his sly little digs. But when I thought about it, he was absolutely right. It is the black psyche which has suffered most. And that is the key to the "spirit." Isn't that what "Black is Beautiful" was about? Trying to restore the black psyche? Way back then the "buy and sell anything," just "get paid" philosophy was beginning to supercede the old code and morals. If Rico could get you to sell your woman, getting you to sell anything else would be easy. We are today at the "anything else" point.

Milner's plays challenge traditional white perceptions of black people, and some perceptions blacks have of themselves. *Wine-Sellers* has a fantastic rapport with audiences. In every city where the play was produced, the audience was convinced it was their city, their neighborhood. At Chicago's Schubert Theatre, the play ran an unprecedented fifteen weeks. As a matter of record, the national tour from 1974 to mid-1975 was the highest grossing production up until that time, playing to 95 percent black audiences.

Worldwide, audiences truly love Milner's characters. In 1998, *Checkmates,* starring Ruby Dee and Ella Joyce, was invited to the Bermuda International Arts Festival and was clearly the event of the gathering. *Checkmates* had made a two-year journey from Chicago's 200 seat ETA Theatre in 1996 to 46th Street Theatre on Broadway in 1998. It starred Denzel Washington, Ruby Dee, Paul Winfield, and a young actress from Atlanta's Jomandi Theatre, Marsha Jackson. At every step of the way, Milner worked to improve *Checkmates.* Milner explained:

> *Checkmates* was my attempt to answer my own question of why and how we, as African Americans, even during slavery and in some of the worst times after, were able to maintain and sustain, not only central, but extended families. And now when we enjoy so much more freedom of choice and movement, so many more material things to give and share, why is it now that we are having such a hard time holding marriages and familial units together? It is about the difference of the older "we" generation approach where the family was the major concern and the younger "I" generation where self-fulfillment is the main aim. How the changing times have shaped these approaches.

Checkmates takes us into comedy as well as drama while contrasting the lives of two black couples, generations apart in age and attitudes. The play speaks particularly to the crisis faced by today's young educated folks obsessed with upward mobility. In contrast, the elder couple is bonded by a life together, dedicated to the survival of each other, prone more to compromise than to competition. The opening two scenes with the younger couple shows the underlying tension growing between them, brought on by changing outside influences. We see both of them rushing home with wine and flowers to celebrate their respective promotions, going happily to the bedroom to consummate the celebration.

Immediately after the lovemaking, the skirmishing starts over how he is to get his "damned meals" while she is out of town moving among strange new men carrying out her promotion. They speak jokingly. But is it really humor they are after? There are generational disputes, as the older field and factory worker Frank talks about the young salesman Syl: "Fieldwork. What that mean? Work when you *feel* like it? . . . Fieldwork. Hmmph. One day's work in a real field would kill him." Or young Syl's later retort, "Uh, what we want is to be in the game, pops. And it's not like coming outta' the fields and renting the outhouse. The games all in the big house now. It's penthouse or nothing. A whole new ballgame. Different strokes! . . . You got to have five-hundred-dollar suits and BMWs just to stay in this game! Too complex for you, pops!"

The elder Mattie gives advice to young Laura, who is contemplating taking on a lover: "people with problems get to thinking they can subtract by adding, and wind up multiplying." Whereas the young Syl tells the older Frank what has become of today's women:

> Naw, naw, they don't need us like they did, pops. You can see it in their eyes! "I can hunt good as you, so, tell me what I need with you?" And now they got all this birth control and abortion stuff. *They* just *decide* if and when, and what they want us for. If they're going to extend and continue us. I mean you see those looks, and you realize, the only way to stay the hunter is to outhunt, outhustle *them*—and then they, her, your wife is now part of the competition. So, now where you go for—for—for—for what? Shit, it's all fucked up!

According to Milner, *Checkmates* is the most perfectly balanced of his plays, "Everyone is right at this moment, wrong the next. Once it starts it just rolls on like a wheel, taking the actors and the audience with it."

Written in the late 1970s, *Jazz-Set* had brief runs at both the New Federal Theatre in New York, and at the Mark Taper Forum in Los Angles. Though not widely produced, *Jazz-Set* is much admired and emulated. Much like Milner's a cappella musical *Season's Reason*, *Jazz-Set* has become somewhat of a legend in the theatre. After a 1979 run at the Taper Theatre, *Jazz Set* was chosen by Los Angeles Drama Critics as one of the ten best plays of that year. Milner views this play as a tribute to the music for which it's entitled:

> *Jazz-Set* was my way of paying tribute to the most creative and purely honest art form there is—jazz. Giving something back to that tremendous source of inspiration. While at the same time taking on the challenge of trying to do a play not just "about" jazz or "about" jazz musicians. But to do a play as jazz that worked like/as jazz works, where the musicians and the music are one, where his/her life experiences, memories, [are] being "played" (acted out here) as music.
>
> So from a cap being tossed from actor to actor like a "note" of music, we see, in the first "tune," musical reactions, impressions of friendship, loyalty, betrayal. Then the tune is over. The actors spin, bow, say thanks. And now the tone, setting, theme switches to the second tune. But this is not just a series of "jazzy" little vignettes called songs. This is an actual play. So we also see the musicians in the dressing room and out in the "club." We see how, who, and what they are offstage determines what they "play" onstage.
>
> We also quickly see that the main theme, the real drama, is between the egotistical, individualistic alto-player, with his predilection for the personal blues, and the real leader of the group, the spiritually rooted tenor player with his faith in a collective, harmonic sense of things. The tenor player's piano-playing wife is a basic fulcrum for these two, while trying to protect and establish her own identity. The same could probably be said for the bassist and drummer, as well as for the elderly trumpet player, with his deep southern roots.
>
> I feel it is an exciting, innovative concept. I loved writing it, seeing it. Like a parent, I have a special feeling for this most difficult and misunderstood offspring.

In his play *Urban Transition: Loose Blossoms,* Milner examines how the drug subculture had risen to the top and woven its way into mainstream culture during contemporary times. *Urban Transition: Loose Blossoms* is so current we can actually see it reflected in everyday life. Young boys too young to drive own Mercedes Benzes and BMWs, support mothers, grandmothers, and siblings—young boys who would consider working at MacDonalds for $4.35 an hour but who know that they can hustle fifty times that in an hour by making a delivery and picking up a package for drug traffickers. Milner forewarned us about those pickups and deliveries back in 1973 with *What the Wine-Sellers Buy.*

Milner explains the historical continuum:

> Rico's "just get paid" philosophy is now the mode of the day. How can a society that pollutes the air and water in the name of profit

sneer at these youngsters selling poison in the name of the same creed: to get paid?

In *Blossoms,* the father, Earle, after long years in the factory, has managed to achieve a "middle-class" plateau. He and his social worker wife, Cheryl, have obtained a two-car garage, which for a while even housed a boat they co-owned with a friend. They have a daughter in college, a son in high school, and a younger daughter enjoying the benefit of being the baby with affectionate siblings.

Then, starting with Earle Sr.'s accident in the factory, all the middle-class underpinnings of the "decent" way of life begin to come undone. First, "common labor" is no more—one must learn a new technocratic skill or become part of the "downsizing," the phaseout for the millennium. Yet, the mortgages and tuition must be paid. A proud man like Earle would have it no other way, but he begins to sink under the weight. Having watched his father's seemingly useless struggle, Earle Jr. goes to the street for solutions and returns home with the bottom line—the "get paid" philosophy. As one member of the family after the next accepts the money, unbeknownst to Earle Sr., a new value (less) system is being established.

How do we answer Earle Jr. when he says to Bert the policemen, friend of his father:

> You gon' pay to keep my sister in college! . . . Yeah. Uh-huh. And when the—the—mortgage. And—and—taxes . . . And all the other . . . Whatchacallit? . . . Middle-class! Yeah! All the other middle-class stuff, they been tryin' to pump all these years. All comes due. All the bullshit notes. You gon' slide some paper on my mother, *then*? So he don't be drinkin' and cryin'! Goin' to pieces! You gon' stop him from goin' all the way out this time? Out to where maybe he can't never get back? Back up to where he was? Where he spose to be? You gon' do that? Huh, Sheriff? . . . What? You want me to make your day, Clint? This ain't no movie, man. This is real. Like Big John say, This is America! Land a' the rich! I'm just trying to get with the country, man!

Earle Sr.'s answer is simple, yet true enough:

> Shouldn't have to think about it. When you're in a game and a play come up, if you have to think about it . . . you're lost. It's supposed to be already *in* you what to do. You've practiced it, and practiced it, until it's in you what to do. It's in me! And I thought it was in you. And in our kids! Don't have . . . shit to do with no drugs. No drug money, drug cars, drug clothes . . . If it takes drug money to

> keep this house up . . . let the sonofabitch fall! . . . That's it. That's all . . . Y'all just got weak for that money! That's all . . .

Earle is still responding to a time when it seemed that everyone at least knew what was right. They might have chosen to do otherwise, but they knew what was correct. But today everything is negotiable and validated by the dollar.

The plays herein represent a major departure from the black literature of the past. In Milner's art, the characters must negotiate space, must already know who they are or they will be destroyed. The plays in this collection are not about self-destruction, losers, or images beyond reality. They are instead deeply rooted in the reality of black lifestyles and black music. These works represent the dynamics of Ron Milner's aesthetics.

As we read this collection of plays, we should note that Ron Milner ran a theatre company and wrote plays amidst the anger and frustration that led to the 1967 Detroit riot. At the same time, he was in contact with other writers and artists in New York, Newark, Los Angeles and elsewhere during the turbulent 1960s. He knew firsthand the passion that led to the riots in the inner cities after the deaths of Malcolm X and Martin Luther King. All of that is reflected in his writings.

Ron Milner is one of America's foremost playwrights. I feel that it is a good sign that after years of resisting, Milner has agreed to greet the new century with the publication of this collection of plays.

Checkmates

CHARACTERS

Frank Cooper: Mattie's husband: mid-sixties; urbanized ex-southerner. Still a soldier; waning in strength, but still proudly erect.

Mattie Cooper: Frank's wife: early sixties; background same as Frank's; very "quick" in mind and spirit; a tough lover and nurturer.

Sylvester Williams (Syl): Laura's husband; late twenties–early thirties; salesman, charmer; views self as streetwise in-fighter, protecting vulnerability.

Laura McClellan-Williams: Syl's wife (but wouldn't particularly relish being introduced that way, thus "McClellan"-Williams); striking appearance hints that glamour and fashion are her business; determined to be a self-defined independent woman.

TIME

1980s

LOCATION

Detroit/just about any other American metropolis.

SET

Ideally should be a double-decker suggesting a duplex, STAGE LEFT are stairs leading from lower apartment to upper with the suggestion of a foyer with the main door being off LEFT. The (UPPER LEVEL) is the apartment of SYL and LAURA: centrally it is the living room, chic modern furnishing, principally, couch, chairs, lamps, sound system, and bar; glass and chrome/aluminum might dominate. There is a computer DOWN RIGHT. REAR CENTER is draped entranceway OFF REAR; suggestion of closet. The (LOWER LEVEL) is that of MATTIE and FRANK; centrally it is a kitchen set, a mixture of old and new, say, a microwave, a well-kept old stove, new refrigerator, with old, handmade cabinets. Entrance to rest of house UPSTAGE. DOWN RIGHT is screen door; bench, flower box—sense of backyard.

ACT I

(Lights up on Mattie on Lower Level, entering as offstage Car Horn sounds, Car Door closes, Syl comes running in from left, carrying flowers and bottle of wine. Comes down hallway as Mattie comes to peer out glass top of imaginary door)

Mattie: Frank? . . .

Syl: Hello, Miss Mattie! . . .

Mattie: Oh. Hello Mister Sylvester! . . .

(He goes on upstairs, enters)

Syl: Hey, babe! I'm home! . . . Laura? . . .

(He goes off through draped entranceway, rear on Lower Level. Mattie goes to imaginary door stage right)

Mattie: Frank? Come on in! . . .

(Frank comes in, right, as Car Horn sounds. Car Door closes. Frank joins Mattie, as Laura comes on left, also carrying wine and flowers. She rushes into apartment, hiding wine and flowers behind her)

Laura: Syl? . . . Baby? . . .

(Syl comes on beaming, wine and flowers behind him. They meet center. Both extending wine/flowers)

Laura/Syl: Da-Da-Da-Dowww! . . .

(They laugh; kiss)

Syl: The promotion?

Laura: You are looking at Burden Department Store's newest buyer. You, too? The bonus?! . . .

Syl: Damn right! . . .

Laura: I don't believe it!

(They laugh, shout. He lifts her off feet; kisses her more seriously as he lowers her to her feet. Downstairs, Mattie serves Frank iced-tea; sits on his lap; obviously listening to upstairs sounds)

Laura: Oh, we definitely have to go out and celebrate . . .

Syl: Yeah, but we don't have to rush right out . . . .

Laura: No. We'll drink my wine now. And yours when we come back . . .

Syl: Uh-huh. Put yours here. And mine: in the bedroom . . .

(She kicks off shoes, puts her arm around his neck. Jumps up to grip his waist with her legs. He carries her rear)

LAURA: So what did they say? . . .

SYL: Can't talk with my mouth full . . . *(Kissing. THEY cross)*

LAURA: *(Offstage)* What about wineglasses? . . .

SYL: *(Offstage)* Damn glasses. *(Shouts)* Naked bodies! And naked bottles!

(Pops cork. THEY exclaim, laugh)

LAURA: *(Offstage)* Shhhhh . . .

SYL: *(Offstage)* Shhh what? *(Shouts)* We're married!! And succ-cess-fullllll!! . . .

LAURA: *(Offstage. Giggling; quieter)* And hornyyy . . .

(DOWNSTAIRS, MATTIE and FRANK listen to the obvious sounds; look at each other pointedly)

MATTIE: Told you it would be good having young folks up over us again.

FRANK: *(Clearing throat)* They are kinda' inspirational, aren't they? Look at us. And in the middle of the afternoon.

(Giggling, MATTIE gets up and leads him by the hand out of the kitchen. OFF LEFT, to bedroom area. Black.

Lights up on UPPER LEVEL as LAURA, wearing dressing robe, comes through archway; followed by SYL half-dressed in half-buttoned shirt, fresh pants, and stockinged feet)

LAURA: If you don't want me take the new job, just come out and say so . . .

SYL: Now who said that? I just asked how often you'll be going out of town, and for how long?

LAURA: As often as necessary. For as long as it takes . . .

(SHE snatches up her shoes)

SYL: It's answers like that—in that tone—that get shit started . . .

LAURA: It was a clear and simple answer: whenever and for as long as necessary to complete the job . . .

SYL: It's not just what you say. It's your damn tone . . .

LAURA: How do you think I like your tone? When I'm trying to tell you about my promotion, and you start talking about how you're going to get your damned meals . . .

SYL: All I said was, I guess I'd better get used to hanging out for my meals again. A little joke . . .

LAURA: I know when you're joking. Hanging out . . .

SYL: Alright, maybe there was a little jab in it. I mean, your wife's gonna' be outta' town. Staying over in hotels, alone, with strangers. Mostly drunk salesmen. Yeah, maybe I did have to work up a little spit to keep that down.

LAURA: *(Coming to couch)* Oh, so now we're getting down to it, right, Syl? I'm supposed to turn down this opportunity, so that these imaginary temptations won't have you feeling threatened, huh, Syl? . . .

SYL: *(Stuffing out cigarette)* There's that damned word. Hold it right there. You can put that word on ice. Just cancel it right on out of our conversations . . .

LAURA: Cancel it? What am I? One of your order clerks? Yeah, can tell you're a sales manager, alright.

SYL: Uh-huh. And I can tell a programmed keyword when I hear one, too.

LAURA: What damned *key*word? . . .

SYL: Threatened. When you're in a hotel with drunk strangers, I'm not threatened. I'm jus' plain straight-out jealous, worried. Normal as hell . . .

LAURA: You mean, typical. And are you sure that it's not the hotel with the drunk salesmen, but the promotion? The new job? The more money? That you find—uh, threatening?

SYL: *(Getting to feet)* Don't bring that *Cosmopolitan—McCall—Ms—Essence—* bullshit in here . . .

LAURA: Meaning? . . .

SYL: Meaning, you just make all the money you can find, baby. Because what's mine is yours, and what's yours is mine. Till death or divorce do we part. Remember? And when you get up to, oh, 50/60 thou? . . . Then I'm getting' my own business, and will be tickled no end that my only investor sleeps with me. Now put that in your next letter to the editoress.

LAURA: *(THEY'VE been to this sore area before)* Letter to the . . . How do my magazines keep popping into this?

(SYL is fixing his clothes)

SYL: Well, you're always using one of those chick's articles against me, so I figured this time I'd go for your weapons first.

LAURA: I don't *use* anything *against* you. When I'm *talking to* you, I'm talking from *me*. What *I* feel. What I think. Those articles are just—just—reference points. Confirmations . . .

SYL: *(Doing snapping Pac-man snaps at her)* Yeah, they're confirmations alright. They confirm the fact that you've joined the pact. That yelping, snapping pact called: Pac-women. Pac-women! Pac-women! Coming soon! To your home! Your office! Your bedroom! Watch out! They'll take your wife! Your secretary! Your daughter! Your mama! Turn them into yelping, snapping monsters! Snapping at your balls! Pac-women! Coming everywhere. Soon! Pac-women! Watch out! Pac-women! . . .

(Laughs, snapping hand at her face. SHE brushes it away)

LAURA: Uh-huh: Laughter camouflaging hostility! . . .

SYL: I must've missed that article. What was it? *Ebony*? *Essence*? Oh . . . I got it: *Psychology Today*. Right? Yeah . . .

(Laughing, HE starts OFF)

LAURA: *(playfully [?] attacks him)* I can't stand you . . .

(HE blocks punches, pins her arms; kisses her. SHE gets up into kiss)

SYL: Damn. You sure we're going out?

LAURA: Very sure. Strap on your credit cards. *(Going out)*

SYL: You bring yours, too. We both got promoted, remember? Equality and all, you know?

LAURA: You're jive. I mean, jive, jive, jive . . .

(HE crosses after her)

SYL: *(Offstage)* Yeah, I know: my money is to go, yours is just for show. Uh-huh.

LAURA: *(Offstage)* Shut up! . . .

SYL: *(Offstage)* Look out, woman. You crazy! . . .

(Black.

Lights up on LOWER LEVEL, MATTIE and FRANK in bath robes. MATTIE goes humming to refrigerator, takes out ham)

MATTIE: Frank? You want a sandwich? . . .

FRANK: No. I'm fine. Thank you.

(HE comes on from LEFT in pajamas; stands watching with amusement as MATTIE, with her back to him, cuts off pieces of ham and eats them without bread)

MATTIE: What? . . .

FRANK: If you ever was to be tippin' out on me, I'd sure know it. When you come back in, you'd head straight for the refrigerator.

MATTIE: Always did make me hungry.

FRANK: *(Turning on coffee pot)* I know. Used to worry about that at first. When we was young. Wondered if it meant I wasn't givin' you enough . . .

MATTIE: *(Giving him look)* Couldn't been wondering too much. I always let you know: Then and now.

(FRANK grins at her. UPSTAIRS there are squeals, laughter; LAURA shouting, "No, Syl, no! . . ." Heavy thumps as someone being thrown on a bed or bumping against a wall)

FRANK: You think we ever kicked up that much fuss? . . .

(MATTIE gives him another telling look)

FRANK: *(Continued) (Smiles)* Yeah, guess we have. Even more than that.

MATTIE: Thank you. Old or not, some things you aren't ever supposed to forget, Frank.

FRANK: *(A beat; tenderly)* I haven't forgotten 'em, baby.

MATTIE: Ummm. Lord, nobody could ever say baby like you.

FRANK: And they bet not let me hear 'em trying to, either. *(He kisses her shoulder)*

MATTIE: You about to get somethin' started in here again, man.

(More shouts, thumps, laughter from UPSTAIRS. FRANK turns to the coffee pot in disgust)

FRANK: Now you know they don't have to keep up all that noise. Don't seem to me that he'd be worth all that.

MATTIE: Worth all what?

FRANK: Just don't seem like there's that much to him, to me.

MATTIE: He never asked *you* to marry him, Frank.

(Sourly grumbling, FRANK pours cup of coffee.

Lights up on STAGE LEFT stairs: SYL and LAURA, dressed for the evening, come running out of apartment; he chasing her, she in mock fear)

LAURA: Nooo . . .

(HE catches her and pulls her to him)

SYL: Now, woman . . . I want you: now . . .

(THEY kiss warmly)

SYL: *(After kiss)* That a promise?

(SHE nods; THEY go out LEFT. Lights off on stairs)

FRANK: Carrying on like that out on the steps.

MATTIE: When you're that young and crazy with each other, stairways and hallways, just mean some other ways.

FRANK: I don't know what comes over you sometimes, Mattie. The way you talk. We were young and crazy too—but we had some sense of decency and dignity. I think he just be trying to show off.

MATTIE: It'll take more than showing off in hallways to reach what we have: Four fine children and forty-six years together.

FRANK: Six grandchildren. Yes, they got a whole lotta doin' to do. A long way to get to this . . .

MATTIE: Yes . . .

(THEY embrace. SHE lays her head on his shoulder; then looks up with a sly grin)

MATTIE: Frank?

FRANK: What?

(SHE takes his hand and starts pulling him out of the kitchen)

FRANK: Woman, you gon' get my back out of wack again! . . .

(Lights out on LOWER LEVEL. Up on STAIRS/HALLWAY. SYL storms upstairs angrily; on into apartment and off UP CENTER to bedroom area. LAURA comes walking in carefully, shakily, dealing with too much alcohol. Goes upstairs. As SYL comes from back wearing slick robe/smoking jacket. SHE sits on couch, carefully. As HE fumes at bar, getting sparkling water drink)

LAURA: They just sat down for a drink.

SYL: And decided to take up residence! We went out to be together. To celebrate. Not to join Louise's traveling freak show!

LAURA: They had a show tonight. They were just feeling good about it: Acting silly.

SYL: That don't take much acting for them. All that posing and carryin' on . . .

LAURA: They're models, they're supposed to pose . . .

SYL: Yeah. Especially that wanna-be-Billy-Dee-Williams dude. Fluttering around you and you playing up to him.

LAURA: It was just a game. He was just—complimenting me. And I'd had that champagne, so I was just—playing, feeling feminine.

SYL: Feeling feminine? With *them*?

LAURA: With them, yes. But for you. If you really want to know it was a kind of foreplay. Yes, for us. For you. A kind of—oh, never mind, you'll never understand.

(SHE starts out)

SYL: Don't give me that you'll never understand shit.

LAURA: I'm going to bed . . .

(HE springs to her, his finger in her face, threatening)

LAURA: *(Continued) (Hands up as to protect her face)* Don't . . .

(SHE stands there, her hands actually trembling at her face. Her eyes closed: It is her Mother-Memory. It seems extreme, out of proportion to the moment. SYL is stopped by the sight, the moment—steps back)

SYL: Baby, don't . . . Don't . . . Look, okay, I'm sorry. Just—calm down.

LAURA: *(Gaining composure)* Give me a cigarette . . .

SYL: You don't need a cigarette. *You* don't smoke. Your mother smokes. It was her that always smoked a cigarette after your stepfather beat her. That was him and her. Not me. Not you. Have I ever—after that one time in self-defense—have I ever hit you? . . . Laura, this isn't fair. Every time I raise my voice you put me with him, and go to pieces. That ain't right. Uh-uh. Ain't fair . . .

LAURA: *(Angrily)* Then why do you do it, Syl? . . .

Syl: What? Raise my voice? . . .

Laura: No! Charge me like that? You should see your face! It's awful! . . .

Syl: Baby, that don't mean nothin'. Me and a dude'll get up in each other's chest, calling each other all kinds of M.F.'s about a basketball game, but it don't mean we're gonna' fight! Just means we feel it! Don't you see, baby? It don't mean nothin' . . .

(He tries to touch her face. She moves away)

Laura: No, I don't see. I'm not some dude. I won't live like that, Syl. Terrorized, like my mother . . .

Syl: I know. I know. Heard it a hundred times. But I'm not . . . Aw, shit . . .

Laura: Please, Syl, I'm very tired, and high. Can I just go on in, please . . .

Syl: Baby, don't sound like that . . .

Laura: *(Confused, irritated)* Like *what*, Syl?

Syl: Like you're scared to leave the room, like you need permission. Like I'm some kind of monster, or something.

Laura: *(Sitting)* If I leave, you'll follow me; say I'm turning my back on you, not listening. And it'll go on and on and on . . .

Syl: Naw, baby, look. We drank that first bottle with nothing to eat. And I was already kinda' high when we got there, dig? So then they came and set down, and—and I got—got scared.

Laura: Of what, Syl? Scared of what? . . .

Syl: Why didn't you tell them to go so we could be alone. If I did it I'd be looking like some kind of jealous chump.

Laura: Louise is my friend and a brilliant designer. We're going to get a shop together with our designs. I want to get out of that department store and get my own thing.

Syl: *(Seeing it for himself)* But, it was like you were holding on to them, to keep something there between you and me. Like you didn't want to be alone with me . . .

Laura: Aw, Syl . . .

Syl: Naw. And watching you, the three of you, talking stuff I didn't know anything about. Blocking me out. I got . . . Yeah, scared.

Laura: Syl, I swear: I was not aware of doing anything like that. If I did, I'm . . .

Syl: *(Cutting her off)* I'm not talking about aware of, I'm talking about what happened. And I was scared because that's like how it always is now: Every time we try to get next to each other, something—something we say, we do—runs us into this—this—cobweb. This invisible something with—with splinters all over it. And we're feeling around each other.

Being real careful and cautious. And that's—scary, baby. Un-natural. I don't want this shit between us. I want to be able to just call, or, reach out, and there we are: Me and you with nothing between us. Like it used to be. Wasn't it? . . .

LAURA: Yes, it was. It still is. You're just high. We're both twisted. Come here . . . Oops . . . *(SHE has started to get up to go to him, but the drink rushes to her head and SHE falls back to the couch)* That wine . . . Come here, Syl . . . Come on. Please? . . .

SYL: Uh-uh. I can't be bothered with no drunk chick.

LAURA: Your drunk chick. Come lay down with me.

(HE comes to couch; sprawls at one end)

LAURA: *(Continued) (Moving to him)* Let me hold you . . .

SYL: Oh, it's my turn to play baby tonight, huh? . . .

(SHE pulls his legs up on the couch, slides herself up to lie on top of him)

LAURA: No, I'm the baby. Hold me . . . *(Squeezing him tighter)* . . . Hold me . . .

(HE does)

LAURA: *(Continued)* . . . Yeah. See? All better . . .

SYL: Yeah, that's why I didn't want to come over here. As soon as I touch you all that other stuff—the cobwebs—disappear.

LAURA: I know. Always been that way. Good.

SYL: I don't know if it's good. Where do the cobwebs go when we touch? And, if you don't know where they go, how do you know where to look for them? And . . . What the hell am I talking about? . . . *(Laughter)*

LAURA: *(Chuckles)* I know what you're saying, drunk. You're right. Once we touch, it's all clear. And words are unnecessary. *(Giggles)* "We tried to talk it over/But the words got in the way."

(BOTH sing last line)

SYL: Masquerade. George Benson, yeah . . .

(Lights fade on them as THEY make their way, giggling, to the back area. Lights up on FRANK coming into kitchen)

FRANK: Hear 'em, Mattie? Come in fussing and banging things around and end up cooing like two doves . . .

(Sound of giggling, whispering from dark UPPER LEVEL. SYL and LAURA get up, she leading him by hand, giggling "—Drunk and naked—" HE laughs)

FRANK: *(Continued) (Listens a beat)* Just listen to 'em . . . *(Chuckles)* Mattie, you remember when . . . Mattie? . . .

(Light fades. MEMORY LIGHT *glows in backyard area,* MATTIE *and* FRANK *come into it as* YOUNG MATTIE *and* YOUNG FRANK, *rendezvousing in the proverbial hayloft)*

FRANK: *(Continued)* Mattie. Mattie. Mattie.

*(*SHE *giggles, lies on her back contented.* FRANK *fixes shirt)*

FRANK: *(Continued)* I'm going to marry you, Mattie . . .

MATTIE: *(Laughs, involved with afterglow, "feeling" herself)* I know . . .

FRANK: Not because of this. Because we've been coming here. Just because I want to marry you.

MATTIE: I know. I always knew you would . . .

FRANK: *(Playfully wrestling with her)* You sure are full of yourself. What you mean, girl, telling me what and when? . . .

MATTIE: Stop!

*(*HE *does)*

MATTIE: *(Continued)* I always knew. I think everybody knew . . .

(Getting up, moving down center, adjusting clothes)

FRANK: They shoulda! The way you was looking at me that first time.

*(*HE *comes up behind her, plays following scene over her shoulder, holding out potato salad.* THEY *sway as if dancing, facing audience)*

MATTIE: I just knew. Knew it was you.

FRANK: I couldn't believe it: Here I am at a church bazaar. Come up to the table for some potato salad . . .

MATTIE: *(Chuckling)* Uh . . . huh . . .

FRANK: And stepped right into your eyes . . .

MATTIE: I couldn't help it. *(Chuckling)*

FRANK: . . . Felt like a fly in a spiderweb. Yo' eyes weren't blinking or nothing; just getting bigger and bigger and hotter and hotter . . .

MATTIE: I couldn't stop it.

FRANK: Downright embarrassing. Me standing there with that paper plate, and you standing there with that spoon fulla' potato salad. I felt like everybody was watching us. What with me holding up the line like that.

MATTIE: Told you: everybody could see it. Everybody knew.

FRANK: Everybody, maybe, but that Avon Carey. Had to 'bout break his head 'fore he got the message.

MATTIE: Avon been waiting a long time. Waiting for me to stop waiting. And then you come stepping up from Mayfield County, and I knew what I'd been waiting for. And maybe Avon didn't know. But my folks did. *(Pause)*

I think my mama and auntie knew what we've been doing out in this barn these last three months too. Uhm hmm . . . *(Breaks mood, moves away)*

FRANK: *(Alarmed)* What?! . . . You, Mattie? But you was a virgin. A good church girl . . . What would make them suspect something like that about you?

MATTIE: I don't know. But I think they know I'm not a virgin no more. Just something about how they look at me whenever your name comes up.

FRANK: And your pa, too? . . .

MATTIE: Hard to tell about Daddy. But he don't talk against me seeing you no more. Guess they all know there ain't no use in that. Me and you was just supposed to be, Frank. That's all there is to that.

(FRANK looks at her a moment, then sits up buttoning his shirt. Stands up. Appears preoccupied, nervous)

MATTIE: *(Continued)* Don't get all worried, Frank. We been careful. Daddy don't have no reason to be oiling his shotgun.

FRANK: With you being just sixteen he's got reason enough . . .

MATTIE: You just eighteen. What happened to my big bad Frank? . . .

(FRANK moves around a beat)

FRANK: Mattie? Remember I told you about my cousin Willie? The one live up in Detroit? Work in that Henry Ford factory? . . .

MATTIE: *(Antennae rising)* Yeah? . . . What about him? . . .

FRANK: Well, looks like the worst of this depression done passed on over up there. They's callin' the men back to work. Mattie, they's payin' five dollars a day up there! . . .

MATTIE: A day? You sure he's telling you right, Frank? Five dollars is a whole lot for a day's work.

FRANK: There's some wrong with Willie—like with everybody else—but lyin' ain't one of his faults. Now, the thing is, he say, since I ain't with no union or nothin', he sho' he can get me a job in that factory. If I come right now. He done already asked about it.

MATTIE: *(Getting to feet)* Right now? What you mean: Right now?!

FRANK: Mean: now. Soon. Right away. Five dollars a day, Mattie. Making that kinda' money, why it wouldn't take no time for me to save up enough to send for you. For us to get married and all . . .

MATTIE: *Send* for me?! That ain't worth what the bird left on the fence, Frank Cooper!

FRANK: Why, Mattie? Shoot, at five dollars a day, I figure, it won't take me longer than three-four months to be ready for you . . .

MATTIE: *(Moving on him)* You gon' be ready for me a whole lot sooner than that, Frank Cooper. Two-three months up there with them wild Detroit gals? In their high heels and silk dresses all mascared up—you won't even remember how I feel, much less what I look like!

FRANK: Aw, Mattie, I ain't gonna' forget about you . . .

MATTIE: Know you ain't! 'Cause I'm goin' wit' you!

(HE takes something from his shirt pocket)

FRANK: Well, this here bus ticket is for leavin' here this next Monday mornin'. 'Course cousin Willie says I gotta' be at that there Henry Ford factory up there, Wednesday morning . . .

(Dumbfounded, MATTIE slumps)

MATTIE: Monday? . . . Monday . . . You really *leavin'* me? . . .

FRANK: *(Jovially)* Aw, Mattie, I'm not leavin' you. I'll send for you . . .

MATTIE: Naw, naw. You're leavin'. What am I gonna do? What . . .

FRANK: *(Bending to her)* Aw, now, Mattie . . .

MATTIE: *(Pulling away)* Naw. I'm jus' gonna' die without you. I know it. Just shrivel up and . . .

(FRANK steps away, then pulls another ticket from his pocket)

FRANK: Guess you could jus' go on and die. But, seems to me it would be a heap better to take these next three days, till Sunday—to get your family and the preacher together. And I'll bring my folks over for the wedding.

MATTIE: Preacher? . . . Wedding?

FRANK: And on Monday we'll use these *two* tickets here and go on up to Detroit—man and wife. 'Course Willie wasn't expectin' nobody but me. But I guess he'll . . .

(MATTIE springs on him, slapping at him with both hands)

MATTIE: You! . . . You! . . .

(FRANK laughs as HE blocks most of the slaps. Grabs her to him to kiss. SHE grabs the tickets and runs OFF)

FRANK: Mattie? . . . Where you goin'?! . . . You got both tickets! Girl! You done left yo' shoes! You cain't . . . ! Lord . . .

(HE snatches up her shoes and runs laughing after her. MEMORY LIGHT out)

(MEMORY LIGHT goes out. FRANK goes back into kitchen area, chuckling to himself. MATTIE calls from Offstage)

MATTIE: *(Offstage)* Frank? . . . You alright? . . .

FRANK: *(Going into hallway)* You alright? . . .

MATTIE: *(Offstage)* Yes, Frank, I'm alright . . .

FRANK: *(Offstage)* If you're alright, then, I'm alright . . .

(Fade on LOWER LEVEL. Up on UPPER LEVEL, daytime. SYL is on the phone. It is a SYL we haven't seen/heard before: HE speaks comfortably, though comically to us, in a "white," business, frat brother lingo. A tough, locker-room veneer, over a "Hi-guy" foundation, with the term freaking being the main adverb, adjective, add-all, as in freakin'-ay! Freakin'-right! Freakin' crazy, etc. . . .)

SYL: *(Normal voice)* On hold. Aren't we always . . . *(Voice change)* Yeah, I'm here. Well, run it by me. Let me hear it for myself . . . Old Polish and Italian neighborhood. So? I don't care if it's freaking Israeli and Saudi, Dan, I can handle it . . . What's his name? . . . Said don't send him no freaking blacks, huh? Well, God'll punish him. So skip his two freaking markets. Give me the rest of the district. Surround his old ass with so many better deals, services, and prices, he'll be . . . As he goes, the district goes? . . . In other words, what you're tellin' me is the only way I can get into the freakin' district is through a freakin' hundred-foot stone wall! Is that it!? . . . Dan, I can understand it when you play hardball. But from you to me I don't expect no curveballs . . . No *fuckin'* curves, Dan! We've been through some deals, Dan! I've made freakin' money here! Even turned a few under the table! . . . I'm not saying that. I know you've thrown me deals! . . . What damn guilt trip?! . . . Dan?!! Dan?!! . . . Dan! *(Checking himself)* . . . Listen to us, Dan. Freakin' fightin'? Me and you? Fighting? Hey, come on. We don't want this. Alright? I'm sorry. You're sorry. Okay, look: Let's draw a line and toss some pennies, okay? Here's the deal: I sell this old guy and his two markets and I've got the district. If I don't—I don't. Cool? A deal? . . . Dan, I love you! I freakin' love you! . . . *(HE hangs up phone)* Fat ass bastard. . . .

(Begins to check computer for address. Phony Italian accent)

SYL: *(Continued)* Corsini—Corsini—Corsini—Where uh—are'aduh you, Frankie?! Eh, Frankie? Eh? Time for the Italiano to help the Afri-cano!! Eh, Frankie? One paisano to another. Eh? . . .

(Chuckling, HE begins to dial cell phone. Light fades on him as HE goes off.

Up on MATTIE and FRANK, having lunch in the kitchen)

FRANK: *(Indicates upstairs)* What kinda' job he got allows him to come home in the middle of the day so much? . . .

MATTIE: Don't know. She says he's out of the office and out in the field a lot. Fieldwork.

FRANK: *(Grunts)* Fieldwork. What that mean? Work when you *feel* like it? . . .

(SHE chuckles)

FRANK: *(Continued)* Fieldwork. Hmmph. One day's work in a real field would kill him. You remember what being in those fields was like, Mattie? Huh?

MATTIE: *(Staring, seeing)* Yes, Lord, from before day, till day died.

FRANK: Yes, and sometimes that sun be putting you and the day in a race for life or death.

MATTIE: Hmmm. Sure did feel like it sometimes. I wasn't no more than a baby, six-seven years old, when I had to get out there and do my part.

FRANK: Uh-huh. Do your part; me too. And you didn't feel much like no baby, now did you? . . .

MATTIE: *(Clearing plates)* Wasn't much time to be no baby; work to do . . .

FRANK: That's what I mean! We had to get out the nest and get started early! Not like these days, stay up under their folks' wings right on up to college, graduate school, and all. Almost thirty years old before they get out on their own to find out what it means to try to be grown.

MATTIE: *(At the sink)* Guess it takes more preparation these days, Frank.

FRANK: Guess so, since these days they start out with such inferior equipment.

(THEY BOTH laugh)

MATTIE: *(Laughing)* Maybe you got a point. Bible says each generation will get wiser and weaker! . . .

FRANK: Yeah, we had the big muscles. They got the big heads.

(SHE chuckles)

FRANK: *(Continued)* Yeah, if you ask me, if heads is houses, they got lots of room, but not much furniture.

(MATTIE moves to sink with dishes, studies him for a moment)

MATTIE: That just go for that boy and girl upstairs? Or does it include our sons and daughters, too?

FRANK: Well, them two boys of yours do get beside themselves sometimes, now that they done took my company from me.

MATTIE: My boys now, huh? Roy is off doing his own thing, thank you. And Frank Jr. didn't take nothing from you. You retired, remember?

FRANK: I had a lot of help making up my mind. Lots of nudging from my wife.

MATTIE: Getting a check without sweating for it, seems just fine to me. And I guess you don't have nothing to say against the girls, huh? Since they still Daddy's two darlin's, all over you.

FRANK: Once or twice you tried to ruin 'em, but fortunately I was here to straighten y'all out.

MATTIE: *(With coffee pot)* You want this in your cup? Or on your head?

(FRANK laughs. Lights down on them.

Up on SYL UPSTAIRS, on the phone, pacing, laughing. UPSTAIRS laughter and DOWNSTAIRS laughter provide the transition)

SYL: . . . Yeah, uh-huh, you remember, don't you now, Frankie: all those laughing and drinking Afro-Americans going up and down the river. What was it? Twelve, fourteen trips a day? That's a lotsa' of money-ay for an Italiano' to be making off an Afro-American festival. Especially when the Afro-Americans were supposed to get first crack at all the concessions . . . Vaguely, my ass. You remember quite vividly I'm sure. 'Cause you had the deal, but you only got that concession 'cause the black Sylvester here agreed to front for you. Uh-huh; sure you do. And I didn't want no money, just the right to choose the people on the job. Uh-huh, I'm sure you are. You're welcome. But you see the way I was figuring there would be more action on your side of the street than on mine: Not just a little money for one day, but lotsa' money and lotsa' jobs for a lotsa' days. Yeah, so, the thing is, I'm ready to cross the street now, Frankie, and I'm thanking you in advance for your kind assistance in this endeavor. *(Bowing like a performer)* What? Crock of shit my ass. Come on, man: *It's payback time!*

(Laughs. Lights fade on his laughter.

Come up DOWNSTAIRS on the laughter of FRANK: HE and MATTIE sit with coffee, laughing)

FRANK: Lord, I wouldn't let well enough alone. I jus' kept beggin' that ol' Polack, Zeke, to put me to work in that foundry. Hell, could make five-six more dollars a week in there. And you about to have the baby and all; shoot, needed that extra. Sam and them other old boys kept tellin' me, "Frank, you better let that foundry alone, boy. You ain't growed enough ass for that job yet, youngblood." Shoot, that was the worst thing they could've said to me. Hell, I was much man as any; and about to be a daddy too? Shoot, I worried, and buttered up that ol' Zeke so, till he had to put me on in there. Well, sir, he walked over there that morning and turned me over to ol' Big, Black Jim.

(MATTIE shakes her head, chuckling)

FRANK: That's what we called him.

(MATTIE nods; THEY have relived this together hundreds of times)

FRANK: *(Continued)* . . . Well, ol' Jim flung me those goggles and gloves and that shovel—Lord—and he opened that furnace . . . and he said: *(HE has gotten up now, acting it out)* . . . and he said: "There's the hole, and there's the coal. Fill the hole with the coal. And jus' keep that fire jumpin' at the sky." Then, Lord, that whistle blew, and all them big fellas, and little me, went at that coal with them shovels. Scrape and chunk. Scrape-chunk; scrape-chunk. And, Lord, my back ain't never gon' be straight no more. And that fire! That heat! Lord, if Hell is any hotter than that foundry then the Devil's got to have air condition. Scrape-chunk, scrape—Oh, Mary, Joseph and Jesus. Trying to breathe up in all that heat, behind them dark glasses, with that mountain of coal multiplying itself every time you take a chunk. Scrape-chunk-scrape—and you tryin' to keep up with the rest of the Devil's crew, and they goin' like they gettin' paid by the shovelful. Scrape-chunk-scrape-chunk. And sometimes, do Jesus, prayers do get answered. That bell rang, and my back bent at a hundred and eighty degrees, I stumbled over to my lunch pail. And, bless you, Mattie, you had boiled eggs, too. But I jumped on that lemonade first; was all set to get into them pork chops, when I noticed them others all leaning on them damned shovels, grinning at me. Jim say, "Little fella', what you think you doing?" "What you think?" I said, "Eatin' my damned lunch." "Lunch? Boy, that bell gives you a five-minute break. Lunch. You ain't worked but an hour and a half." An-hour-and-a-half? I knew damn well I had been working *at least four* hours. But, naw, back to that: Scrape and chunk, scrape and chunk. And, Mattieeee? By the time that shift was overrr . . .

(Extending the word, HE *goes to slump heavily in his chair, staring vacantly.* MATTIE *comes over to him)*

MATTIE: I know. I took one look and said, "What's the matter? What's done happened to you?"

*(*THEY *laugh as* SHE *sits in his lap)*

MATTIE: *(Continued) (Laughing)* What did they *do* to you? . . . What did they do? . . .

FRANK: Lord, that foundry. That foundry . . .

(Light dimming on them as MEMORY LIGHT *comes up* STAGE RIGHT. MATTIE *and* FRANK *move into it as* YOUNG MATTIE *and* YOUNG FRANK*)*

MATTIE: *(Incredulously)* You did what? . . .

FRANK: I don't know what come over me, Mattie . . .

MATTIE: What? . . .

FRANK: I seen those white fellas goin' in there. No older than me, Mattie . . . and then some of us goin' too . . .

MATTIE: You joined the *army*?! . . .

FRANK: Well Mattie, I had a couple nips, and, it looked like everybody but me was going to do they bit. And—and, I don't know, Mattie, 'fore I knowed it I'd—done it.

MATTIE: Well you just go back and un-done it. Go back down there and tell 'em you was drunk. Tell 'em you done changed your mind. Tell 'em anything. Frank Jr. layin' in there and another one growin' in me. Naw. No. You ain't leavin' me here.

FRANK: Mattie . . .

MATTIE: Those white folks' war don't have nothin' to do with you and me and these kids. We'll fight right here. Right now. You and me. I'm not gonna' have it, Frank. You ain't gonna' do this to me. You hear me? I don't wanna' hear no more about no damned war. No damned soldiers. No—nothin'. You . . .

FRANK: *(Thundering)* Mattie! I gotta' be a man. Not no damned mule! *(Pleading)* Mattie, sometimes I look down our section of that assembly line—with us all bent, sweating, and straining, and them, in they shirtsleeves carryin' them damn clipboards, snarlin' at us like we dogs, mules, anything but men—and it's like I'm still on the plantation sharecroppin', Mattie. Like I never come North. Like there ain't no North for me, Mattie.

MATTIE: *(Turning away)* I don't care about that, Frank. You hear? I . . .

FRANK: *(Turning her to him)* You've got to care, Mattie. I won't be able to face Frank Jr.—and our new baby—feelin' like this. Don't you see? I got to stand side by side, toe to toe with 'em. Show 'em, Mattie. We all do. Then when it's over, they got to give us our due, Mattie. They got to! And I ain't forsakin' y'all, Mattie. Government be sending you money every month . . .

MATTIE: *(Pulling away)* Damn that money and damn you, too! Damn everything but me and my—my babies . . .

(SHE cries. HE goes to her, embracing her from behind)

FRANK: Mattie, I gotta' go. I just got to. Mattie, Please. Please, Mattie. Please . . .

(SHE leans her head back against him, crying silently. MEMORY LIGHT dims. MATTIE and FRANK come back to kitchen, laughing at the factory incident)

MATTIE/FRANK: That foundry . . . that foundry . . .

(They cross as lights fade on LOWER LEVEL. Up on SYL on UPPER LEVEL, still on the phone)

SYL: *(Laughs)* The deal's like I said, you get your one-deal fee, return your favor, and earn my eternal respect . . . Meet you with the papers, tomorrow? Ten o'clock? God's gonna' bless you for this, Frankie . . . Ciao . . . *(Hangs up)* Ciao, ciao, ciao. Get 'em, Sylvester baby. Yes-suh . . .

(LAURA comes UPSTAGE LEFT steps, carrying flight bag, samples of apparel material, etc. SYL dances over to phonograph, puts on Kool & Gang's

"Celebration"; dances, singing. Suddenly grabs suitcase from couch, rushes out door—as Laura *comes up steps.,* He *grabs and kisses her)* Hey, lady!

Laura: Well, well, aren't we up today . . . Where you goin'? Want to talk to you . . .

Syl: Be right back. Going round the corner. Get some champagne. We celebrating.

Laura: Celebrating what? . . .

Syl: Right back! . . .

Laura: I have something important to tell you!! . . .

Syl: Be right back.

*(*He *crosses.* Laura *goes up stairs, enters.* She *puts down bag. Turns music down. Dials phone)*

Laura: *(On phone)* Louise? . . . Talked to Shirley. The material is absolutely gorgeous, Louise. Better even than I expected . . . Yes. And listen: I got her down to five! Five thousand. Yep. Be picking up your half of the money in about two hours . . . And, Louise? I won't be needing that doctor's number . . . I decided to have the baby . . . Yes, you will be a godmother . . . I know it's the only way you'll be a mother. Unless somebody catches you drunk, between pills. Never mind. What? Never mind what I said before I'm having a baby. Now! No, I haven't told Hercules yet . . . Of course he'll be happy . . . Think I hear him coming now. Yep. Get that check from the non-bouncing account. Call you when I'm on my way. Bye! . . .

*(*She *rushes off as* Syl *comes running back in with a bottle of champagne. Turns music back up loud. Pops cork, pours wine.)*

Syl: Hey, foxy, Mrs. Williams. *(Singing)* Celebration . . . Howwwww!!

Laura: *(Enters)* Syl? . . . Will you . . . Well. What's got you so up? . . .

Syl: Mr. Williams has that northeast district in the bag! Mrs. Williams. In the bag!

Laura: *(Taking off shoes; glad for him)* Really, baby? . . . When? Wow . . . How'd you work it? . . .

Syl: Just now, today. They put up a white wall, so I dropped in a white Trojan horse. Before they know it, the gates will be open and I'll ease in smooth as black silk and smelling like Lagerfeld . . .

Laura: Smooth, baby! Who's the Trojan horse? . . .

Syl: *(Coming to embrace-dance-kiss)* Frank Corsini. Remember the New Year's Eve party? You liked his wife? He owed me one for the Afro-American festival.

Laura: Oh, yeah. *He's* fronting for you, huh. Beautiful, baby. Great.

(They touch lips. Syl wants to get a good mood going)

Syl: Uh-huh. I've been dealing and you've been working, so, no cookin' tonight. I'm taking you out. Spend some of that extra bread right now. Write it off, too . . . Come on. Go get casually sharp—cele-ahh-bray-shun!— *(Singing, then)* Yeah, celebration . . .

(Turns music back up. Dancing. Laura stands)

Laura: Syl? Baby? I can't go to dinner with you . . .

Syl: *(Not hearing her)* What? . . . You what? . . . Whatever . . . Go get ready . . .

(She turns music down)

Laura: I said I can't go to dinner with you. Syl . . .

Syl: What? What do you mean? Why not? . . .

Laura: I have to do some buying for the store. Catching a plane in . . . *(Checks watch)* . . . three hours for Philadelphia. And I also have to pick up Louise's half of the money to do some buying for us—you know building for the boutique. I'm sorry, baby.

Syl: *(Deflated, disgusted)* Louise. Look, I pulled off a big one. Can't you go in the morning? What the hell you gon' do there tonight? Everything'll be locked up when you get there.

Laura: Syl, my appointment's at 9:30 in the morning. If I catch that morning flight, I'll be rushing through two airports, taking chances on delays and all that, then going into the appointment all rushed. That's not how I want to do it, Syl . . .

Syl: Aren't there any later flights to Philly? . . .

Laura: Only on weekends. I checked. Don't put me in a thing, Syl, please . . .

(He turns away, disgusted; sits on couch. She goes to sit on arm, embracing, rubbing his back)

Laura: *(Continued)* Baby, I'm sorry, really. Look, all I have to do is shower, and grab a few things. You run me by Louise's for her money, and we'll go on to the airport. If we hurry, we'll have maybe an hour. Celebrate with a couple of drinks. You can eat later. I want to talk to you about something very important . . .

Syl: *(Pulling away, rising)* Like what? Next year's fall colors? I'm not loanin' you and Louise any more money if that's it. Eat later, huh? Uh-huh. Maybe you and Louise don't need no food in you all's wrist-kissin' business. But it's real tough dodgin' the bullshit over here. Going out to get me somethin' to eat. And come back and go to bed . . .

(He stomps out. She goes to door to holler after him)

Laura: Wrist-kissing, my ass! My work is just as hard as yours!

SYL: Yeah? Well your paychecks sure don't show it! . . .

(HE goes off. SHE stands frozen for a beat with the low blow. Then whirls and storms into the apartment furious; turns record off. A beat, then goes to phone, dials)

LAURA: *(On phone)* Louise? Look: I'll be by for the money in forty minutes. You'll have to drive me to the airport . . . No cute shit tonight, Louise. Okay? . . . Do you have to ask? He's up in orbit again. Where else? Just be ready. What . . . No I didn't tell him. Changed my mind. I'm not stopping my career to have no baby! . . . Not slowing it down, either. Abortion, yes! . . . I don't have time. I'm not going to be dependent on nobody's *(shouts at window)* big paychecks! . . . Nothing. Be there in a half hour . . . Louise? And have that doctor's phone number ready . . .

(SHE slams phone down. Then slams front door as SHE goes by it to exit to the rest of apartment. Up on LOWER LEVEL. FRANK/MATTIE come into kitchen as upstairs door slams)

FRANK: Goddamnit! Now he don't have to be slammin' doors like that! . . . Always actin' like a big man. He's rentin' from me, ain't he? . . . I'd like to show him how big he ain't. Uh-huh. And I just might do that: Wait up till he comes marching back in here—and meet his little fancy ass out there in the hall.

MATTIE: You ain't gonna' do no such a thing.

(HE turns to her startled)

MATTIE: *(Continued)* You just leave that boy alone. You hear me, Frank? I mean that now . . .

FRANK: Woman, who you talking to?

MATTIE: Talking to you. I'm about sick of this now. You got a bug about that boy. Like you jealous of him or something. Some kind of sour taste in your mouth, making you ugly. And I want you to stop it now. You hear me? . . .

FRANK: *(A beat)* Yes, I hear you. And I'm gone tell you something. Your son looks something like me. But he don't live here no more. Now, if you want to talk to a man like he's a child, I'll get you his phone number.

(SHE clucks her teeth with disgust)

FRANK: *(Continued)* Suck your teeth all you want, but don't be talking to me just any ole kind of way . . . Jealous of him. You mean that little ol' gal upstairs?—Aw, Mattie, I swear sometimes you get so far out the way I can't even see you.

MATTIE: Uh-huh. But I can see you . . .

FRANK: Mattie, I swear 'fore God. It's a good thing I ain't young and foolish no more. Else one of these days I be done hurt you before I know it . . .

MATTIE: Oh, I'd let you know it alright. Pain for pain. And hurt for hurt . . .

(HE moves to fridge door; beat, HE hits door. MATTIE flinches. HE goes to cabinet; takes out a bottle and glass. HE pours glass half full; takes a sip. MATTIE easily takes glass from his hand. Goes to sink)

FRANK: *Now* what you think you doing? . . .

MATTIE: This is too much. I'm gon' take a little of it, make us both a toddy. Then I'm pouring the rest back into that bottle . . .

(SHE runs water into teakettle. HE glares at her a moment, then comes to fridge door again. SHE puts the kettle on the stove, flinches again as HE opens and slams the fridge door once, twice, three times)

MATTIE: *(Continued)* —Frank—?

(HE slams it again and again, and SHE crosses to him, gently putting a hand on each shoulder, rubbing, leaning against him)

MATTIE: *(Continued)* Your pressure, Frank, your pressure . . .

(HE finally stops; breathing heavily; composing himself)

FRANK: You's right, Mattie. Damn you. You's always right. *(Goes to screen door)* But it ain't about that little ol' high-strung gal . . . Mattie, that boy up there, and our boys, our sons—Mattie, they got things so clear and open for *them*. They've got so *much* that they can do. And they act like they *supposed* to have it like that . . .

MATTIE: Well, Frank, they are supposed to. Just because we didn't have it.

FRANK: Naw, Mattie. Naw. They act like they did it for themselves. Like we ain't had nothing to do with it. Like they's smarter than us. Better than us . . .

MATTIE: *(Going to stove)* Aw, Frank, now, our kids don't feel like that. They appreciate all we did for them.

FRANK: Naw, not always. Sometimes they look at me just like that boy do. Like they know something I don't know. An' like it's my fault I don't know it . . .

MATTIE: Aw, Frank . . .

FRANK: If I'd a had the chance to learn it like they did. Mattie, they got so much possible for 'em. And they ain't doing so great such a much. Not like I woulda done if I coulda gone on to school . . .

MATTIE: There was some comin' along with us who went on to school. And haven't done nearly as good as we have.

FRANK: Not coming from where we was. And not having babies fast as we was.

MATTIE: *(A beat)* Oh? And now what you trying to say . . .

FRANK: I didn't mean nothing like that now, Mattie. Don't try to get me wrong now.

MATTIE: I sure guess you didn't mean nothing like that. 'Cause I sure don't remember you poppin' up off of me, saying, "Stop, Mattie. I got to go to school."

FRANK: Mattie, I swear, the way you talk sometimes. But see? That's another thing: that birth control pill. A little thing like that can make all the difference in the world.

(MATTIE crosses with tea, lemon, etc.)

MATTIE: Yeah, don't have babies, have cancer. Shut your mouth, man, and drink this toddy.

FRANK: Him, lookin' down at me with his chest puffed out. Shoot, I'd a had the chances they got, I wouldn'a been workin' in no factory or office either. Woulda' owned factories and offices. Shoot, I mean, I woulda' had me something. You know how I was, Mattie: Quick and smart and handy. All the good ideas I had. Just couldn't get far enough ahead to work on 'em all. One thing's sure, I woulda' ended up with more than a construction company and two-three little piecea' houses.

MATTIE: Oh? It's a little piecea' house now, huh? Guess you want one of those villas you talked about so.

FRANK: *(Anticipating)* Aw, Mattie, now, just . . .

MATTIE: With your *(Mimicking)* "Mon ami, my Frankie. Leave your colored fam-uh-lee, stay here in Paree and be white with meee." . . . Hmm-mmph . . .

FRANK: *(Getting up, hiding smile)* Now don't start with that, Mattie . . .

MATTIE: Wish I could've caught her over here, mon Frankee . . .

FRANK: *(About to laugh)* I don't even want to get into this . . .

(HE leaves kitchen area)

MATTIE: Oh, goin' up front so you can laugh at me. I would've told her, "Frank-eee belongs to Matteee, and don't you for-get-ee."

FRANK: Aw, come on, leave that stuff be, Mattie. Come sit up front with me . . .

MATTIE: Call France. Let her sit with you.

FRANK: Mattie, come on now . . . *(As crossing)* Parlez vous Francais? . . .

MATTIE: Enough to know you about to get knocked down.

(HE laughs, as SHE goes after him with the dishcloth. THEY exit, both laughing. Lights fade.

Come up on UPPER LEVEL. SYL comes on from OFF REAR, hurt, upset, steaming. HE is carrying a small suitcase. LAURA follows him)

LAURA: You're not being fair, Syl.

SYL: Was it fair what you did? Was it fair for you to talk it over with Louise, but not me? Why, Laura? Why did you do that?

LAURA: I don't know. I felt I had to talk to someone . . .

SYL: Someone? Anyone but me, huh? . . .

LAURA: No. Syl, will you sit down? Please? . . .

SYL: For what? Why not me? I mean it was my baby, right? So why discuss it with her? . . .

LAURA: Don't say: baby. It wasn't a baby, yet. It was a—a—conceivement. A fetus . . .

SYL: Okay then my conceivement. My whatever the hell you want to call it! It was mine, right? So why you have to discuss it with her? Huh?! Why!? . . .

(HE shouts this last; seems about to jump at her. SHE recoils)

LAURA: Because she was—safe. I mean, she wouldn't be trying to make me—telling me to—do one thing or the other. She would just—listen. Discuss it . . . .

SYL: *(Packing papers)* I bet. Yeah. Just the good old sisterhood, right. No boys allowed, right?

(SHE sits on couch watching him apprehensively)

LAURA: Syl, baby, I've been waiting—looking for the right time. I thought that since we were feeling so good today. So close. That today would be the right time.

SYL: The right time, Laura, was when it was happenin'. But naw, then you were talkin' to home-girl. But then that's where it's at, right? The sisterhood and white boys. I mean I can't tell you what, when, or, how, to do nothin'. But one of them in France tells you what to wear. Another one in Hollywood tells you how to fix your hair. And another one, somewhere else—New York maybe—tells you how to smell. Yeah. Hell, you're their woman, not mine!

LAURA: Stop it! *Their* woman. Your woman. I'm my woman, understand? First and last, I'm mine! Your baby. You're not concerned about not having the baby. You're concerned about not having the final say!

SYL: Hey, listen . . .

LAURA: What? That's exactly why I talked to Louise. So I could hear myself think. Get some opinions, ideas, not declarations! I knew if I talked to you I would get the emperial design. Yeah, your baby, with your little woman, waiting at home for your *big* paychecks. Well it's my body, my life. And my career, too! And I decide what to do with it all. Me. Myself. For myself. Do you understand that?

SYL: *(A beat)* Oh, you're damned right I do . . .

(HE storms OFF REAR. SHE tries to appear calm, but apprehensively moves a safer distance to the bar. HE comes back on with a pile of her women's magazines. As HE reads the cover story titles HE throws each one to the floor)

SYL: *(Continued)*

Doing it for your-SELF.
Loving your-SELF.
Enjoying your-SELF.
Realizing your-SELF.
Pleasing your-SELF.
Self! Self! Self

(HE throws the remainder to the floor) All about you all getting to yourselves! And you're really getting to it, baby. So, if it's all about your life, your body, your thing? Then what the hell am I here for? To assist you in masturbation—

LAURA: You son of a bitch!

SYL: From what I hear all you need is some batteries!

LAURA: Kiss my ass! . . .

SYL: Yeah, well, I was just gonna' take a couple days to cool out after this abortion news. But I don't want no more days, no more nothin'. You can have your 'new thang' I guess I was born too old for it! . . .

(HE goes out slamming door. SHE runs out to shout at him)

LAURA: Who the hell cares? I don't need you! You hear me? I don't need you !! . . .

SYL: Yeah! You've got batteries! . . .

(FRANK is coming into the house as SYL reaches the bottom of the steps. SYL brushes past him, jostling him off balance)

FRANK: Just go on and knock me down! I wish you would! . . .

(SYL continues OFF. LAURA storms back into living room, slamming door. MATTIE gets up in kitchen and crosses LEFT)

MATTIE: Frank? What's the matter?

(FRANK turns at her voice, then grumbling, slowly follows SYL's wake.

LAURA fumes a moment, kicks at magazines, then rushes to invisible front window, LEFT, and raises it)

LAURA: *(Shouting)* Come back and clean up this mess! I'm not your damned maid!!

(Sound of car backing out, roaring OFF. LAURA glares after it. MATTIE looks up at sound of her movements. FRANK enters their apartment)

FRANK: Got the whole world opened to 'em and can't get a hand in a glove.

(Laura closes window, moves Center, stands gripping her elbows, back to audience. Mattie looks from Frank, back upstairs. Frank crosses. Fade on Laura/Mattie both standing in separate spaces, backs to audience, staring upstage: two question marks)

ACT II

SET

Same as Act I, with the changes in decoration, furniture arrangement, etc., that might naturally occur within a two-week period.

(Lights up on Lower Level. Mattie comes from stove with teakettle. Laura is seated at table. Her bags, jacket, etc., lie in chair, denoting that she is coming in from work)

Mattie: I had a miscarriage once, and that was bad. But I guess in some ways an abortion is even worse.

Laura: Yes. This poem by Gwendolyn Brooks says . . . Well, the point is that you can have nine children but you'll always be missing the one you didn't have . . .

Mattie: Lord, keep that poem away from me 'cause it sure is the ugly truth . . . But, honey, even though you all weren't seeing eye to eye right then, still, was an abortion the only answer? . . .

Laura: With him acting like that, and me pregnant, all I could see was my mother and stepfather . . .

Mattie: Your mother? . . .

Laura: Yes . . . *(Moves to screen door)* Have you ever walked up on one of those ravaged little street dogs? The way they look at you so vulnerable; so hopeful of mercy, and kindness. But knowing better than to really expect it, so, all set to cry and duck . . . Well, that was my mother, facing him. Every single day. And she stayed there like that, in that—just, stayed there.

Mattie: Well, now, honey, maybe she had her reasons . . .

Laura: Umm hmmm. The three of us she had before she met him, and the two she had with him . . . Mattie, I would actually think that if I could just stay awake until they went to sleep just concentrate on that bedroom wall, pray hard enough, then, I could keep him from hitting her. Wouldn't have to wake up to her falling against that wall, crying, begging.

Mattie: Lord, today . . .

LAURA: *(Coming to table)* So, I sold my way into Aunt Cheryl and Uncle Mac's house. That was my first sale: I begged 'em to let me come stay with them. They knew what was going on so they let me come. And, Mattie, I was like, "I Dream of Jeannie"!

MATTIE: How you mean?

LAURA: I mean if they thought it, I did it. Before they could ask it.

MATTIE: You was right smart around there, huh? . . .

LAURA: Almost too smart. She told me one day: "Sugar, now you're about to make me look bad in fronta' my man. Leave me something to do. Least let him finish his cigarette before you empty the ashtray."

MATTIE: *(Laughing with her)* Whoa, mule! *I'm* runnin' this show! . . .

LAURA: Yes. But I wasn't taking any chances on being sent back—*home*. And by the time I was sixteen, I was making my own money. Paying my own way.

MATTIE: Well, strut, Miss Lady . . .

LAURA: *(Moving to door)* Yes, I knew how to get a job. I mean, I was cute, sexy, intelligent and knew how to present the package . . . *(Posturing, ala, a model)*

MATTIE: Well, alright, the truth is the light. Look like you still know how to present it, too . . .

LAURA: *(Looking out into hallway)* That's a matter of opinion. Think I'll have just one more . . . *(Coming to table for cookie/cookies)*

MATTIE: *(Continued)* Honey, why don't you go on and call him? Before you blow the roof off this house. And he blow a hole in wherever he is.

LAURA: Just what do you mean? I'll have you know that I'm in perfect control of my—my drives. Besides, that's exactly what he wants: for me to be calling him like I can't make it without him—him and his *big paychecks*. Mattie? You hear me? First with Miss Louise, and then on my own—I'm going to have my own company, own say-so, own power. You hear me? . . .

MATTIE: Yeah, I hear you, and, *see* you too.

LAURA: Please, spare me. Power. Yeah, that's what I did—mess with his sense of power. You know: A man's home is *his* castle? Yes, and he has dominion over all therein including you? At the very least, you know, he should be able to decide whether or not his wife is going to have a child, you know . . . *(Pacing)*

MATTIE: Sounds reasonable to me . . .

LAURA: Oh, sure. Just like his cows, chickens and dogs, should all mate and foal when he wants them to mate and foal. Aw, Mattie, you all are hopeless. It's that kind of man-based thinking that has women like you and my mother chained from the waist down, locked up in the dungeons of the Dark Ages! . . . *(Pacing)*

MATTIE: *(Growing peeved)* So, that's where I been all this time. Down there with your mama, huh? . . .

LAURA: *(Pacing)* I'm afraid so. I'll loan you some books. Power. That's all it is. *(As if quoting)* Those who have little or no power are constantly in danger of being either seduced, or dominated, by those who have. Yeah, those with the big paychecks.

MATTIE: And since he's obviously already seduced you, it's the domination's got you worried now, huh? . . .

(LAURA looks at her)

MATTIE: *(Continued)* Now, you hear this: I don't know about your mama, but when it comes to me and Frank? I think I did the first seducing, and when it comes to dominating it was just a matter of who had the best grip on the rope at the time. Understand? . . .

LAURA: Mattie, I'm sorry, I didn't mean . . .

MATTIE: Whatever you meant, Miss: You can climb just as high as you have to, but don't worry about kicking no dirt down in my face, honey, 'cause I know I'm standing on high ground. Four fine children, and six fine grandchildren? The near forty-six years I've been wrestling with my Frank to get 'em, keep 'em, and send 'em out proud and straight? Well, Missy, I'll stack that up against whoever, whatever, wherever.

LAURA: *(Affected; embarrassed)* I don't blame you, Mattie. I would too. I'm sorry. I'd better go.

MATTIE: Sorry ain't allowed in here but once, and you been here a few times. You ain't going nowhere. Just sit your little butt down there, and get some more tea . . .

LAURA: *(Taking Kleenex from her purse)* I have to go, Mattie . . . I'm so, ashamed . . .

MATTIE: Don't allow shame in here but once, either. So sit . . .

LAURA: Aw, Mattie . . . *(Moves to screen door)*

MATTIE: Aw, Mattie, what? . . .

(LAURA looks out screen door)

LAURA: Nothing . . . There's your Frank: Working at his flowers . . . I feel utterly ridiculous . . .

MATTIE: Well, that's better: Sorry and shame ain't welcome, but ridiculous is in and out of here all the time, honey.

LAURA: She's sure here now, Ms. Ridiculous: Trying to tell you what's what, after you've built all you have, you and Frank. So much understanding. Forty-six beautiful years. I can't stand it.

MATTIE: You see the parade: the marching bands with the medals and polished boots. But, now, you didn't see the war. *(Laughs)* Even the crippled and the crazy look good in the parade! But the war, now, honey, that was something else altogether! . . .

(LAURA joins in her infectious laughter. Lights dim on them.

Up MEMORY LIGHT. MATTIE moves to join FRANK in STAGE RIGHT area. Drinking from a pint bottle FRANK has on WWII jacket and boots with dungarees)

FRANK: . . . And I seen these polacks, eyeing my jacket, my medals. Lookin' like they wanted to spit on 'em. I said, "Why don't you snatch it off me, why don't you? Like they doin' them boys in Mississippi! And Texas! And St. Louis! Come on! Take it off me!" Wish he woulda'. Fought an' bled for this. Earned it like a man. Gone wear it till I die. Whipped out my knife and dared 'em, the sonofabitches!

MATTIE: But what about the job, Frank? What about the job?

FRANK: Wasn't no job for no man, Mattie. Nigga' job! Sweepin' they flo's. Cleaning they toilets. Wouldn't accept it. Won't accept it . . .

MATTIE: *(Stunned)* Won't accept it? Well, what you gon' do? Now the war's over they put us women outta' the factories. We got these babies in there. We got to take what we can get, Frank.

FRANK: I ain't got to take no nigga' nothin'! We went over there and fought, and died, and killed, for this place! Understand me! Done fought and killed for it! Now they gon' give the white boys they jobs back? And tell us to take low? Step down? Clean they damn toilets? Well I ain't acceptin' it!

(HE turns away from her, drinking)

MATTIE: Some of the whites can't get they jobs back, man. Listen to me. I gotta' go out there and do day work! Clean they whole houses, wash they dirty draw's. Everyday! For these babies. So, don't tell me what you won't accept! *(SHE flails at his back in frustration)*

FRANK: Get off me! . . . *(HE slaps her, then grips her shoulders)* . . . You want to keep me a nigga'! Well, I done been places! Seen things! Been treated like a man, woman! A man! And I ain't gon' take being treated like no nigga' no more! Hear me? . . . I can't stand being no nigga' no more! . . .

(SHE sobs/screams more from the intensity of his change than from pain. HE pushes her away as though SHE were an affront. CHILDREN [OFFSTAGE] cry, call for their mother)

FRANK: *(Continued) (To children, OFF)* Shut up! Shut 'em up, dammit! . . . I can't stand it! Gotta' get outta' this—nigga' house! . . .

(HE exits. MATTIE consoles unseen CHILDREN)

MATTIE: Hush. Shhhh. It's alright. It's alright. Daddy jus' drunk. He didn't mean it. Go on back to bed, now. Go 'head . . . *(SHE moves to shout OFF RIGHT as if to FRANK)* Frank? . . . Frank? . . . Where you gon'? . . . You comin' back? *(Tearfully)* You comin' baaaackkk? . . .

(Lights fade as SHE crosses, consoling the CHILDREN.

Up on MATTIE and LAURA in kitchen, laughing. Obviously MATTIE hasn't told LAURA any of what we've just seen. MATTIE comes back into room)

LAURA: I swore I would never get married. Should have kept my promise to myself . . .

MATTIE: Those kind don't count; not by young girls.

LAURA: Guess not. Scared of getting married didn't seem normal, right. So now what? So now I've done it twice. The first time I barely got through two and a half years—and now looks like I won't make one.

MATTIE: Oh, I think you two will be alright. Must've been awfully young that first time.

LAURA: Yes. But then, too, Curtis thought of himself as some kind of charm bracelet: we women were the charms, and the more of us he could have dangling, the better he looked.

MATTIE: I've seen plenty them kind.

LAURA: Then whenever I would confront him with anything, he would become my stepfather.

MATTIE: Oh?

LAURA: Yes, Curtis liked to holler and hit too. What right did I have to complain about anything: He was bringing in good money, while I was "Playing School," he called it. Sometimes after he had hit, belittled, and intimidated me, I would sit up all day and night thinking of ways to kill him: castration, burning . . .

MATTIE: Oh, my . . .

LAURA: One night I just got dressed, got the gun—he had bought me for the house. He was sleeping. I got up on the bed and grabbed his hair. *(Doing actions on/across kitchen chair)* Stuck the gun in his face and said, "Wake up, Curt! You see this? I'm leaving. One of us has to go before they have to carry both of us out of here."

MATTIE: My . . . Does Mr. Sylvester know about that? I mean about the gun? I hear him raring up pretty rough up there sometimes.

LAURA: No, he doesn't know about that. But he knows something. Feels something. When he start going up, and he sees me getting all trembly and everything, he stops himself. Cools out. I think he doesn't want to be identified with all that, my stepfather and Curtis, you know.

MATTIE: Well how did Mr. Sylvester get through all that to get you to do it again and marry him?

LAURA: I don't know, I think the truth is: I'm gonna' have a man, one way or another . . .

MATTIE: Uhh huhhh. A hot box like me and my youngest, Emily.

(THEY laugh)

LAURA: Oo, Mattie! Yes, he came bopping around with that salesman's smile. Yes, but when he came with that engagement ring. I hit the pause button again: He looked for all the world like a mischievous cowboy coming with a rope and a branding iron. But I sure didn't want anyone else to have him . . .

MATTIE: So, ride cowboy ride, huh . . .

LAURA: *(Laughter as SHE moves to door; staring down hallway)* So I should just march on over to Jeff's and give Syl his orders to come home, huh? . . . Tell him three weeks is long enough, huh?

MATTIE: Yes, mam. Tell him you need some work done at the house and he's the only one who can do it right. *(Winks)*

LAURA: *(Laughs)* I'll think about it. I'd better get upstairs and at least *look* at this work I brought home.

MATTIE: Alright, honey. Thanks for dropping in.

LAURA: Thank you—for listening.

(THEY BOTH stop as THEY hear car door slam. SYL comes in front door, goes up steps, knocks at their door, finds door unlocked, goes in, calling for LAURA, goes OFF REAR. LAURA looks to MATTIE. FRANK is coming in back door with a flower, freshly picked)

MATTIE: Remember, honey: Advice is cheap, it's action makes a payday.

FRANK: Well, I brung one pretty flower for one beautiful lady, and now I need two. Should I give it to the one who lives here? Or the one who's the guest?

LAURA: I'll take mine next time, Mr. Cooper. Thanks, Mattie.

MATTIE: Go head now . . . .

(LAURA exits to hallway. FRANK offers MATTIE flower)

FRANK: Well that makes the decision for me.

MATTIE: *(Bowing)* Thank you, sir . . .

FRANK: You're welcome, mam . . .

MATTIE: *(Coyly, exiting)* Think I'll put this in the bedroom . . .

FRANK: Let me help you find the spot for it . . .

(THEY exit kitchen. LAURA has entered apartment on UPPER LEVEL. SYL comes from back, comes down. THEY stare across at each other. HE reaches into inside suit pocket, pulls out red rose, offers it to her in truce. SHE runs over to kiss him/wrap her legs around his waist, HE carries her off to bedroom.

Lights up on MATTIE in robe coming to sink to drink, picks up large, ancient butcher knife; stares at it as SHE moves to upstage side of table)

FRANK: *(Offstage)* Mattie? . . .

(SHE doesn't answer)

FRANK: *(Offstage, continued)* Mattie? . . .

MATTIE: *(Lower)* What? . . .

FRANK: *(Offstage)* —Mattie?—

MATTIE: *(Louder)* What? . . .

FRANK: *(Offstage)* What you doin'? You alright? . . .

MATTIE: I'm alright . . .

FRANK: *(Offstage)* What? . . .

MATTIE: I'm fine! Leave me alone! Go on back to sleep! . . .

(FRANK stands in MEMORY LIGHT, hat in hand, HE wears crisply pressed work clothes under his army jacket. MATTIE walks to him wearing a sweater over her housedress, carrying the large butcher knife, SHE comes calmly)

FRANK: Hello, Mattie.

MATTIE: Hello, Frank.

FRANK: Why you got that butcher knife?

MATTIE: Cutting chickens.

FRANK: Could've left it to come out.

MATTIE: Thought it might help you get it in your mind that I ain't takin' no more whippins from you. Don't deserve none. Ain't takin' none.

FRANK: I'm sorry about that, Mattie. Just back from the war, wasn't in my proper mind.

MATTIE: Yes. And Tim and Cora ain't takin' no more of your kickin' in their screen door either. You owe me money for that.

FRANK: Well they had my family locked up in there.

MATTIE: Your family asked to be here.

FRANK: And did you have to tell everybody down home about our troubles? First my family calling, then yours. Making me feel like I killed Jesus or something.

MATTIE: That's what family is for, to come to the aid. Family is about all we got.

FRANK: I know, Mattie, I know. That's why I come back. Had to. You and the kids. But I had to hold on to what I had over there. I didn't want to forget what it felt like.

MATTIE: What? Your Frenchwoman? . . .

(HE looks)

MATTIE: *(Continued)* Yes, I found your letters. And burned every damned one. The whore! . . .

FRANK: *(A beat, turns away)* She wasn't no—whore, Mattie. No, she wasn't. And it wasn't her. It was me. Me over there. They put their arms around my shoulders, Mattie. White men, Frenchmen—and looked me in the eye, and invited me to their tables, their homes. I stood up all the way straight for the first time in my life, and that old nigga' stuff just fell off—didn't fit no more. And then I come back home, and . . . Anyhow, I ain't gon' never forget how it felt. How it's supposed to feel.

MATTIE: *(A beat)* If it takes a white man's arms around you to make you feel like somebody, then I guess you gonna' be in a lotta' trouble over here, Frank.

FRANK: *(A beat)* You always was a smart-butt wasn't you?

(SHE smiles)

FRANK: *(Continued)* Well, look. See that truck there? Belong to Buck Johnson, my partner. You take that butcher knife back to Miss Cora and bring my kids outta' there. I'm gonna' show you this place I can rent—make up for the one I made us lose. If you like it we can move in this evening.

MATTIE: You workin', Frank? . . .

FRANK: Yeah, I took one a them sorry jobs at the factory. But ain't having it long. Another thing I found out over there is I can build anything once I see how it works. So me and Buck gonna' have a construction company. But before that, we got this janitorial service started. And till we can afford a crew, you and his wife, Alma, gonna' be working right alongside us. So, time's a wasting now, if you comin', come on . . .

(HE crosses. SHE stands stunned)

MATTIE: *(Hands on hips)* Well, I'll think about it, Mr. Cooper. *(Turns and runs off)* Frank Jr.! Ellie!—Get ready! . . . We goin' wit yo' daddy! . . .

(MATTIE chuckles as MEMORY LIGHT fades. SHE crosses back into kitchen)

FRANK: *(Offstage)* Mattie? What you doin' out there this time a' night? Come on to bed.

(MATTIE puts down knife; goes off)

MATTIE: Well, I'll think about it, Mr. Cooper.

FRANK: What?! . . .

(Then THEY BOTH laugh in memory.

Lights up on UPPER LEVEL, next morning. Laughter, playful shouts. SYL comes running from OFF bedroom area carrying Sunday papers, wearing only pajama bottoms, dragging blanket with him. Flops on couch)

LAURA: *(Offstage)* Come back here! . . .

SYL: Nooo. I've gotta get some air! Take a break. God. Read my papers out here, where I can get some peace! P-E-A-C-E . . . not P-I-E-C-E!

(LAURA comes on)

LAURA: Creep . . .

SYL: I'll be creepin' and crawlin' too, I stay back there with you . . .

(LAURA sits across arm of couch, prods him with her foot)

LAURA: Coppin' out . . .

SYL: Uh-huh, now I know how you're gonna' punish me for leaving you: you gonna' screw me to death . . .

LAURA: Just can't handle it. Getting old on me already . . .

SYL: Listen, I've put your lights out—two—three—times, counting this morning. I'm trying to take it easy on you. Don't want your heart to stop beating . . .

LAURA: Aw, jive ass . . .

(LAURA plunges on top of him)

SYL: Look out, fool! Tearing up my paper! . . . Trying to see what time the games come on . . .

LAURA: Oh, no! No T.V.! I'm the game today . . .

(SHE comes over the back of the couch to lay on him, snatch the paper. HE manages to sit up, pin her down across his lap)

SYL: Quit. Stop! Be still! Wild hussy! Go call yo' Mama, or somethin' . . . *(Takes paper back; reads holding her down)* That damn Jordan and the Bulls, playing my Pistons. Hill and the boys gon' get 'em this time . . .

LAURA: Let me go, Creep! . . . *(Gets up, goes around to back of couch)* Gonna' ask my friend the psychologist what it means when a man would rather look at other men in shorts, than his own naked woman.

SYL: I'll tell you what it means: Means he's tired! That's what it means.

LAURA: Uh-huh. Losing your grip, that's all.

SYL: Challenging my ego won't work either.

LAURA: Well it's really not worth all this effort anyway.

(SHE starts out, nose in air, looks back and laughs at his look)

SYL: Ain't what you said last night! . . . *(Turns to paper)* Utah at Utah. Ought to give 'em thirty free throws before the game starts. Let everybody know it's crooked. *(Phone rings)* . . . If that's Jeff or one of them, tell 'em I'm not here! . . . Gonna' just relax: be with my Pistons and my lady . . .

(LAURA is heard on phone . . . "Just a minute." Then SHE peeps through rear drapes/curtains)

LAURA: Think maybe you'd better take it.

SYL: *(Irritated)* I told you—who is it?—

LAURA: Dan, says he want to make sure you come into the office in the morning. For the meeting? . . .

SYL: *(Getting up)* Dan? . . . The Monday morning meeting? That automatic bullshit? *(Crosses to phone in living room as LAURA exits out behind curtain)* Hey, Dan . . . Know this must be fricking traumatic. Messing with my Sunday, and my Pistons . . . *(To LAURA)* . . . I got it, baby! . . . *(Listening)* Sure, I can make it. But, Dan, what's the deal? Those Monday morning things are for rookies and fuck-ups, Dan . . . Alright. Alright. I'll be there. But come on, Dan, give me a freaking peep. What's up? . . . I know I'll know when I get there. I wanna know something, now. Yeah, Dan, and milk grows on trees . . . Huh? . . . Come on, Dan, prep me on this meeting now.—Bullshit, Dan. Come one, now . . . *(Looks at receiver, indicating a hang up)* Fat ass.

(Slowly, thoughtfully, puts receiver down. LAURA comes in with towel, wearing shower-cap)

LAURA: Brunch at the Harlequin? I'll leave the water running for you. Or are you man enough to join me?

SYL: *(Crossing to couch)* I've gotta do some thinking . . .

LAURA: Oh, I've really scared you, haven't I? I promise not to be so aggressive in the future.

SYL: *(Looks at her)* Please. I'm serious. The referees about to put some do-do in the game.

LAURA: The Bulls and the Pistons?

SYL: Naw. Those snakes at the office. When they want everybody at a Monday meeting they're about to drop a hammer on somebody. Who? Who!—Jackson? Naw, they've already got him stuck on nothing but those jungle routes. Riding around behind his trucks, carrying a pistol. Jarrett! Naw, his nose is browner than his ass . . . One of the white boys? Who? Naw, it's got to be me. What? Where?

LAURA: You sure you aren't being a little premature? Just a little paranoid?

SYL: *(Stands to look at her)* Look, I've told you about using those words with me. I ain't no paro-nothing. I'm aware of what is going on around me. What I'm dealing with. And that makes me nervous. Yeah, uh-huh. So, if you can't come with nothing better than that para-bull, then "help the bear."

LAURA: Help the what? . . .

SYL: Help the bear. That means if you see me and a bear fighting and you can't come with something better than that paranoid—something good and strong—then help the bear, 'cause you ain't no help to me.

(HE comes away from her)

LAURA: Oh, I see. I'm no help to you, huh? Well you and that bear can both go to hell.

(SHE exits out. HE starts after her)

SYL: I didn't say you were no . . . Shittt . . . *(Stops. Sighs. Exits to telephone table. Looks through address book. Dials number)* Jarrett? . . . Syl Williams, brother, what's going on? What are they cooking up for this meeting tomorrow? . . . Aw, man, you know you're in with the white folks.

(LAURA, literally growling through the curtains, wearing a fur coat, wielding a pillow. Throws it at him. HE blocks it. SHE growls again, snatches pillow from couch, throws it at him)

SYL: *(Ouching)* What the hell? . . .

LAURA: Grwwww . . . I'm helping the bear! . . . Grr-rr . . .

(SHE beats chest growling)

SYL: *(Chuckling)* Jarrett, I'll call you back. Gotta deal with a bear . . . Call you right back . . .

(Growling, SHE whips off the coat and whacks him with it, once, twice, then runs laughing around the couch. As HE pursues)

LAURA: I quit. I quit. Half-time . . .

SYL: *(Blocking her at head of couch)* Aw-naw! First I'll deal with you. *(Looks at phone)* Then I'll get back to that bear.

(Squealing with laughter SHE runs out. HE runs off after her. Black.

Lights up on LOWER LEVEL, a few weeks later. MATTIE is cutting out supermarket coupons as FRANK enters from LEFT. HE comes to MATTIE at table, taking check from his shirt pocket; shows it to her, puts it back in pocket)

FRANK: That boy up there give me they rent. Bet most of it come from her much as he's been laying around the house here lately . . .

MATTIE: I don't think they have much trouble paying the rent, Frank. Rarely been late . . .

FRANK: Probably thanks to her.

MATTIE: He carries his rightful weight seems to me . . .

FRANK: Hmph. Then how come he spends so much time sitting round here lately? Somedays he don't even have on them funny shirts and ties no more. Looking like a bum . . .

MATTIE: Frank, ain't in no mood to hear you picking at them young people up there, today, now.

FRANK: Not them, him! It burns me up, Mattie.

MATTIE: *What* burns you? . . .

FRANK: It don't make no sense, Mattie. Folks paying him good money to sit around doing nothing and men out here—good men—just dying for something to do. Some kinda' work. Burns me good.

MATTIE: *(After beat)* Well if *you're* dying for something to do, you can get that step out back there.

FRANK: I got that step this morning. Could run a fourteen-wheel truck over it and it wouldn't even squeak.

MATTIE: Thank you.

FRANK: She said there was a leak up there, must be coming from the roof. Maybe I'll go up take a look . . .

MATTIE: You're not going up on that roof! Now that's the end of that.

FRANK: Hmph. That's what I'm talking about. Paying him for nothing and don't want a man to keep on at his own business! Too old, hmph. My own son, young puppy, telling me to stay away from my own business.

MATTIE: Didn't tell you, he asked you. And me and the doctor both agreed with him.

FRANK: Know you did, all ganging up on me.

MATTIE: If youda' went down there and stayed in the office, handled what you could, like somebody with some sense, it would've been alright. But naw, you wanta' go out with the crews, run everything, just like you did twenty-thirty years ago.

FRANK: Aw, you don't know what you talking about.

MATTIE: Don't? And the strain, the stress, had your blood pressure knocking you down every other week. It was time for you to let go, Frank. You still get a percentage. And by God's grace, we don't need the money. So why you in such a hurry to make me a rich widow? . . .

FRANK: Aw, woman. I'm tireda' talkin' to you. Goin' go—Go on deposit this rent check at the bank.

MATTIE: You don't have—

(HE looks at her)

MATTIE: *(Continued)* Well, wait a minute and I'll go with you.

FRANK: I don't need you goin' with me. I look like some schoolboy to you? The bank ain't moved. In the same place it was the last time I went. I'll find it there again. Don't need you tagging along like a shirttail.

(HE starts out, stops, pulling pockets, as if looking for something)

MATTIE: The check's in your shirt pocket. Your key's on the ledge there.

(Glaring at her, HE gets his keys)

FRANK: I swear one of these days I'm gonna' cover your mouth with masking tape. Have me some peace around here—

(Grumbles. HE exits kitchen)

MATTIE: You drive careful out there.

FRANK: Goin' do eighty all the way! Drive all the way to Paris . . .

(Laughs. HE goes OFF. MATTIE gets up from table and comes to kitchen door)

MATTIE: Hey, old man! Just let me tell you one thing! . . .

(HE slams front door. MATTIE stands with fists on hips, staring. Lights dim on LOWER LEVEL.

Up on UPPER LEVEL. SYL comes through rear curtain carrying phone)

SYL: Well, when you hear from him, you tell Mr. Dan that he can reach me at home. Tell him we have to get a few things clear. And the clearer the better, okay? Thank you, Maggie. Bye-Bye. *(HE hangs phone up, places it on stand. Goes over to turn on radio to jazz station. Goes OFF REAR, comes back with beer. Phone rings. HE answers)* Sylvester Williams, here . . . Hey, Jeff. Way I answer during business hours. You dig . . . What? . . . Oh, yeah? . . . Naw, I don't think so. I've got a lot on my head right now. I'll tell you what . . . Wait a second . . . Think I hear my old lady pulling up . . . *(Sound of car door)* . . . Yeah, that's her. I'm going to pass, man. Whatever. Talk to you later . . .

(Hangs up. Sits at desk intently going over papers. LAURA comes up the stairs, carrying her now proverbial apparel bags and paraphernalia. SHE enters, dropping bags, and immediately removes shoes)

LAURA: Hi . . . Get your business straight? . . .

SYL: *(Look)* I'm getting it straight.

LAURA: Really? What's the move? . . .

SYL: *(Glad to air plans)* Okay, now they didn't expect me to get into that district, right? But I did. So they pull me back in the office with a bullshit title and a bullshit raise. To do what? Supervise Jackson. Yeah, since "You came from that district." Damn right I did, and I'm not going back. Jackson doesn't need a supervisor. He needs a fifty-man security guard. It's a setup. That's what it is.

LAURA: For what? . . .

SYL: For phase-out. This new deal, outstate new district that they're *thinking of, maybe,* having me develop—is all too vague . . .

LAURA: So, baby, your move is? . . .

SYL: Make 'em make the district and the deal clear. And if a familiar odor comes rising from it, then I'm letting 'em know I'm going to the Fair Employment Commission and file a case. Damn good one too: all the sales increases, the money, I've brought in this year. Shit. I got a case.

LAURA: Yes. But, Syl? Baby? They know about the sales and the money, too. Right? . . .

SYL: Hell, yeah, they know.

LAURA: Well, I mean, they're not stupid. Not going to hurt their own business. Maybe they're sincere about the promotion. The new district.

SYL: *(A beat)* Now when you tell me about bullshit being dumped on you at that store, I automatically assume you know what you're talking about, and get on your side . . .

LAURA: *(Anticipating)* Oh, Lord . . .

SYL: But I can tell you that I got into it with a junkie on some corner, and you'll say, "Maybe the man had a point." I've always got to be wrong. Why is that?

LAURA: I didn't say that you were . . . I just . . . Forget it, okay? Just forget it . . . *(Goes to bar for a bottled water)*

SYL: Yeah, forget it. I damn near created a whole new district over there. Me. Scheming, maneuvering, hustling my black butt off. Yeah, yeah, a black ant in a bowl of milk trying to make some butter. And now they're going to take it? And give it to some blond dust mop? Who can't do nothing but put up corny displays. And talk like T.V. commercials. Guess I'm supposed to forget that too, huh?

LAURA: Syl. Please. All I was saying was that maybe they truly recognized and appreciate how good you are—and, maybe, just possibly, the promotion and the new district are real. That's all. A positive attitude . . .

(SHE goes to her samples, garments, begins looking through them. HE comes to lean on couch)

SYL: Positive attitude! Listen: If they start their cut-back game and I'm sitting there supervising a district that doesn't need any supervising, I could be out. Gone! From top salesman to zilch. Understand? They're trying to take money out of my pocket! Out of our joint-account pocket! . . .

LAURA: You don't have to holler at *me*, Syl. I wouldn't like that any more than you would. So if there's anything I can do to help, just tell me . . .

(SHE snatches up garb and goes OFF)

SYL: *(To himself)* A sympathetic attitude might have helped. But you blew that.

(HE fixes himself a drink, as we hear her moving about; turning on the shower. Kitchen sounds: rattling dishes; then—cussing. SHE comes through rear curtain)

LAURA: *(Frustrated; near tears)* Syl? You've been here all day and you haven't washed a dish?

SYL: *(A beat)* I did have a few other things to do. You know? . . .

LAURA: Don't we all. But I called you from work; asked you to thaw the meat out. Not cook it—though that would have been feasibly considerate. But, no, just thaw it out. That's all I asked. And you couldn't even do that?

SYL: I had a few other things on my mind.

LAURA: *(Holding breath)* If the situations were reversed and I told you that—how would you feel, Syl? What would you do? . . .

SYL: Probably cuss and grumble for a minute; then I'd go on out and get me something to eat.

LAURA: You're right. Absolutely right. Won't even shower. Just wash up, and go.

SYL: Go where? . . .

(SHE exits. HE seems about to follow her; then goes to bar. Phone rings. HE answers)

SYL: *(Continued)* Sylvester Williams, here. Oh, hey, Jackson . . . Hold it, Jackson. Hold it. Let's not play gladiators for the Romans, okay? . . . I mean, don't dump all this shit on me . . . Hold it. You know and I know that you don't need no supervising. It's not you, but me, they're putting the screw on, okay. So, let's just play straight, alright? Cover your ass with reports. If I have any questions on it, I'll call you, cool? . . . Sure, we can have a meeting if you want one. *(Pause; then wryly)* Jackson? I'm not over or underestimating your understanding of the situation, am I? . . . Nothing. We'll meet tomorrow. Take care . . . Yeah.

(HE lowers the phone sighing, shaking his head. LAURA comes through rear curtain; blouseless in a strikingly sexy skirt and net stockings outfit; becoming more striking as SHE takes high heels from bag left on couch and slips them on. Watching her SYL is affected both positively and negatively—the latter because she is leaving.)

SYL: *(Casual)* Where you goin'?

LAURA: *(Straightening stocking seam)* To tend to my business.

SYL: I asked you where you're goin'? . . .

LAURA: And I told you: to take care of my business.

(SHE starts REAR. HE springs after her, grabbing her by shoulders and turning her to face him)

SYL: I said where the fuck you goin'? . . .

(SHE is instantly into the Mother-Memory; body hunched; eyes closed, hands raised as to ward off blows. HE sees it and releases her shoulders, tries to touch her face, frame it, reassuringly)

LAURA: Don't . . . Don't . . . Please . . .

SYL: Baby, Laura . . . Laura . . . Baby, you know I ain't gonna' hurt you. Do nothin' to you . . .

LAURA: Don't touch . . . Don't . . . Move . . . Get away . . . Get . . . Away . . .

SYL: *(Moving away)* Laura, I didn't . . . All you had to do was tell me where you were going . . .

LAURA: *(Difficult breathing)* I'm going—going to do—this show—for Louise . . . Possible investors . . . Can't afford two models . . . So—I'm modeling for him. Is it alright, sir. Can I . . . Daddy? Can I go out? . . . Cigarette . . .

SYL: Don't need no cigarette. Laura. Look, it's all these pressures from the job. I can't get it all . . .

LAURA: Don't talk to me about pressures, Syl. 'Cause when I'm under pressure I'm still supposed to wash and cook, and be polite, and listen to you carrying on about *your* pressures. I'm still supposed . . .

SYL: Alright! Okay! I know the whole damn speech, okay! I said I'm sorry. And you got somewhere to go! So go 'head on! Go on take care of your business! And I'll take care of mine.

(HE turns record player on high, it is Duke Ellington's '56 version of "Diminuendo And Crescendo In Blue." HE keeps turning it higher as HE looks at her)

LAURA: Talk when you want to talk. Listen when you want to listen, huh? . . . Well . . . *(Shouting)* Okay—*Sir*! Okay . . . *Daddy*!

(SHE goes out; starts downstairs. HE rushes over, seems about to open door; then slams fist against door, hurting his hand)

SYL: Fuck! . . .

(Shaking hand HE goes over to turn record player off. SHE hesitates hearing knock against door, the cussing. Goes back upstairs; opens door)

LAURA: You alright? . . .

SYL: Just get whatever you forgot and go 'head on! . . .

LAURA: *(Beat)* I forgot I didn't have anything to come back for.

(SHE goes down steps. SHE slams downstairs door behind her. HE goes to phone, dials)

SYL: Jeff? . . . Those people still there? . . . Well tell her to stay there till I get there . . . Naw. Just tell her to wait . . . Tell her to wait!!

(Hangs up. Lights lower on music—Paul Gonslavez' mounting sax solo. Lights up on LOWER LEVEL [daytime], kitchen area. MATTIE and LAURA sit)

LAURA: And he asked me to wait. To have a drink with him afterward. Just he and I, and I did. It's the third time now we've been out alone. Lunches before, now this.

MATTIE: Ummm. And what's his name. This big businessman?

LAURA: Ralph. Ralph Richardson.

MATTIE: Ummm. I know some Richardsons.

LAURA: And I know that part of the reason I agreed to go at all, to model and all that, was because I knew he'd be there.

MATTIE Kinda like him, huh, this Ralph?

LAURA: *(Shrugs)* Curious. Interested. Yes, I like him. I don't really want to. But I guess the truth is I do. Mattie, he's—I mean he's a hard businessman, and all that. But he is so sensitized to everything, so understanding. Mattie, he really listens to me. You know? He *listens*.

MATTIE: Hunters always listen, honey. It's after they've been well fed that they start to falling to sleep on you. You haven't fed him yet, have you?

LAURA: *(Mock indignation)* Mattie, that is *not* your business. No . . . I haven't—fed him. Yet.

MATTIE: Good. 'Cause you want to think about it real good, honey.

LAURA: I know, I know.

MATTIE: Ummm hmmm. 'Cause people with problems get to thinking they can subtract by adding, and wind up multiplying.

LAURA: What? Would you repeat that, Mattie? I'd like to remember that . . .

(THEY laugh. Lights up on FRANK going to upstairs door, wearing overalls, perhaps carrying tool box. HE knocks at door. SYL enters from rear drinking morning-after cup of coffee)

SYL: Laura?! . . .

FRANK: No. It's Mr. Cooper from downstairs. Wanna look at that leak your wife's complaining about.

(SYL makes a face, goes reluctantly to open door. FRANK comes in, closes door, stands waiting, watching SYL as HE goes to look at work papers on the desk. FRANK drops tool box. SYL looks up with questioning look)

FRANK: *(Continued)* Where is the leak?

SYL: Oh, in the kitchen. Right up above the cabinet.

(FRANK goes OFF REAR. SYL holds his heavy head. Goes to pick up papers from coffee table. FRANK comes back ON)

FRANK: *(Goes to tool box)* I see it. Got some of this instant sealant, downstairs. Just mix it with some water. Goes on like plaster. But won't stop it long. Just come in somewhere else. Gotta get on the roof.

SYL: *(Absently)* Yeah, I know. That's what I told Laura.

FRANK: Yeah, I see you patched one spot. Didn't think this kinda work be in your line. Since you can't do it on the telephone.

SYL: Oh, Lord, I think that chick was right. Bad karma. Need to meditate, or pray, or something. Now which of my cosmic errors brings you up here?

FRANK: What—what brings me up here?

SYL: *(Takes a beat to focus)* Forget it, man. I read your little dig about the telephone. Since I don't leave here every morning wearing overalls. And carrying a lunchpail and a pick and shovel, I'm not working. Right? But your rent's all paid up, right. So, I really don't have to be listening to you, talking to you, now do I?

FRANK: Let me tell *you* something, boy. Long as you're renting from me, you gon' talk to me, if I want you to.

SYL: *(A slow beat)* That chick was a prophet.

FRANK: *(Defensively)* What you say? . . .

SYL: Somebody told me at a little party last night, that my spirit was in turmoil. Bad karma. Aura like porcupine quills she said must've set out some cosmic error. But if I'd be still, meditate, pray, then the forces would send me a messenger as a sign. Some incident. Some person. And if I was attentive, aware, I would get . . .

FRANK: What? . . .

SYL: *(Salesman's charm)* No problem. You drink Strohs, don't you? Yeah? A Strohs man. I've seen you. Just sit tight and I'll get you one out of the fridge. Give you a six-pack to carry out.

FRANK: What? Aw, naw, I'm gon' patch that leak and leave you in your foolishness.

SYL: *(Half serious, half filling time)* Aw, you can't do that, pops. You're the messenger from The Forces. I'll get the Strohs. Then you just sit back and lay it on me. *(HE exits rear)*

FRANK: *(A beat)* The forces?? . . . A damn devil worshipper. That's what he is: a damn devil worshipper.

(As lights fade, HE goes OFF REAR to spy on SYL in kitchen. Lights up on LOWER LEVEL. LAURA standing looking out back screen door. MATTIE sitting at table with flowers)

MATTIE: So what did Syl say when you come in last night? . . .

LAURA: This morning really. And that was funny: He wasn't home. So right away I stopped resenting him and started missing him. Worrying about him, about us. But when he finally did come in, about an hour or so later, I pretended I was asleep. And when he took a pillow and went out to sleep on the couch, I was—relieved. Because I—I wasn't sure how I would feel if he—touched me . . .

MATTIE: That bad, huh?

LAURA: Sometimes. I guess this all sounds pretty awful to you, Mattie. I mean you've been with Frank forty-five years—

MATTIE: Forty-six.

LAURA: *(Continues)* And here I am barely in my second marriage, talking about meeting some other man.

MATTIE: Well, it doesn't sound good.

LAURA: I know, but well it was different for your generation. Mattie, your whole focus, orientation, was the home, neighbors, church. But nowadays we're out there in the world, the marketplace. Meeting all kinds of new people everyday. Just like the men do. All kinds of new—people. I mean the comparisons, the interactions are inevitable.

MATTIE: Well. When we went to work in those factories during the war, *all* men weren't overseas fighting. There were plenty of them in the plants with us. Like you say, all kinds—interacting and comparing. And some of our husbands and boyfriends were gone a long time. An awful long time, for young and healthy as we were.

LAURA: How did you handle that, Mattie? I mean, young and healthy as you were? . . .

MATTIE: And *that* is none of your business. Put those flowers on the table for me.

LAURA: Yes, mam . . .

(As LAURA moves to cabinet, MATTIE tends to pot on the stove. MEMORY LIGHT glows DOWN FRONT, MATTIE stares at it, moves into it as YOUNG MATTIE. As SHE begins SHE mimes putting clothes back on)

MATTIE: You know what I'm trying to say? . . . War is like some kind of tornado . . . shaking up and splitting off everything. Half the house end up in another county. Woman here, man—over there. I just got to feelin' like . . . like I was gonna' shake to pieces, going dizzy, crazy. You think maybe they just not tellin' me? You think that he's in a hospital somewhere, hurt, and they just not tellin' me? . . . No! . . . *(Pushing, fighting off)* No! . . . No. Just—sit down! Get away! . . . Get . . . Leave me be . . . No, now . . . You don't know. You don't know . . . No, you . . .

You don't even have a—a face no more. You're just something that happens to me in the dark sometimes, when I close my eyes . . . And when I open my eyes? I hear my babies cryin'—'cause I ain't home. No, I'm not gonna' let this war rip up this family . . . No. I'm sorry if I hurt you, but I got to go, Got to go . . . *(She starts to leave; then struggles against a touch, an embrace)* No. No, now. Stop . . . Going where? Going home . . . To what? To my babies . . . Noo. Nooo . . . Ohh, naw, naww . . . Noooo . . . Noooo . . . Just this one last time . . . One more . . . Then no more . . . No more, you hear? Just this one last—

(She goes into embrace . . . Then she leaves Memory Light as it fades; moves back into the present with Laura who watches her as she stands at stove, staring out, remembering)

Laura: *(Suspiciously)* What you thinking about, Miss Mattie? About how young and healthy you were? Huh? . . .

Mattie: If you wasn't there, then I guess you musta missed it, little ol' gal . . .

Laura: *(Going to chair)* Well, excuse me . . .

(They laugh. Lights lower on them)

Mattie: Help me carry these flowers up front.

Laura: Yes M'am . . .

(Come up on Upper Level. Syl sits in chair across from Frank on couch. There are two cans of opened beer)

Frank: So what's your pay? How much you make a week?

Syl: *(Pause)* You're the messenger. You're supposed to be telling me things.

Frank: Bet it's more than five dollars a day. That's what Ford was paying us. Five a day. That's what we made. Now how much you getting that you think ain't enough?

Syl: Well it's a lot more than five. But then my rent's a lot more than yours was, right? . . .

Frank: *(Chuckles)* Well, naturally the cost of everything done gon' up since then.

Syl: Yeah, so when you gonna tell me something I don't know, messenger?

Frank: *(Considers)* You tell me something.

Syl: . . . What's that? . . .

Frank: How come lately you been sitting around here looking like some kind of bum? . . . Mean you used to go out here looking all crisp with your briefcase and all. Make a ol' horse like me feel good. Feel proud . . .

Syl: *(Surprised)* Proud? You? About me? . . .

Frank: *(Somewhat embarrassed)* Well, ones like you, you and my sons, going out to work with white shirts, ties, make us old-timers feel like we done something. I mean, we paved the way, you know. Built up that ladder y'all climbing up on, you know.

SYL: *(Touched)* Yeah. So you all—uh—identify with us, us young group, huh? Proud of us.

FRANK: Well, y'all ain't done so great such a much. But—Well, like they say in church, we's all one family. There's a communion, a connection . . . Yeah, makes us feel good to see y'all doing good.

SYL: That's . . . that's nice, Mr.—Cooper. Yeah. My old man used to say things like that to me before he—passed on—

FRANK: *(After a beat)* Yeah, well bet he wouldn't like the way you been sitting around here lately. Makes us feel like we's falling back: backsliding.

SYL: Yeah, I guess that's one way of putting it, backsliding.

FRANK: What church you go to?

SYL: Mostly, I don't . . .

FRANK: Ummmm Hmmmm. And who do think is the Lord? . . .

SYL: I haven't worked my way up that high, yet.

FRANK: How's that? . . . *(A bloodhound on the scent)*

SYL: See, it's like you're my *landlord*, here. Right? And at work, I've got some more *lords*. And they tell me they've got a lord somewhere. And it goes on that way, up to where people say there's a Lord up over the whole thing—the earth, the galaxy, everything. I haven't worked up that high, yet. Heard a lot about He, She, or It . . . But I've never met Him, Her or What, yet.

FRANK: Well if you don't know the boss how you going to know the rules?

SYL: The rules, huh? Sure need some around here. Mr. Cooper, maybe I need to talk to you more often . . .

FRANK: Ummmm Hmmmm. You oughta start looking up insteada' down.

SYL: What?

FRANK: You gotta lot to be thankful for.

SYL: Oh, yeah. Like what?

FRANK: Like that good wife you're about to worry to death, for one thing.

SYL: Naw, messenger, you got something wrong there. They worried back when you were making five a day. Now they make adjustments. She's just figuring out her adjustments, that's all.

(Lights down on UPPER LEVEL.

Up on LOWER LEVEL. MATTIE is putting food from pot into bags for freezing)

LAURA: Oh, Mattie, our marriage is all so vague and disconnected now. It's like . . . like you've got these pieces of something in your hands but you've forgotten why—what you were making with them, trying to build. I think we missed—a connecting point with the abortion. I feel this ache, this gap. But I just couldn't give him that kind of—of: grip . . .

MATTIE: Grip?

LAURA: Trap. The baby.

MATTIE: Lord, in my day, children was a woman's glory—today they a trap . . . Lord . . . Today . . .

(Lights down on THEM.

Up on UPPER LEVEL*)*

SYL: See, it used to take all kinds of strength, muscle, to pull a bow back far enough to send a stick through the ribs of a tough, snorting animal. Run up on him and ram a stick through him. Dodge those claws, and teeth, and shit. Took stamina to be on the run, in the sun, for days, without much water, cutting through jungle-bush with a eight pound knife all day long. Took strength, stamina, courage for that kind of hunting, see, and everybody knew it, see.

FRANK: Yeah, so?

SYL: So when a woman saw a dude walking up wearing a—a leopard skin and a eagle's father, she knew he had stabbed a leopard and wrestled with an eagle. She knew right away who he was, what he was. What he could do with an enemy, could do for her and kids, see?

FRANK: Sure, alright . . .

SYL: Then—*(*HE *drinks beer.* FRANK *stares fascinated)* Then comes the machines. See, everybody talks about the Machine Age, the cotton gin, Henry Ford, all that. But they don't talk about the main machine, the one that turned it all around for Western Man, for the world. No, don't write about that main machine in the history books . . .

FRANK: And what's that?

SYL: The pistol. That's the one turned it all around. Yes-sir, that's the one. No more so much strength-stamina-courage—Just finger-finger, boom-boom. Yeah, wasn't for that pistol the Zulus probably be running that continent over there. And the uh—uh—Seminoles and Cheyennes probably be running this continent. 'Cause ain't no way those dudes with their snuffboxes and silk handkerchiefs, those sailors eating all that rotten food, and those exiled gamblers, indentured slaves, and thieves come over here—no way they gonna handle Zulus and Comanches, strength to strength, stamina to stamina, knife to knife. Sheet! Don't believe me, check boxing, the box scores, the Olympics. Yeah . . .

FRANK: So what? So you're saying all that to say what? . . .

SYL: I'm saying that the women still look to see what you're wearing, showing, checking for alligator shoes, Mercedes. Seeing if you can hunt. But the hunting is different now. You're hunting for little green pieces of paper. Don't take strength-courage-stamina—takes this *(Crooks finger)* and this—*(Jams finger as if in computer keyboard)* This is today's labor. Computer finger, you dig? All it takes, is some brains, some training, and some fingers. And going for those green sheets sometimes the best hunter is just the best whore!—

FRANK: Boy, your thinking is pitiful—

SYL: Naw, naw, they don't need us like they did, pops. You can see it in their eyes! "I can hunt good as you, so, tell me what I need with you?" And now they got all this birth control and abortion stuff. *They* just *decide* if and when, and what they want us for. If they're going to extend and continue us. I mean you see those looks, and you realize, the only way to stay the hunter is to outhunt, outhustle *them*—and then they, her, your wife is now part of the competition. So, now where you go for—for—for—for what? Shit, it's all fucked up! *(Drinks)*

FRANK: What's fucked up is y'all.

SYL: What?

FRANK: Yeah, worrying about what the women thinking. What the white man thinking. Just worry about what you thinking. Yeah, the whole bunch! Whole generation of you. Just like the dumb dog running round and round barking at the tree 'cause he thinks he still tied to it. Well, the rope been broke a long time ago, sonnyboy. Ain't nothing still tied to that ol' tree but yo' *mind*, boy.

SYL: *(Up)* Cool it, ol' man. Watch your pressure now.

FRANK: Cool it my black ass! All, y'all young ones—All it takes to stop the bunch of you is a stop sign! Well, like the fella told the policeman: "Sign say stop: don't say stay." *(FRANK becomes very animated, accenting each point with body language: waving, stomping)* Overcoming the *hardness* of it is the *glory* of it. The glory of being a man! They wouldn't even let us walk on the sidewalk. You hear me? When we see them coming we had to get off the walkway. Out into the dirt. But now? Nowadays you got the laws! The equal opportunity! College degrees! Black folk with money all over the place! Whole other countries to go and do business with! Can even get on up into space! Lord, God, boy, what do you want?! . . .

SYL: Uh, what we want is to be in the game, pops. And it's not like coming outta' the fields and renting the outhouse. The games all in the big house now. It's penthouse or nothing. A whole new ballgame. Different strokes! . . .

FRANK: Different nothin'! . . . Got two, three cars in the garage, and a closet fulla' fancy clothes and still sitting, waiting by the phone, like that dog sitting by the victrola—waiting for his master's voice. Aw, boy . . . Start your own business!

SYL: You got to have five-hundred-dollar suits and BMWs just to stay in this game! Too complex for you, pops! . . .

FRANK: I got your complex . . . *(Grabs groin area)*

(WOMEN, DOWNSTAIRS, look at each other and start for the front door)

SYL: I'll show you to the door.

FRANK: You don't have to show me the door, I built that door.

SYL: Yeah, then you know how it works.

FRANK: It works to keep a wise man away from a fool like you . . .

SYL: Find a tractor or something to work on.

FRANK: Don't be talking to me like that. Reach in this toolbox and come up with my hammer.

MATTIE: Frank? What is the matter? Come on down here where you belong now . . .

LAURA: *(Going up)* Syl? . . . Will you stop this? Please! . . .

FRANK: *(To MATTIE)* I belong where I please! . . .

SYL: He's the one that flew over the cuckoo nest. Not me . . .

LAURA: Syl! . . .

MATTIE: *(As FRANK reaches her)* You come on and cool down. Know how your pressure is.

FRANK: My pressure's fine, don't be . . .

SYL: Yeah! You might be missing *Hee Haw* or *The Waltons*. Something you know something about.

FRANK: Keep on you gon' meet my hammer.

SYL: You mean onea' them Flintstones tomahawks? . . .

(LAURA pulls him inside)

FRANK: *(At doorway)* Hey—boy, let me tell you somethin'—

MATTIE: Frank, go on in the house. *(SHE pushes him inside and closes the door)*

LAURA: You should be ashamed, Syl. That nice old man.

SYL: Nice old man. We got to move away from that old gate mouth. He's nuts! . . . *(Goes OFF REAR)*

LAURA: Shhh. I'm crazy about 'em both.

(DOWNSTAIRS, FRANK stands glowering, catching his breath)

FRANK: Just like them boys of yours. A clipped poodle. I'm going to call 'em right now. *(Starts toward phone in bedroom)*

MATTIE: Going to call *who*? . . .

FRANK: Call 'em tell 'em bring my grandchildren over here so I can start teaching 'em up right. *(Dialing)* Get 'em some uniforms, learn 'em drill formation. Discipline. Precision.

MATTIE: *(Smiling)* The girls too? . . .

FRANK: Yep. Ain't gon' take no chances.

(Lights dim on him and MATTIE.

SYL and LAURA enter UPSTAIRS)

SYL: Them ol' dinosaurs think that 'cause they've sent off and got their G.E.D.'s now we're supposed to walk in and take over General Motors. *(Phone rings. HE answers)* Sylvester Williams, here . . . Who's calling? Hold on. *(Holds phone out)* . . . Ralph Richardson . . .

(Surprised, LAURA waves that SHE doesn't want to talk)

SYL: *(Continued) (In phone)* She's busy at the moment. Can she call you? Or you wanna call later—Right—*(Hangs up)* Say you can call him. Who is that? . . .

LAURA: A buyer. One of Louise's people.

SYL: Oh, one of them. *(Stomps on floor. Shouting)* Hey, down there!! Old Farmer! You got a proposal? A perspective?! Something I can take to the bank?! . . . *(Then: HE smiles at LAURA. Then stands shaking head, looking out. SHE slowly looks from him to phone and back)* I gotta' meet with Jackson . . . *(Grabs coat)* That ol' guy: Deep stuff goin' on all around him and he don't know what's happening . . .

(HE exits. LAURA moves to phone, picks it up, begins to dial. Fade. Lights up on LOWER LEVEL: FRANK is on wall phone)

FRANK: . . . Frank Jr.?! Now listen boy: I want you to get all my grandchildren together and bring 'em over here! . . . Huh? This weekend! I'm gon' get 'em straightened out! . . .

(HE hangs up as lights fade. Up on LAURA upstairs on the phone)

LAURA: *(Laughing)* No! You fool! I can't! And don't call me here anymore! Byyye! . . . *(Hangs phone up, chuckling, starts out. Phone rings again. SHE considers as it rings again, decides to answer.) (Playfully)* I told you . . . Oh, sorry. No he isn't. May I tell him who . . . Yes, it is. I mean, I am . . . Oh? . . . Uh-huh . . . Uh-huh. Uh. *(Sits on couch)* Who am I talking to? . . .

(As SHE listens, lights fade . . . On LOWER-LEVEL, FRANK, in his old Army Uniform marches back and forth across space beyond kitchen doorway. HE gives out with the drill: Hup-Two-Three-Four/Hup-Two-Three-Four-Hup . . . SYL comes rushing in, seeming to be moving to FRANK's martial

rhythm. In fact, slamming apartment door behind him right on FRANK'S *last: Hup!* LAURA *is sitting solemnly on couch.* FRANK *exits downstairs)*

SYL: Modeling, huh?

*(*SHE *gives him stoic glance)*

SYL: *(Continued)* Since when does modeling include dancing all over some dude at the club 80! Huh?! Kissin' him! In fronta' everybody!! Hey!! . . . *(*HE *rushes over to pull her to her feet.* SHE *pulls away and backs to edge of couch)*

SYL: A friend of mine saw you. Goddammit! Kissin'! Guess you just want everybody to know you're tippin' on me, huh?!

LAURA: *(Defiantly)* Maybe. Maybe you're right!

*(*HE *lunges to slap her down on couch)*

SYL: *(As* SHE *gets up)* They say y'all left together around one o'clock. How come you weren't home here when I called at three in the morning!!? . . .

LAURA: *(On feet)* And where were you, Syl? I don't care anymore, you hear? About you, about us. I don't care, so don't ever hit me again. You hear!! . . .

SYL: Bitch!! . . .

*(*HE *moves for her.* SHE *moves to couch, reaches into bag and comes out with pistol.* HE *backs up)*

LAURA: You ready to listen now, Syl? Debra, Syl: Debra. She called. We had a long talk . . .

SYL: *(Watching the gun)* What? . . . Debra what? Debra who? What you . . .

LAURA: You know who, nigga'. Is she going to have an abortion, too? Or are you all going to have the baby, huh? What're you fathering this time, Syl? . . .

SYL: *(Mind whirling)* What? Debra? . . .

LAURA: Shit, what is this? . . . Look, we're in different places. It's over. Okay? *(*SHE *sits in chair. Puts gun on table; holds head in hands)*

SYL: A gun? . . . Laura? . . . Look, look, okay. So, I'm staying with Jeff. Mad at you about that abortion. So, she comes by. We get into a little thing for a minute.

LAURA: *(Gets up, pointing pistol)* You disgust me, Syl. I talked to her. You and her have been going on longer than that, much longer. Oh, fuck. I've gotta get outta' here. *(Exits. Sound of door closing, locking,* SYL *stunned)*

SYL: *(To himself)* She told me she was already having an abort—. I don't care what she—She can't come in here messing—*(To Laura)* And what about that dude at the Club 80!? Huh? . . . What about that . . . *(Stops, lost. To himself)* A gun? She pulled a gun on me? . . . *(Going* OFF*)* Hey, baby? Laura, we gotta' talk, baby? We gotta talk! Baby!! . . . *(Exits)*

LAURA: *(Offstage)* Stay away from me, Syl!!

(Lights cross-fade. Up on LOWER LEVEL, CENTER. *Dark pacing/marching* FIGURE *becomes* FRANK *in uniform, with French officer-like riding crop, sounding off—Jodie marching song)*

FRANK: Ain't no sense in going home. Jodie's got your girl and gone/sound off. Hup two three four, Hup two three—

*(*MATTIE *comes on, worried, yet bemused look on her face)*

MATTIE: Frank? Now you know they ain't gonna' bring those kids over here for you to be drilling.

FRANK: They have theirs orders. Have to tighten up the troops! Hup two three four, Hup two *(Continues)*

*(*MATTIE *watches a moment)*

MATTIE: Hey now? Hey? What's this? Your change of life? You going senile? I got to put up with that too now? Huh? . . .

FRANK: *(Marching)* Once a year, Mattie. Once a year. Gon' do this once a year. Remind myself. Remind everybody.

*(*HE *marches on, back/forth. After beat,* SHE *falls in behind him, half parading/half joining. Then* HE *turns and marches into the hands-on-hips solid reality of her.* THEY *stare a beat. Then* MATTIE *salutes)*

MATTIE: Private Cooper, sir, reporting for duty, sir.

*(*FRANK *slumps, shakes his head)*

FRANK: Mattie, Mattie, Mattie. What would I do without you?

MATTIE: I wouldn't let you do without me . . .

FRANK: Mattie, Mattie, Mattie.

*(*THEY *embrace as lights fade; go off together through yard space in fading light.*

Up on two spots UPPER LEVEL. SYL *in one,* LAURA *the other)*

LAURA: Maybe Syl was right about the self thing. I went to a disco—and the dancers were all dancing into the mirrors, for their images, for themselves. Nobody touched; just looked at themselves. It was awful. I remembered how when I was a kid, a teenager, how the moves, the focus, were into, toward, your partner: How we flowed into one another. Now, they dance to the mirror . . . to themselves.

SYL: She was right, you know: the promotion, the new district, were real, you know. But these people are so shrewd, so cold, you just never know how you stand. You know. Yeah, I got scared. Paranoid, she calls it. Yeah, I got—scared. I just couldn't come weeping home, laying my head in her lap, again, "Mama, they cheated me again." I mean no matter how much they gang up on you, after a while all she sees is the bruises, all she sees is a loser, and your woman's eyes can hurt you more than any mirror.

LAURA: His frustration. His rage. I remember my stepfather. And I know he might explode on me any minute. And I can't handle that. I—But he brings that same intensity, that same need, when he comes to me. Lays with me. God—It's an awful thing for me to say. But I feel—Yes, this is where it all comes together; this displaces all the rest. Awful, isn't it? Modern me feeling like that's it? That that's the summation? Yes, the words do get in the way. Because it's all too much to try to say.

SYL: Look, I wouldn't come to no counselor, whatever you are. Her idea. But the barbershop, and poolroom, and corner don't help—help no more. Never was into witch doctors, priest—Never mind, look: Help me. Help me.

LAURA: *(As on phone)* You called? . . .

SYL: Uh, yeah . . . I just wanted to make sure that no matter—where we go—we stay in touch . . . Be friends.

LAURA: In touch? Friends? Do we know how to do that? . . .

SYL: We should try . . .

LAURA: Yes. We should . . . try . . .

(By this point the lights have changed to show them in the living-room. THEY struggle with/against their emotions. But, SHE has a suitcase, sitting beside the couch. HE picks his up from behind the couch. HE goes out door and downstairs to sit in hallway on suitcase. SHE sits on arm of couch, her suitcase beside her. Light holds them dimly as THEY sit unable to go. THEY both turn right to sound of TRIUMPHANT FRENCH ANTHEM:

MATTIE/FRANK come dance/marching from rear, old, golden goblets with wine in hand. HE sits, SHE sits on his lap—THEY raise gleaming goblets triumphantly as SYL/LAURA listen/watch them)

(END)

Urban Transition: Loose Blossoms II

CHARACTERS

Earl: Father. Fifty-ish, has worked in the factory 28 years, now at an impasse.

Cheryl: Earl's wife and high school sweetheart, a social worker.

E. J.: Earl and Cheryl's son, a bright, aggressive young teen.

Gail: Their oldest daughter, a college student, overachiever, pride of the family.

Sherrie: Their youngest, seven or eight years old, a charmer.

Eric: E. J.'s best friend, being left behind in the old "ghetto" neighborhood.

Bert: Earl and Cheryl's lifelong friend, a compulsive cop and problem drinker.

TIME

Now

PLACE

Any American metropolis.

ACT I

(Lights up on CARTERS' living room. Christmas decorations over (fake) fireplace, around walls, and (if visible) windows. Christmas tree well decorated; abundance of presents in bright boxes with elegant ribbons.

CENTER STAGE, MR. AND MRS. CARTER, EARL and CHERYL, are doing slick, deep-dipping, nostalgic ballroom dance—Astaire/Rogers with a sepia sensuality—to the Orioles' doo-wop, "Christmas in Heaven."

THEY end with chuckles and a grand dip; a kiss. Record changes to Orioles' "Thrill Me."

And now the "slickness" is gone from their dancing, leaving only the slow sensuality inside the rhythm: the touch of their bodies is the music they hear, follow, slide inside of. HE giving short chuckles, and "Yeah babys," of approval, as SHE purrs with her head on his shoulder, her tongue playing over her bared teeth.

Their 15-year-old son, EARL JR. (E. J.) appears at the entrance to the hallway STAGE RIGHT, motions, and their two daughters, GAIL, 18, and SHERRIE, 8, come to see)

SHERRIE: Mama!? . . . Look at you! . . . What you doin'?

EARL: *(Dancing)* Doin' what we used to do before you crumb snatchers come poppin' up to be spyin' on us all the time . . .

(CHERYL laughs as THEY execute another turn and a funky "dip")

GAIL: Break it up! . . . Break it up! . . . No ol' timey belly rub in here! . . .

E. J.: Yeah. Enough of that. It's Christmas Eve—not Soul Train!

SHERRIE: Yeah! Stop that! Ugh! . . .

(THEY run laughing to pull their parents apart.

Blackout to the Drifters' "White Christmas")

DRIFTERS:

I-YI-YI-YI'M DREAMING
OF A WHITE
CHRISTMAS! . . .

(Sounds of party reveling; party horns; shouts of "Merry Christmas!" . . . etc.

Lights back up on set: Presents are now open under tree, drink glasses on tables, etc. EARL, drink in hand, sits with CHERYL on his lap in easy chair. Across from them on the couch sits their lifetime buddy, LT. BERT CHILDS, Vice Detective. GAIL sits alongside BERT. SHERRIE lies sleeping on floor near tree. EARL JR. is showing his friend, ERIC, to the front door hallway, DOWN LEFT)

ERIC: Check you tomorrow, man. Don't forget. . . . Good-night, Mr. Carter! Mrs. Carter . . . Gail! . . . Merry Christmas, everybody! . . . You too, Mr. Bert! . . .

(EVERYONE gives him waves/Christmas wishes)

EARL: Eric?! . . . You gon' come have some Christmas turkey with us tomorrow ain't ya? . . .

ERIC: Yes, sir! Be here early! . . .

CHERYL: Be careful out there this time a' night.

(E. J./ERIC go off into hallway)

CHERYL: *(Continued)* Who is that pickin' him up this late? . . .

GAIL: Some cousin of his who was at some party over this way. Surprised he didn't try to spend the night. Get breakfast . . .

CHERYL: *(Eyes closed)* Be nice, Gail . . .

EARL: Yeah. He's had it rough. Just likes being around a real family. Probably helped him get through.

BERT: No doubt about it.

CHERYL: We sorta adopted him.

GAIL: Who adopted who? Seems like he followed E. J. home from kindergarten one day and he's been here every day since. Especially at meal time . . .

CHERYL: Be thankful we had enough to share.

EARL: Right. Good thing we were around. His daddy o'deein'. Mother out there strung out. Well, wasn't no way his grandmother gonna handle him, his little brother, and sister, too, without some help from somewhere. Good thing we was able . . .

BERT: Amen. Everyday I got to be checkin' the ones that didn't get that kinda help nowhere . . .

EARL: Uh-huh. Everybody ain't lucky enough to have me for a daddy . . .

GAIL: Oh Gawd . . .

EARL: And a chick smart enough to choose me for yo' mama. You three knuckleheads came here lucky! . . .

CHERYL: Whiskey's speaking now.

GAIL: Uh-huh, he'll be cryin' in a minute.

BERT: *(Laughing)* Yeah! That's what we used to call him, "Cryin' Earl" . . . Get happy, he cry. Get sad, he cry. Get *mad,* he cry. Be puttin' a Joe Louis/Sugar Ray whippin' on a dude, and he be cryin' like he the one hurtin'! . . .

CHERYL: *(As BERT and GAIL laugh)* Y'all leave my baby alone . . .

EARL: When I get filled up, I jus' boil over.

(E. J. comes back in)

E. J.: What y'all laughin' about now? . . .

GAIL: Daddy's cryin'.

E. J.: Oh. You started, Dad? We was wonderin' how long it would take you to get it goin' . . .

EARL: Wanna see somebody cry? Keep lookin' in that mirror and come a lil' closer . . .

E. J.: Child abuse. With the police sittin' right here.

BERT: Off duty. Ain't seen a thing.

EARL: That ain't no policeman: That's my buddy.

E. J.: Oh, okay. I see.

CHERYL: E. J.? Why don't you put your sister in bed for me. Just lay her on the bed. I'll get her into her pajamas later.

EARL: Yeah, boy. Shut yo' mouth and earn your keep.

(E. J. crosses to bend to SHERRIE)

E. J.: Come on, Grandma . . . *(Lifting her)*

SHERRIE: What? . . . What? . . . Let me alone. I ain't sleepy . . .

E. J.: *(Carrying her out, RIGHT)* Naw, you ain't sleepy: You sleep.

(A beat of contentment passes)

EARL: Yeah, Detective Bert! Glad you came by, fella! . . .

BERT: Oh. Time for me to go, huh? . . . *(Getting up)* . . . Well, hell, I was tired of this joint anyway. Just being polite . . .

GAIL/CHERYL: Uncle Bert! . . . Bert! . . .

EARL: Aw, nigguh, you know now I mean it. Sit down. Ain't no holiday if some a' the fellas don't come by. Sit down, fool! . . .

BERT: Just stretchin' these ol' bones, boy. You can't run me outta here . . . *(Stretches, sits back down)*

EARL: Better act like you belong here . . . Gon' kick Jones' ass. Had me buy that jive gin don't nobody drink but him, and then he don't show. Gone get on him and Liz. Yeah. Thought you was gonna bring Myrna by.

CHERYL: *(Getting up)* Mr. Whiskey talkin' again: Don't know when to quit. Come on, Gail, let's straighten up around this tree . . . *(SHE and GAIL cross to tree)*

EARL: What you talkin' about, girl? . . . He said he was . . .

BERT: That's alright, Cheryl. It's okay. Aw, I was gonna bring her, man. Went by to drop off the presents, see the kids. But she had a couple sips and started talkin' mess again. You know: Next year she's gonna have her somebody who's there all the time. I won't be able to be walkin' in and out, like—yeah, dig that—like it's *still* my home! Hell, I'm *still* payin' for it, ain't I? She talks like *I* divorced *her*. Insteada' vice versa, like it went down . . .

EARL: *(Picking up after awkward pause)* Well, you keep takin' your egg nog straight like you doin' tonight, and I'll bet you'll be back livin' there in a quick minute . . .

CHERYL: *(Picking up another botched beat)* Earl . . .

EARL: Earl what? . . .

CHERYL: But I notice you have been spending a lot more time there lately, Bert.

BERT: Uh huh . . . Earl? . . . You, Myrna, and the department can all just . . . I won't say it in fronta' Gail here: But you all know what you can do for me.

EARL: What I say now?! . . .

BERT: I ain't never been no alky.

EARL: Aw, man . . .

BERT: Aw, man, shit. Excuse me, Gail. Look here, fella: I took everybody's advice and went to some of those AA meetings. Hell, those people talkin' bout seein' shit comin' outta the walls and shit. Shakin' all over. I couldn't relate to *none* of that. I stopped just to prove to everybody—myself included—that I could stop.

EARL: That's a good reason.

BERT: Go to hell. Excuse me, Gail . . . *(Getting up)*

GAIL: I haven't heard anything unusual yet.

BERT: Hell, had to have a drink, or two, every day, before I waded out into all that garbage out there. And then have a couple to wash the garbage off, before I could go back to Myrna and the kids. But I wasn't shakin' and seein' things on the walls. But it didn't make no difference when I stopped drinkin'. She still couldn't stand me being a garbage man: A cop. Too hard to get the smell off, you dig? Step in a lot of feces all day long—bound to have some on your shoes when you get home. Know what I mean? But that's what I am: A cop!

EARL: *(Standing)* Damn right! And a damned good one, too! After all, you went to the big NE, didn't you!!? . . .

BERT: Damn right!! . . .

BOTH: Falcons!! Falcons! Falcons!! . . . The big NE! Hah! The big NE!! Hah! The big NE!! Hah!

(THEY throw fast, fake, body punches at each other; then grab each other in headlocks)

E. J.: *(Coming back in)* Oh wow!! . . . That big NE junk!! . . .

GAIL: Yes, Lord. Let me go to bed.

EARL: Y'all just jealous 'cause you was born too late to be in on it. Right, baby?

CHERYL: Right, baby . . .

BERT: They missed out alright. Looka here: When Myrna got ridiculous and ran me outta my ex-house? I thought about you two and came over to lift my glass to you. *(Lifts glass)* With all the feces goin' on today, you two, since way back in grade school, still keepin' in step, kickin' it together. I dig it! Lift my egg nog to you! . . .

(EARL moves to CHERYL, THEY lift glasses)

EARL/CHERYL: Thanks, man. Thanks, Bert . . .

BERT: Now I'm gonna get my coat, and get outta here . . .

GAIL: *(Incredulous)* You mean these two have been together since *grade school.*

BERT: Bout round in there. Junior High at least. Middle school y'all call it.

E. J.: Yeah? What were they like? Back then I mean? . . .

GAIL: Bet she was all over him, wasn't she? . . .

CHERYL: Excuse me? . . .

E. J.: Naw. He was all over her.

EARL: The better to conceive y'all, little boy.

E. J.: Ooo, gross. Chill him, Mama.

BERT: *(Laughing, pulling on coat)* They were all over each other! . . .

GAIL: *(Faking indignation)* Disgusting . . .

CHERYL: What are you telling our children? . . .

EARL: I think he sneaked somethin' in that egg nog.

BERT: Don't get me wrong: They weren't x-rated, or nothin'. Most of the time anyway. They were just like . . . like, every group has its couple. You know, its model. The one that shows you how it's supposed to be. These two were it for me. For us. You dig? . . . And now, I've raised my egg nog to 'em, so now the hell with both the jive turkeys. I gotta go. *(HE starts to hallway)*

CHERYL: Kiss Myrna for me.

(BERT turns to wink and point a you-got-it finger at her)

BERT: See there: She's always been smarter than you, boy.

EARL: What? . . . You mean Myrna's gonna let you back in there, tonight? . . .

BERT: Oh, yeah. She just gets mad at herself, 'cause she still wants me, dig. I just decided to skip the speeches this time. *(Laughs)* She'll be in her Christmas gown, with her hair down . . . Gi' me a piecea' this mistletoe, nigguh! . . . *(HE snatches off a piece of the mistletoe hanging over the doorway. Laughing, HE runs off into hallway, as EARL snatches up a magazine to swing at him)*

EARL: Put my damn mistletoe back! . . .

BERT: *(Offstage)* Bye!! . . . Merry Christmas, everybody!! . . .

EARL: *(Looking down hallway)* Buy your own mistletoe!! . . . Hey, policeman! Be careful! Don't let one of them jitterbugs out there take that pistol and kick your ass! . . .

BERT: *(Offstage)* Go to hell!! . . .

(Door slams with sound of jingling bells. GAIL goes to hug/kiss CHERYL)

GAIL: Dad and all his crazy friends! . . .

E. J.: The nutty Falcons . . .

EARL: *(Examining mistletoe)* Ain't that something: Tore off my stuff.

GAIL: Good night, Dad. Goin' to bed.

E. J.: Me too. See you all on Christmas.

EARL: What? . . . It *is* Christmas. Y'all can't go to bed, yet.

GAIL: Dad . . .

CHERYL: *(Checking watch)* Earl. It's almost . . .

EARL: Naw! Nobody's here but us, now! Family! Get that champagne out! Time for the family toast: to all who came before, and all who are to come. A-men. Come on, Cheryl, get the good stuff . . .

CHERYL: Alright. One family toast, and that's it . . . *(SHE crosses into inner hallway, RIGHT)*

GAIL: Hurry up, Ma. I'm dead.

EARL: *(Mimicking awkward dance steps)* That's how you looked dancing with that Jenkins boy too: Dead! . . . E. J.! Flick on the dooley. Show y'all somethin' . . .

E. J.: Flick on what? . . . The tapes? . . .

EARL: Yeah . . . I'll get it . . . . *(HE dances over to machine, punches button. Bill Doggett's "Honky Tonk" blasts out)*

E. J./GAIL: Awww, man! . . . Oh, Gawd . . .

EARL: Show y'all how to get it . . . *(Takes GAIL by the hand and leads her [resisting all the way!] into classic "bop" moves)*

E. J.: *(Laughing)* Dead stuff, Dad. Dead . . .

EARL: Don't you say nothin'. Saw you too. Lookin' like a scarecrow with the hiccups! . . . Like you tryin' to stomp roaches in a windstorm! . . . *(Releases GAIL to do head-jutting, arm-leg-flaring parody of current youth-dance; going into Americanized MC Hammer/Bobby Brown versions of African "boot dance." As THEY laugh/razz him)* Now, here's how you supposed to get it! . . .

(Light narrows onto him down front doing James Brown-like "chicken")

EARL: *(Continued) (J.B. shout)* OWWWWW!! . . . *(HE spins as lights go black. In dark, his James Brown shout turns suddenly into a painful scream, then a deep moaning: "Oh, God . . . God . . ." In dark)* Man, I don't know how it happened . . . I mean, I've picked up stuff like that, a thousand times . . . You know, over the years . . . Somebody had left one of . . . one of those damn blocks out . . . And I know we ain't . . . Ain't supposed to . . . to pick the suckers up . . . But, hell, I'm trying' to get things . . . things cleared away. So—so I can get . . . get home . . .

(Lights come up on living room, and it is a few days later; and BERT—wearing a different suit—is helping EARL, now dressed in house coat and pajama top, to the couch)

BERT: So you gon' play twenty-year-old Superman . . . *(HE helps EARL ease down onto couch)*

EARL: Awww . . . Thanks . . . Go to hell . . . Told you, picked that shit up before. But I guess I didn't . . . didn't . . . go down right. Get my back straight . . . Just reached over, put the weight on my arms and back. Steada' my legs, you know . . . And buddy, let me tell you. The pain? . . . It was like God had been lookin' to give me a spankin'. And saw me all bent over, tooted up? And sent a bolt of lightin' right on up, through the split, to the top of my neck! Crrack! I felt bones just splittin' apart. Crrack! Felt like a fire was burnin' me in half. Hollered like a baby, Jim. Passed flat out . . .

(He takes out handkerchief to wipe his sweating face. Bert sits across from him in easy chair)

Bert: Damn. Sounds like you really caught one. You sure it's alright you comin' out here? Sure you shouldn't stay in the bed? . . .

Earl: Tired of that damn bed. Everybody tippin' round out here, like I'm dyin'. Come out where I can see . . . see what's goin' on aroun' here . . .

Bert: Well, what the doctor say?

Earl: Nothin'. Didn't know what to say. Told me to take it easy. Take my time. Like, what else am I gonna do? Know what he said? Said if I'da had a heart attack, he could just about tell me what day I would be back to work. But a back is "tricky." Just have to wait and see how it goes. Hmmph. Tricky, ain't the word for it, boy.

Bert: Well, he's the doctor. Just do like he says. Be alright.

Earl: Wait is easy to say, but hard to do.

(Sound of front door opening/closing. E. J. comes in carrying school books)

E. J.: Hey, Uncle Bert. Saw your car out there. Hey, Dad. How you doin'? Feelin' better? . . .

Earl: Yeah. This chump come by to shake his head over me. Got up to show him I can still handle him if I have to . . . *(Sudden pain makes him have to close his eyes)* Ummmm . . . Aw, shit . . .

E. J.: *(Alarmed)* Dad? . . . What's the matter? . . .

Bert: *(On feet)* You okay, Earl? . . .

Earl: Okay. I'm okay. Just get me a glass of water, Junior.

E. J.: You sure? . . . Maybe we should call the doctor? . . .

Earl: Junior. I'm okay. Just onea' those damned flashes. Just get me a glass of water, alright? . . .

(E. J. hesitates, looking from his father to Bert, for reassurance)

Earl: *(Continued)* What you waitin' on, boy? Will you bring me some water? Or you want me to get it? . . .

(E. J. crosses into inner hallway, Right)

Earl: *(Continued)* I don't know about this shit, man.

BERT: Probably just tensed up some muscles. Got to learn how to roll with it. Just relax and be sick for awhile, macho man. Probably should get your ass back in that bed . . .

EARL: When my family come in here, today, I'm gon' be . . . *(Closes eyes, breathes deeply)* Gon' be sittin' up . . .

BERT: Look, fool: They wanna see you layin' back, lookin' comfortable. Not sittin' up, lookin' stupid. Sweatin'. Bitin' yo lips . . .

EARL: Ain't nobody bitin' no . . . Listen: Why don't you go arrest somebody across town somewhere . . .

(E. J. comes in looking anxious with the glass of water)

E. J.: Here you go, Dad. I let it run, get cold.

EARL: Thanks, Junior . . . *(Downs it all)* . . . Ahhh . . . Thanks.

E. J.: *(Taking glass)* Get you another one. Want somethin', Uncle Bert? Coffee, a drink, or somethin'? . . .

BERT: *(Putting on hat, gloves)* Naw, E. J. I'm gonna go arrest somebody. And I hope they give me some lip about it. So I can pretend they're your daddy there, and knock hell outta 'em . . .

E. J.: What? . . .

EARL: Uh-huh. See how my good friends come by to cheer me up? *(To BERT)* Get on outta here. Bout time you earned somea' my tax money.

BERT: *(Moving to doorway)* I'll be back to make sure you're behaving . . .

EARL: Gonna tell Cheryl not to let you in here without a warrant.

(BERT waves a hand at him; crosses, followed by E. J.)

E. J.: Take care, Uncle Bert. Thanks for comin' by.

BERT: *(Offstage)* Yeah. You all do what you can with macho-man! . . .

EARL: *(Grumbling to himself)* Go to hell, Dick Tracy . . .

(HE picks up remote control, begins flicking through channels. [TV is unseen, played as though in DOWN RIGHT audience.]

E. J. comes back in; glances at EARL, then wanders aimlessly around room, as though looking for something. Finally settles in chair with magazine; thumbs through pages, stealing glances at EARL)

EARL: *(Continued)* Quit watchin' me like you tryin' to catch my last breath or somethin', boy . . . Turn on the radio. Ain't nothin' but sad news on this damned TV . . .

(E. J. crosses UP RIGHT to entertainment center)

EARL: *(Continued)* Wonder why they do that? Have five/six murders, tragedies, one right after another? Seems like they could even it up. Have one good thing, one bad, one good, one bad. You know? Act like they wanna keep people scared, uptight . . .

(E. J. shrugs, finds easy jazz on radio. Crosses back to chair and magazine. Earl catches him sneaking looks again)

Earl: *(Continued)* Y'all takin' shifts, right? . . .

E. J.: Huh? . . .

Earl: Huh, nothin'. You watch me till yo' baby sister comes in from school, right? Then I guess yo' mama takes over when she gets in from work, huh . . .

E. J.: Aw, come on, Dad, man. We jus' . . . jus' wanna make sure somebody's around in case you . . . need somethin' done.

Earl: Uh-huh.

E. J.: Okay, I'll go on in the kitchen . . . Do my homework . . . *(He gathers up books from table)*

Earl: Sit down, boy.

E. J.: Naw, I'll go on in the kitchen . . .

(Earl suddenly winces and goes open mouthed with pain. E. J. drops books back to table and rushes to him)

E. J.: *(Continued)* Dad? . . . You alright? . . .

Earl: *(Pointing finger)* Gotcha.

E. J.: Aw, man. Don't be doin' that . . .

Earl: Uh-huh. Sit down, boy. You know I always dig having you aroun', talkin' to you. Why would it be different now? . . .

E. J.: You sure I'm not buggin' you . . .

Earl: Sit down. Let's rap.

E. J.: *(Relieved, pulling chair closer)* About what? . . .

Earl: You name it. Women. New sneakers. That bullshit rap music you listen to . . . That about covers your subjects, don't it . . .

E. J.: Aw, man, I got more on my mind than that stuff. Got lotsa stuff on my mind.

Earl: Yeah? Like what? . . . Come on. What? . . .

E. J.: Lotsa stuff. Just ain't ready to talk about it yet.

Earl: I see. Well, tell me somethin'. You all tippin' aroun' here, watchin' me. Did the doctor tell your mother somethin' he didn't tell me? Y'all got secrets? Is my back worse than he told me it was? . . .

E. J.: Naw, Dad. She said just like you: That he said you have to chill awhile, then you'd be cool . . .

Earl: If I chill I guess I will be cool, huh?

E. J.: That is what he told you, ain't it? The doctor I mean.

EARL: Boy, dealin' wit' you is like lookin' in a mirror. Yeah, chill and I'll be cool. That's what he said.

E. J.: Well, that's all Ma said.

EARL: Hush. Listen to some good music for a change. Might blow somea' that other crap outta yo' system . . .

(A Duke Ellington tune has come on the radio)

E. J.: *(After a few beats)* You know what it is, Dad. We so used to havin' you always proppin' us up, that now that we have to boost you a minute—we don't know how to handle it. What to do, or what not to do. Know what I mean?

EARL: Yeah, I love you too. All y'all. And I appreciate you lookin' out for me. But I'm cool. For real. Just need a minute, that's all. Cool?

E. J.: Cool . . .

EARL: Go on do your homework.

(Sound of front door banging open, slamming shut. Little SHERRIE comes running in as E. J. moves to doorway)

E. J.: Cut all that noise, girl.

SHERRIE: Hey, E. J.!! . . . He sleep!? . . . He alright!? . . . Daddy!! . . . *(SHE runs to couch, falls to her knees, rubs noses with EARL; then gives him a kiss—holding her hands up to not touch him as SHE does so)* Umm . . . Mommie said I can't be grabbin' on you.

EARL: She just jealous. Tryin' to keep us apart. Give me another kiss.

SHERRIE: Ummm . . . I drew you a picture, Daddy. Wanna see it? . . .

EARL: What you think? Yeah, I wanna see what my baby drew for me.

SHERRIE: *(Going into back pack)* Okay . . .

E. J.: *(Gathering up books)* I'll be in the kitchen if you want anything, Dad.

SHERRIE: If he needs anything, I'll get it for him.

E. J.: Shut up and sit down somewhere. *(HE starts out)*

EARL: Junior? Stayin' around the house, doin' your homework. Maybe I need to crack my back more often.

E. J.: Chill, Dad . . . *(HE crosses)*

EARL: *(Calling after him)* Hey! Better hit them books an' get a scholarship somewhere like yo' sister. These damned Republicans ain't gon' make no way for you. You can bet that. Sonofabitches! . . .

SHERRIE: Ooo, Daddy . . .

EARL: Sorry, baby. But Republicans is mean. Remember that when you start votin' . . . Let me see what we got here . . . *(Takes the crayon drawing)* That me? . . .

SHERRIE: Yep. Makin' big muscles 'cause you're all well.

EARL: Aw, yeah. Big muscles. Look just like me. But what's this outfit I'm wearin'?

SHERRIE: A weight-lifting suit. Like it?

EARL: Oh yeah. It's nice. But I have to wear it in the house.

SHERRIE: Why? . . .

EARL: I don't think Mommie gon' let me go out in the street dressed like this. She's jealous you know. But this is a fine picture. Gonna hang it up in my room for inspiration. Give me a hug.

SHERRIE: Mommie said don't.

EARL: Forget Mommie. Told you how she is. Come here.

(SHE hugs him. Then sits on floor with her head against his leg, looking over one of her notebooks)

EARL: *(Continued)* Sherrie, baby? Me and you don't have no secrets, right?

SHERRIE: Right . . .

EARL: Right. So tell me what Mommie said the doctor said about my back.

SHERRIE: Huh? . . . She said the doctor said you have to have rest.

EARL: For a *long* time?

SHERRIE: Uh-huh . . . Naw, a *little* while.

EARL: Oh, a little while. I can handle that.

SHERRIE: Uh-huh . . . I'm gon' get me a sandwich. Want one? . . .

EARL: Naw, baby. I'm fine.

(SHE gets up and starts to hallway)

EARL: *(Continued)* Hey. Make sure your brother ain't just starin' at those books, daydreamin'. Tell him to *study*; turn some pages in there . . .

SHERRIE: Right . . . *(Goes offstage)* . . . E. J.?! . . . Daddy say study! Turn some pages!! . . .

E. J.: *(Offstage)* You better leave me alone. Little creep . . .

(Front door opens/closes. CHERYL comes in)

CHERYL: Earl?? . . . What're you doin' out of bed? . . .

EARL: What are you doin' home? . . . Off early, ain't you?

CHERYL: *(Going to him)* We had a luncheon. Took the rest of the day off. Look at you: Out here sweatin'.

EARL: Tired of that damned bed. A luncheon, huh. That why you look so pretty—and sexy? Give me a kiss.

(SHE bends to kiss)

CHERYL: You said I always look pretty and sexy. Guess I just can't help it . . .

EARL: Well, I don't like it when I'm laid up like this.

(CHERYL sits beside him on couch, playfully touching, kissing him)

CHERYL: Laid up. Sexy. Isn't there some kind of connection there?

EARL: Oh, now you gonna tease me . . .

CHERYL: Tease? . . . Mister, I've been thinkin' about you *layin' up* in that bed, all day long. Wondering if I couldn't maybe do *something* to relieve you a little. Something better than those pills. I'm sure I could think of something that wouldn't—ummm—tax your energy . . .

EARL: What? . . . How many drinks did you have at this luncheon?

CHERYL: One virgin daiquiri. I didn't need anything to drink. The thought of you lying there was enough.

EARL: Girl, you oughta be ashamed . . .

CHERYL: *(Taking off earrings, etc.)* Of what? Wanting to tend to my husband? . . . Can you make it back to the bed? . . . I'll go tell these children that Daddy mustn't be disturbed for the next couple hours . . .

EARL: *(Struggling to rise)* Yeah. Send 'em to the library, or the movie. Somewhere . . .

CHERYL: *(Rising)* You need help? . . .

EARL: Naw, I don't need no damn help . . .

CHERYL: *(Crossing out)* E. J.?! . . . Sherrie?! . . . I'm about to give Daddy a—a massage and—sleeping pill. So you have to keep it down. And stay out of our room! . . .

(EARL gets up with effort, smiling, shaking head)

EARL: Now this is what I call a real private nurse . . .

(HE crosses into hallway. Lights fading to rise of Doggett's "Honky Tonk."

Lights up on E. J. tiptoeing into living room, holding an apple in his mouth as HE slips into jacket. HE listens to CHERYL laughing from offstage bedroom)

CHERYL: *(Offstage)* Nooo! . . . Nooo! . . . Uh-uh! . . . We can't! . . . Doctor's orders! . . .

EARL: *(Offstage)* Awww. Then why you talk all that talk out there then?! . . .

CHERYL: *(Offstage)* Because if I'd said, "Earl, please get back in bed," you'd still be out there arguin' with me . . .

EARL: *(Offstage)* Awww. Got my back all tensed up anyway with the thought; might as well come on with the action . . .

CHERYL: *(Offstage)* Believe me, baby: It's just as hard on me as it is on you . . .

EARL: *(Offstage)* Naw, it's on me! Bout to lift me off this bed!!

(E. J. shakes his head at the two of them; tips toward door)

EARL: *(Offstage, Continued)* E. J.!? . . . If you finished your homework! Bring it in here, let me see it!! . . . If not! Get back in there an' turn some pages, boy! . . .

E. J.: Aw, Dad, I was jus' goin' down to . . .

EARL: *(Offstage)* You heard me, boy!! . . .

(SHERRIE peeks out from doorway)

SHERRIE: You heard him, boy! . . . *(Sticks out tongue)*

E. J.: Shut up, little snitch! You told, didn't you! Gon' get you! . . .

(Chases SHERRIE into hallway. SHE screams for her parents)

EARL: *(Offstage)* E. J.!! . . .

CHERYL: *(Offstage)* Don't you bother my baby! . . .

(As light fades to black, loud hip-hop music displaces "Yakkity Yak." In darkness, ERIC/E. J. dance movements with SHERRIE. Music lowers)

GAIL: *(In dark)* What, Ma?! . . . Why are you buggin' me!? . . .

(Lights up on CHERYL following GAIL from hallway. It is the fall of the following year)

CHERYL: Buggin' you!? . . . I'm gonna do more than that if you don't straighten up and stop being so selfish! . . .

GAIL: Selfish?! . . .

CHERYL: That's right! . . . Sherrie, turn that thing down! Turn it off!! . . .

(SHERRIE turns off the music. ERIC/E. J. each sit in an easy chair)

GAIL: Just what are we talking about here, Mother?

(ERIC/E. J. make faces and gestures aping her formal speech and attitude)

CHERYL: Don't give me that tone. I'll tell you what I'm talkin' about: Give your father a break! . . .

GAIL: What? . . .

CHERYL: Stop tellin' him about all this little brick-brat, bullshit, you *need*. And do something for yourself. For a change!

GAIL: Oh, for a change, huh? That's not fair. I do a *lot* for myself. As a matter of fact that's all I was telling Dad, that I have saved half of what I need from this little summer job. And I'll get some job around school for the rest! That's all I said to him!

CHERYL: Uh-huh. Just enough to have him laying up worrying about it. Trying to figure out how to borrow some more for you. You know what his situation is . . . *(Paces)* . . . The first few months, when he was on full pay, everything was—alright, the same. Then it went to eighty per cent. Then sixty. And now . . . Well, it's not like it was before. And you know how he feels about you and your education. We already talked about this, Gail: You're no longer a little girl runnin' to Daddy because Mommy won't let you have new pair of jeans! . . .

GAIL: *(Near tears)* That's not fair, Mother. That's not fair at all . . .

ERIC: *(Laughs, mimicking)* That's not fair, Mother. Wooo! . . .

(Perhaps HE expected E. J. to laugh with him. At any rate HE misjudges the moment: EVERYONE turns to him with familial hostility and protectiveness. HE is an electrified outsider)

GAIL: *(Charging to him)* What're you laughing at! Get out! This is none of your ghetto-ass business!

SHERRIE: Yeah! Go home! . . .

CHERYL: Gail! . . . Sherrie! . . .

ERIC: *(Getting to feet)* Hey. You know what you can do with that ghetto talk. I'm here with your brother, like always. Alright? If I jumped outta turn, I'm sorry . . .

GAIL: Get out! . . .

E. J.: *(Rising)* You right, you jumped outta place. So it's time for you to hit it. Come on, I'll walk you to the stop.

CHERYL: E. J. . . .

ERIC: You serious? You gon' come on me like this?

E. J.: You got it. You get silly enough to step between my mother and sister, then it's time for you to air out. I'll walk and rap with you.

ERIC: *(Picking up jacket)* Hey, you don't have to walk me nowhere. I got over here, I can get back!

GAIL: Just go! . . .

SHERRIE: Knock him out, Jun'! . . .

CHERYL: Everybody just shut up! E. J.!? Eric!? You two just cut it out! Right now! . . .

(EARL comes in from front door area, carrying bottle in brown paper bag)

EARL: Cut what out?! . . . What's all this hollerin'?! . . . What's happenin' in here?! . . .

CHERYL: Nothin', Earl . . .

EARL: Nothin'? . . . E. J.? . . . Eric? . . .

ERIC: *(Eyes on E. J.)* Nothin', Mr. Carter. I was jus' bouncin' up outta' here . . .

(With a facetious "butler's bow," E. J. extends a hand toward the door, moves aside. ERIC crosses out)

E. J.: *(Relenting)* Hold up, man! . . . *(Crosses)*

ERIC: *(Offstage)* Skip it, man. Forget it . . .

E. J.: *(Offstage)* Aw, man, hold up! . . .

(Sound of front door opening/closing.

EARL looks questioningly at his three females with the befuddled focus of the inebriated)

CHERYL: In the kitchen, Gail . . .

GAIL: Mother, you can't be ordering me around like a little child! I am not . . .

(Exasperated to tears, SHE nevertheless marches off to kitchen. CHERYL follows her)

EARL: Cheryl? . . . Gail? . . .

(HE turns to SHERRIE who starts for kitchen)

SHERRIE: Come on, Daddy. Mama and Eric jumpin' on my sister.

EARL: Yo' mama and Eric??? . . .

(THEY go off to kitchen)

CHERYL: *(Offstage)* We don't need you two in here! . . .

EARL: *(Offstage) (Comically)* Now, wait just one damned minute! I may be out of work! But this is still my damned house! . . .

(Lights up on E. J./ERIC DOWN LEFT in street area)

ERIC: Man, you don't know how bad I feel about this man . . .

E. J.: Skip past it, man. It's over. You stepped up on the bad foot, and I pulled your coat. Forget it . . . Where's the damned bus? . . .

ERIC: Man, how come Gail always so down on me? . . . I mean the resta y'all always been cool, and she's always been N.G. on me . . .

E. J.: Hey, she's Gail, my sister. What can I say? Maybe she goes for you. That what you want me to say? . . .

ERIC: Aw, man, I don' even think about her like that.

E. J.: Yeah, right . . .

ERIC: Come on, man, it ain't like that . . . *(A beat)* . . . Know what I think? It's like I'm part of the old neighborhood. And she wants to get as far away from that as she can. Don't never come back and hang like you do . . .

E. J.: *(Looking down street for the bus)* Since my grandmother died, none of them go back much. Pops used to make us go so we'd remember where we came from before we moved over here . . . Damn! It's a bitch, man!

ERIC: What?

E. J.: The way things are at the house all the time now, man. Everybody always wack about—money. Pops getting' all—all bent outta shape.

ERIC: Ain't no thang, man. He just used to being Pops Carter. You know, the big fella. He'll pump it up.

E. J.: Wow, glad you told me that, man. Now I don't have to be worryin' on it no more, right? . . . Where the bus? . . . Some damn money. What's up with that? My folks workin' straight all they lives, and all twisted up. And dumb-butt doo-doo's like Skeet and Slim got fat pockets, ridin' in Beemers and Benzes. What's up with that? . . .

ERIC: Hey, they workin' wit' Big John. He got 'em wit' them bankrolls and rides . . .

E. J.: Yeah. He still after you to get with him? . . .

ERIC: Naw, not much no more. Everybody know I run with you. And you don't go that way . . .

E. J.: Got that right. Dad would bust me down hisself.

ERIC: Yeah, I run with you. You got a paper route. Got me one. You start workin' in the malls and stuff. Me too. Helped me keep my thang together. Down with all y'all. The whole family. Gail too. Go to the wall for her too. That's why it bugs me so, her dissin' me like she do. Talkin' that ghetto random, and shit . . .

E. J.: Aw, man, don't go back there again. Please . . . Where the bus? . . .

ERIC: Yeah, why don't the bus come, so you won't have to be tryin' to hear what's happenin' wit' me. Right? . . .

E. J.: Right . . . *(Smiling)*

ERIC: Yeah, you think you know, but you don't know. I can tell you somethin' you don't know.

E. J.: *(Looking for bus)* Like what?

ERIC: Like those times y'all be getting' up in the mornin'? And I'd be right there at the door when your ol' man be leavin' for work? I'd be right there at the door? Remember? . . .

E. J.: Yeah. So? . . .

ERIC: So sometimes I never went home. Sleep in onea' them ol' cars ol' Jake be fixin' in that lot across the street from y'all. Or that ol' abandoned building on the corner . . .

E. J.: What? . . . You did what? . . .

ERIC: You heard me. Had an alarm clock. And Bull. Remember the dog I had back then? Bull? Kept the rats and junkies and shit off me . . .

E. J.: Wait. Hold it. You bullshittin' . . .

ERIC: Naw. Sometimes I'd go by home first. Change clothes. So I wouldn't be so funky. Always ask to use the bathroom first. Remember? Sneak and brush my teeth with my finger. So I wouldn't be makin' that brushin' sound, you know, what a brush makes . . .

E. J.: Hold it. You actually slept in ol' Jake's funky cars? With Bull? . . . Why, man? What was up with that? . . .

ERIC: Come on, man. You seen what I was livin' in. Would you wanna be up in that? Your grandmother tryin' to work past two junkies, your mother and your uncle? And they arguin' about some dope, smellin' like . . . She shooin' them around like—two dogs in the way. My little brother and sister caught up in it. Think you wanna take that to school wit' you in the mornin', every day? . . . Hmmph, sometimes I couldn't make it. So I go hang with y'all. People sittin' aroun' a table, talkin' and carryin' on, like—people spose to. I'd take that to school . . . Yeah, take y'all to school . . .

(E.J stares at him, then turns away with embarrassment)

E. J.: Damn . . . Thought you was just tryin' to get up on some breakfast.

ERIC: Yeah, Gail be crackin' like that, "If you already had breakfast, how come yo' stomach growlin'?" But it wasn't all about no breakfast. Know what it was like? Was like, y'all house was some kinda dream; and mine was the real deal. But I wanted it the other way: Let that shit be the dream. Bad dream. Yeah, just wake up somewhere else . . . Yeah, and she still be crackin', with her jive, stuck-up butt . . .

E. J.: Yo. Hold it. See there: Some dudes don't never learn. Don't be dissin' my sister—chump! . . . *(Hits him hard on the arm)*

ERIC: What?! . . . Okay, chump! Downin' yo' ass! . . .

(THEY go at it with shots to the arms, slaps to the face. It is clear that E. J. is the superior fighter, faster, more aggressive, and, finally, stronger. HE rushes ERIC; lifts him in air with an arm under/between his legs; other hand gripping his collar; turns him upside down, head pointing to ground—coins fall out of his pocket)

ERIC: *(Continued)* Yo! Let me down, fool! Let me down! . . . Losin' my bus fare! . . .

(E. J. puts him on ground, laughing)

ERIC: *(Continued) (On knees, looking for coins)* One of these days, I'm gon' kick yo' jive ass . . .

E. J.: Been sayin' that since we was nine. And I'm still downin' you . . .

ERIC: I'm short a quarter! . . .

E. J.: *(Laughing)* Better find it. Don't think Gail gon' vote for you to spend the night here . . .

ERIC: To hell wit' Gail . . . Here it is . . .

E. J.: You gettin' lucky. Here comes the bus . . .

(ERIC scrambles to his feet, dusting himself off; starts off)

E. J.: *(Continued)* Check this: We need some money. See if Big John let us work some of his legit things.

ERIC: He ain't got nothin' legit! . . . *(Goes off)*

E. J.: *(Calling after him)* Heard he had some stores! . . . Them dudes always got some kinda legit fronts! . . . Check him! . . .

ERIC: *(Offstage)* Alright! . . . Later! . . . Yo! . . . Hold that bus!! . . . Yo! . . .

(E. J. waves, laughing; then as the bus sounds dim, HE turns toward house; hesitates, then walks thoughtfully, aimlessly, up and off.

Lights up on living room. EARL coming from hallway, pouring drink from bottle in brown paper bag. CHERYL/SHERRIE/GAIL follow him in with wearied expressions to take seats)

EARL: Now I want you all to come in here and sit. 'Cause I got somethin' to say . . .

CHERYL: Well, say it then, and get it over with . . .

EARL: *(A hard look)* Right there. That's what I mean . . .

CHERYL: Oh, Lord. What?! . . .

EARL: No respect! That's what! . . .

CHERYL: Oh, God . . .

GAIL: Dad, listen. We . . .

EARL: Naw, y'all listen. I don't care what those people out there be tryin' to put on me. Cuttin' my money almost in half. And . . .

CHERYL: *(Wearily)* Earl, it's regular workman's comp. It decreases.

EARL: I know that, Miss Social Worker. But how come I'm on comp anyway? Huh? I been tellin' 'em I'm ready to come back to work for a year now. And what they say, huh? . . .

CHERYL: The *doctor* said you couldn't go back to your old job. Not with your back liable to go out any minute.

EARL: So how come they haven't found me another job? Huh? . . .

CHERYL: All those old jobs are being phased out. That's why they wanted you to go to school . . .

EARL: School! . . . Computers. Went to those damned classes. I felt like . . . like . . . Sherrie here startin' kindergarten. Pushin' those damned buttons, keys: Click-click. Clack-clack . . . Shiiit . . .

GAIL: That's what's happenin' now, Dad, computers . . . *(Shrugs)* Once you get into them . . .

EARL: *You* get into 'em. I been doin' a man's work since I was a boy! Ain't gon' start doin' some woman's work now, when I'm just as good as I ever been! Or, just about as good . . .

CHERYL: *(Noticing her nodding off)* Sherrie. Go to bed, baby. Go 'head . . .

(SHERRIE hesitates, looking to her father)

EARL: Go on to bed, baby. Past yo' time.

SHERRIE: Y'all ain't gon' be hollerin' down here, are you? . . . *(Crosses to kiss CHERYL; comes to EARL)*

EARL: *(Bending to her)* Naw, sugar, won't be no more hollerin' . . .

SHERRIE: You sure, Daddy? You gon' be alright? . . .

EARL: Yeah, Daddy's gon' be cool . . .

SHERRIE: Okay . . . *(Starting out)* . . . You comin' up in a little while, Gail?

GAIL: Yep. Get the bed warmed up for me.

(SHE crosses as E. J. enters. EARL pours another drink from the bag/bottle)

EARL: Junior! Good. Glad you back. Want you *all* to hear this . . .

E. J.: Huh? What's up now? . . .

CHERYL: That damned bottle is what's up! . . .

GAIL: *(Aside)* Too many times, if you ask me . . .

EARL: Don't you worry about this bottle. I can handle this shit. *I'll* tell *you* what I can and can't handle. Sit down, Junior.

E. J.: Think I'll stand, Dad.

EARL: Alright. Now: I can handle them tryin' to jugg me out there on the job; with the damned union droppin' its drawers and getting' in bed with management. Playin' me cheap with sweet talk about retraining, re-this, and re-that. Like they gon' redo *me*! I can stand anything they throwin' on me out there. What I can't stand—*(Pauses to control his emotions)* . . . What I can't stand, is comin' in here and shit's flyin' off the walls from everybody! And when I come in, it don't stop! Don't make no difference me being here. Used to make a difference when I walked in here. Family sat up and took notice. And now? I don't make no damned difference?! . . . Uh-uh . . .

CHERYL: Earl, listen . . .

GAIL: Come on, Dad . . .

EARL: . . . Naw! . . . Uh-uh . . . I know I can't make a damn difference out there! They can call me what they want out there! A has-been ass failure out there, if they want! But ain't nothin' changin' in here! You hear me!? . . . *(Has started to cry)* . . . I-still-make-a-difference—in here! Hear me! I make a . . .

(CHERYL/GAIL start to him)

CHERYL: Don't start this now, Earl . . .

GAIL: Come on, Dad, now . . .

EARL: *(Crying)* Naw, get off me! . . . Out there's one thing! But in here?! I'm holdin' these walls up! The floor down! And that damned roof on! . . . You got that?! . . .

(The TWO WOMEN *have him between them now)*

CHERYL: Earl. Honey. Stop it . . .

GAIL: Dad. Dad . . . Please . . .

EARL: Naw! . . . I'm somebody in here! Understand? I worked for it! Earned it! Gon' have it! . . . Hear me!? . . . I mean that shit! I . . . aw, shit . . . shit . . .

CHERYL: Earl . . . Don't, baby . . . Don't . . .

GAIL: Dad, we *love* you . . . We love you, Dad. Please . . .

E. J.: *(An eruption)* Let him go!! Let him go! . . . Cut that out, Dad!! You hear me!? Don't do that!! Don't cry like that, man!! Don't you cry like that! . . .

*(*HE *has backed near the door; near angry tears himself.* EARL *straightens under E. J.'s condemning look; pulls away from the* WOMEN, *takes a step toward his son)*

EARL: Earl Junior, now you listen here . . .

E. J.: Naw, man, you nix this! . . .

EARL: Hey! Now you listen to me! I been one to cry all my life! Ask your mama. But it ain't never been outta no weakness! Feelings, yeah! Weakness—hell, naw! . . .

E. J.: Naw! . . . I know the difference, man! You hear? I know the difference. So you cut the shit! . . .

*(*HE *runs out.* EARL *goes to doorway to holler after him)*

EARL: Boy!? . . . E. J.?! . . . You come back in here! . . . You hear me?! You come . . .

*(*HE *turns back to wife and daughter.* CHERYL *gives him a disgusted look as* SHE *snatches up the bag/bottle from the table and exits.* GAIL *averts her face from him as* SHE *sits sideways on the couch.* EARL *starts first after* CHERYL*; stops and turns toward* GAIL*; then turns and comes to audience as light fades around him and spot narrows in on his face)*

EARL: *(Continued)* They got it all wrong in the Bible: It ain't by the sweat of your brow. It's by the sweata' your back. That's how you make your bread. Make your children. Make your way. You don't believe me, then try to do somethin', anything, without usin' your back. Those muscles all up and down back there. Try to raise something. Make love. Hold on to something—without usin' those big back muscles. You can't do it. Not and do it strong. Do it like . . . like, a man. Naw, that sweata' yo' brow stuff is for them pushin' them keys. Up in those offices. Wearin' those white shirts. Yeah *(Pause)* I maybe coulda been onea' them workin' it by the sweat of the brow. Uh-huh. I mean I wasn't no dummy in school. But

I loved this woman here. Her and anything coming out of her. Yeah, she was gonna have my baby. And, hell, we'd done waited long enough. All through my army bit. Wasn't no sense in waitin' through college. Hell, I didn't want no college; no white shirts. I wanted her. Always wanted her. And I didn't need nothin' but the brains I was born with and this strong back to get into that factory. It was the best, fastest way to take care of her, me, and anything we could make together. And I ain't complaining. Fact I bragged about it: House. New cars. Even had part ownership in a little boat. Don't have it now. But I had it. Oh, yeah, I used to throw all that this ol' back gave me up in the faces of the dudes goin' after those white shirts. Hell, took them years to catch up to me in my overalls. Yeah, hell yeah. But now—now I've got to carry my back, like it used to carry me. And . . . well, my mind's been leaning on my back so long it's gotten lazy. Can't shift gears fast enough to catch on to all these clack-clack keys, and classes—and bull. Naw. All this new stuff is comin' too late for me. But, y'all . . .

(Lights come up full as HE *moves back to sit in chair across from* GAIL *on the couch; speaking as though the monologue had all taken place to her)*

EARL: *(Continued)* . . . you, and your brother and sister. Y'all gon' be hip to it all. Gonna be like drivin' a car to y'all. So I don't want you to be worried about your school money. 'Cause I'm gon' see to it . . .

GAIL: I'm not worried, Dad. Really. But I can go to work for awhile . . .

EARL: Hey! That's what your mother said. Before . . . Before babies and other good things started happenin' so fast, she didn't never get back to school. Now, she can't get no promotions . . .

GAIL: Nothing will keep me from goin' back. It would only be for a little while . . .

EARL: *(Getting up)* Hey! What did I tell you: You do your part an' keep that scholarship; and I'll do mine, and see that you have everything you need. Right? Ain't that what I said? . . . Well, that's what gon' happen . . .

*(*HE *holds out his hand;* SHE *takes it and gets up to share hug/kiss on the forehead)*

EARL: *(Continued)* That's my smart girl. You go on upstairs. I'm gonna sit out here awhile; wait for that boy of mine to come back.

GAIL: *(Crossing)* You two aren't gonna be at each other, now, are you?

EARL: Naw. Gonna tell him he was right: There is a difference. And, like your mama said, it probably comes from that bottle.

GAIL: Good night, Dad . . .

EARL: Good night, sugar . . .

(SHE exits. HE settles onto couch; light fades to a blue glow as HE sinks into sleep. CHERYL comes out with blanket; carefully puts it over him; starts to give him kiss, then waves away alcohol aroma, and goes back out.

E. J. comes in; sees him on couch; hesitates, then goes to nudge him awake; sits next to him)

E. J.: Hey, Dad. Hey. Wake up . . . Ma lock you out? . . .

(EARL sits up)

EARL: Don't know . . . Ain't tried the door yet . . .

E. J.: Dad? I'm sorry. I was out the box. Out of place.

EARL: Yeah. But right as rain. And, look here: Whenever you see me comin' outta that po-mouth, sorry little boy shit—you check me. Hear?

(E. J. smiles, nods)

EARL: *(Continued)* Okay. Now help me up from here . . .

(E. J. starts to help him up; EARL grabs him by his jacket collar, pulls him down, wraps legs around his arms, his waist)

EARL: *(Continued)* But don't be checkin' me too damned tough! . . . Understand?! . . . Understand?! . . .

E. J.: Hey, Dad, chill! . . . Gon' hurt your back . . . Okay. Alright. Alright . . .

EARL: *(Releases him)* Alright then. Now help me up, *Junior*.

(THEY move to hallway)

EARL: *(Continued)* Good night, son. Don't worry, I'll be cool.

E. J.: I know. See you in the mornin' . . .

(THEY enter hallway; E. J. going LEFT, EARL, RIGHT)

CHERYL: *(Offstage)* Don't know where you think you goin'! . . . Don't feel like smellin' no alcohol tonight.

EARL: Know you ain't lockin' no doors on me! This my damned house! . . .

CHERYL: *(Offstage)* That ain't all I'm lockin' . . .

EARL: *(Tapping on door)* Baby, come on. I got mouth wash in there . . . You know that couch bad for my back. Come on, Cheryl! . . .

SHERRIE: *(Offstage)* E. J.!? . . . What they hollerin' about?! . . .

E. J.: *(Offstage)* Nothin'! Go back to sleep! . . .

GAIL: *(Offstage) (Sleepily)* It's called foreplay . . .

SHERRIE: *(Offstage)* What? Play? . . . Mama?! Can I play too!? . . .

CHERYL: *(Offstage)* Yeah, baby! Come on! Mama'll open the door for *you*! . . .

EARL: *(Offstage)* Naw! Naw, Sherrie! . . .

SHERRIE: *(Offstage) (Running)* Yayy! . . . Come on, Daddy!! We gon' play!! . . .

EARL: *(Offstage)* Awww, Lord . . . Cheryl, you oughta be ashamed . . .

(Lights fade on EVERYONE'S laughter—except EARL'S.

Lights up on CHERYL at her desk area of living room. It is a year later. SHE is dressed in winter clothes; looking harassed, haggard, as SHE goes over pile of bills. SHE paces; comes back to desk; picks up bills, an open, already read letter; turns suddenly toward hallway)

CHERYL: E. J.! . . . You heard me, boy! Get-in-here! . . . E. J.?! . . .

E. J.: *(Offstage)* I'm comin', Ma! . . . Chill . . .

CHERYL: *(To herself)* I've got your chill . . .

(SHE leans against desk, arms folded. E. J. enters with slight, "street" swagger; wearing a baseball cap, with his jacket tucked under his arm as HE rubs lotion on his hands, face)

E. J.: What's up? . . .

CHERYL: Don't give me that what's up mess. I'll tell you what's not up: your grades. And what is *up* is the number of times you've been absent this term. Why, Earl Junior? . . . *(Holds out letter and report card)* Your report card. Since you conveniently lost the one you alleged we had signed, the school decided to mail us one. Why, Earl Junior? Why do you want to hit him with this kind of mess now? . . .

E. J.: Him? . . . I ain't tryin' to do nothin' to him.

CHERYL: No? Look at this! *(Picks up pile of bills and drops them back on desk)* Bills! Just rainin' down on him! Piling up like—like snow! And—and, Gail's in trouble. And it's been almost two years now since he's had a decent pay. And now here you come with this mess! . . .

E. J.: Gail? What kinda trouble she got? . . .

CHERYL: What kind you think? Money trouble. We don't have the money for her next term. So she might have to come home and work for awhile. You know how *that's* gonna make him feel. And now here you come with some delinquent shit. Why? . . . Why? . . . Answer me, dammit! . . .

E. J.: Just hold it a minute, Ma. Calm down. Be done woke him up . . .

CHERYL: *(Lowering voice)* Don't tell me to calm down. Answer my question. What's goin' with you and your grades? . . .

E. J.: I don't know. Guess I jus'—jus' lost my concentration.

CHERYL: What else you got to do but concentrate on school? Huh? . . .

E. J.: Whole lotta things goin' on, Ma. I mean, I see what he' goin' through. What's happenin'. I see everything.

CHERYL: Don't you try to put this on him too. This is your responsibility. Yours, Earl Junior. He's got enough on his plate.

E. J.: I didn't mean it like that, Ma. I'm just sayin' you ain't the only one see what's happenin' with him. Me too. Look: I jus' got off the track. Okay? Like, school just lost it with me for a minute. You know?

CHERYL: Lost it with *you*?

E. J.: I mean with all that's happenin' all around, school just wasn't like up on it. You know? Like they talkin' about things that's dead. Or things that's gonna be. They ain't up with me on what's happenin' now. Understand? . . .

CHERYL: Just shut up. What's happenin' now is you're adding to his problems. Do you understand *that*?

E. J.: Yeah, Ma, I understand. Look: Cut you a deal. Okay?

CHERYL: Do what? . . .

E. J.: Listen: You don't tell him about this, and I promise I'll bring my grades back up. I swear, Ma. I'll get 'em back up. Okay? A deal? . . .

CHERYL: *(A beat)* Where you get this deal talk? . . .

E. J.: Okay, Ma? Swear. I'll get 'em back up. Okay?

CHERYL: You better get 'em up . . . I'll think about it.

(SHE picks up bills)

E. J.: Thanks, Ma. Gotta go . . . *(Puts on jacket. It is an expensive looking, leather and suede item)*

CHERYL: Go where? . . . You always runnin' out in the street. You need to be getting' on some homework! Right now! . . . That a new jacket? Where'd you get that jacket? . . .

E. J.: This Eric's jacket. Sharp, ain't it. He let me wear it. He got mine. That's onea' the things I gotta do: Take him his jacket. Get mine.

CHERYL: Keep your own clothes from now on. Alright. But you come straight back here and get in those books. Understand? . . . *(SHE goes to sit at desk, picks up bills)*

E. J.: Yeah, Ma. Be right back . . .

(HE hesitates; puts on scarf, zips up jacket, pulls on new-looking leather gloves. HE watches her as SHE drops bills, picks up official-looking paper)

CHERYL: Gail's keepin' her grades up, bless her heart. But my credit union said no more. Sooo, there's just—no way. *(Pushes bills away; puts fingertips to temples)*

E. J.: She just *have* to come home?

CHERYL: Yes! And get a job and pull her weight. While you're—you're—Just go on, Earl Junior. Go on . . .

(Her tone strikes him; gives him the impetus for his decision. HE hesitates; looks to hallway)

E. J.: You sure he's sleep in there? . . .

CHERYL: What he calls sleep nowadays. I can't remember him ever talkin' in his sleep before. But now? All night long, mumbling and moaning. Last night, I finally figured out what he's been saying. Sayin': Don't worry, I got it. I got it. Don't worry. Over and over. Like it's one long word. God. I just don't know what to do for him no more . . .

E. J.: How much is it, Ma? . . .

CHERYL: Huh? . . . What? . . . How much is what? . . .

E. J.: All that on the desk. All the bills. Gail's stuff. Everything. How much is it, Ma. Huh? . . .

CHERYL: Why? What difference does it make? Lot more than we can handle all at once like this. That's how much.

E. J.: How much? Just wanna know. Just—curious. How much, Ma?

CHERYL: Alright. How much? All of it? The mortgage, car insurances, regular ol' bills, and the half we'd have to pay on Gail's money? . . . Oh, about—thirty-five hundred dollars.

E. J.: That's all? . . .

CHERYL: What? Is that all? Boy, get outta here before I throw somethin' at you. Is that all? Just—go on somewhere.

E. J.: Naw. I mean, we goin' through all this. And that's it? Thirty-five hundred? . . . Hold on. Jus' hold on . . .

(HE crosses into hallway, purposefully)

CHERYL: Don't you wake him up . . . Where're you goin'? Like father, like son: Crazy! "Is that all?!" I swear . . .

(SHE stands wondering; picks up a letter, paces, reading it. Goes back to sit at desk.

E. J. comes back in, hands in jacket pockets; goes to desk, puts thick roll of bills down in front of her)

CHERYL: *(Incredulous; picking it up)* What's this? . . .

E. J.: It's money, Ma. Thirty-two hundred dollars . . .

CHERYL: *(Counting)* Thirty-two hun . . . ??? . . . E. J.? Whose money is this? Where'd you get all this money??? . . .

E. J.: It's mine, Ma. Ours. I hustled for it.

CHERYL: *(Stunned, registering)* Hustled for it? . . .

(SHE stands slowly and moves toward him, shaking her head with disbelief and pained realization)

E. J.: *(With a nervous chuckle)* Ma . . . Ma, listen . . .

CHERYL: Hustled for it? . . . That jacket. Riding up here in those expensive cars all the time . . . E.J . . . . E. J. Uh-uh! Uh-uh . . .

E. J.: *(Keeping his voice down)* Ma, listen to me now . . .

CHERYL: No, E. J., no! . . . *(Like flicking off a deadly bug* SHE *flings the roll against his chest with a flip of her wrists. Fierce whisper)* Take-this-shit-out-of-my-house!

E. J.: Ma, listen to me. Listen! . . .

CHERYL: Pick it up—and get it *out* of here.

E. J.: *(Gripping her shoulders)* I know what you're thinking, Ma. Think I'll mess aroun' and get shot or somethin'. Right? . . .

CHERYL: Boy, did you hear me? Did you hear any of the things we tried to teach you all these years? Huh? Who *are* you? . . .

E. J.: *(Holding her wrists)* I'm me, Ma. Your son. His son. And I heard you before, and I hear you now. Everyday. Moanin' and groanin' about money. Gettin' all bent over 'bout a few limp dollars. Both'a you . . .

CHERYL: Turn me loose! . . .

(SHE pulls away from him, one hand raised as to slap him. HE stands frozen before her—his entire body imploring understanding, acceptance)

E. J.: . . . Y'all getting' all punked out bout a few greens! You and Dad. My folks. While dumb-ass dudes out there scoopin' it up off the streets like it's fallin' off the trees! . . .

CHERYL: I don't care what they're doin' out there. You. In here. That's what I'm talkin' about. You get that stuff up out of . . .

E. J.: Ma, I understand how you feel. But, listen . . .

CHERYL: No. Naw. You don't understand. Uh-uh. You couldn't. 'Cause if you did, you couldn't be doin' this. Standin' there sayin' this . . . E. J., you got to back away from me. I need some air. You took all the air out of this room . . . Out of me . . .

(As SHE *says this last,* SHE *leans against a chair; first waving her hands before her face, then touching her temples)*

E. J.: Ma, listen, you thinkin' about hits and shootouts, and like that. But I ain't into nonea' that . . .

CHERYL: Just what are you into, E. J.? Huh? No. Don't tell me. All you can do is pick that up; take it back where you got it; come back in here and don't ever go back there. That's all you can do for me. That's all.

(SHE moves around chair to slide down into it, shaking her head)

E. J.: Ma, it's not just the rollin', dealin'. There's all kinds of soft stuff goin' on *aroun'* the dealin'. Understand? Pickups. Delivering. Packaging. Hey, just showin' folks to what they want. Understand? . . .

CHERYL: *(Incredulous chuckle)* Pickups. Packaging. You sound like you workin' in a department store . . . Lord, none of this is really happening. Not all that money on the floor. Not you standin' here tellin' me about pickups and packaging. None of this . . .

E. J.: Oh, it's happenin', Ma. And for a while it's gonna keep on happenin' . . .

CHERYL: What? . . .

(HE bends to scoop up money; then moves to desk, taking rubber band off and dropping batches of bills down as HE talks)

E. J.: My sister's gon' stay in school . . . My pops gon' get that hump out. Hold his head up again . . . And my ma's—my ma's gonna quit walkin' the floor at night, talkin' to herself . . . Then I'll ease on out the game. And get down with school and all that, again.

(SHE stands up. THEY stare at each other; SHE incredulous, HE determined. Offstage THEY hear EARL coming, singing)

EARL:

SUGAR PIE/HONEY BUNCH

(Repeats)

YOU KNOW THAT I LOOOVVVE YOU!
CAN'T HELP MYSELF/I LOVE YOU AND
NOBODY ELSE.

(At the first sound the TWO BOTH jump. E. J. sweeps money into desk drawer, then backs to door)

E. J.: It's already here, Ma. I can't take it back. Best you use it for somethin' good . . . I gotta go . . .

(HE turns and goes out door. CHERYL crosses to doorway)

CHERYL: *(Keeping voice down)* You take this shit outta here!! . . . E. J.?! . . . Come back here . . . I'm gonna throw it out in the yard! . . .

(Outer door slams. EARL enters)

EARL: Gonna throw what in the yard? . . . Who's that goin' out? . . .

CHERYL: E. J. . . .

EARL: E. J.? . . . This timea' night? Where's he goin'?

CHERYL: Who knows.

EARL: Huh? . . . Aw, don't worry. Can't be goin' far this timea' night. Knows he's got to get ready for school tomorrow. Just young, restless . . . Just had a idea. Listen: Hard times like these, what do people want to do? . . .

CHERYL: *(Moving to desk)* What? . . . Get some money? . . .

EARL: Well, yeah, naturally. I'm comin' to that. Definitely. But think: What do they wanna do?! Party! . . . Forget their problems and have a good time! Right? . . .

CHERYL: *(Absently)* I guess. Yeah . . .

(SHE stares at desk drawer, pulls it out slightly)

EARL: Damn right. Ball and forget it all. Okay. But our crowd, folks our age, what they gonna do? Where they goin'? Somewhere with rowdy young jitterbugs, hip-hoppin' and DJ's scratchin' on the records? Huh?! Where . . . What's all that? . . . *(Points to pile of bills on the desk)* All bills? . . .

CHERYL: *(Startled; closing drawer)* Huh? . . . Oh, ummm. Old bills . . .

EARL: Old bills? And they still here? Let me see 'em . . .

CHERYL: They're dead now, Earl. Don't worry about 'em. *(SHE sweeps them up, and puts them into drawer)* . . . We've paid 'em . . .

EARL: Paid 'em? All of 'em? . . .

CHERYL: *(A beat, staring at money)* Yeah . . . All of 'em . . .

(Taking handkerchief from sweater pocket for a shield, SHE takes roll of money from drawer, slips it in handkerchief into her sweater pocket)

EARL: *(Relieved)* Well, alright! See?! Things is lookin' up! And I got this idea, see? What our crowd needs is the old house parties! See? . . .

CHERYL: *(Moving from desk, absently)* House parties?

EARL: Yeah, pay your little bread at the door. Cop you a nice cheap drink. And do your thing with the kind of music we wanna hear. Like: OOO WEE OOO, BABY, BABY . . . *(Croons Smokey's "Baby, Baby." Pulls her into ballroom dance step. Dancing)* Got that shit all paid up, huh? Alright, way to go. Baby, you somethin' else. Don't know how you stretch that little we got comin' in now, to cover everything. You somethin' else . . . Gail too? . . .

CHERYL: *(Hesitates; then)* Yes. Gail too . . . *(SHE moves out of dance; HE twirls alone for a moment)*

EARL: Yeah, The old house parties. But not at houses now. We all got too nicea' places for Negroes dancin' wit' drinks and cigarettes in their hands. Got to get some cheap hall, rec center or somethin'. Three or four of us go in together on this . . .

CHERYL: Earl? . . . What're you talkin' about?! . . .

EARL: We fixin' to go into the ol' house party business. The Oldie but Goodie business, baby. Aw, yeah, gon' take off like a spaceship. You think we payin' off some bills now, wait till this thing gets started! . . . Hey, girl! *(Sings)*
YOU CAN'T KEEP A GOOD MAN DOWWWN
NO YOU CAN'T KEEP A GOOD MAN DOWWWN! . . .
AW NAW! . . . YOU CAN'T KEEP

(HE comes toward her comically, in a wide-legged, shoulder-shaking caricature of a transplanted fertility dance. SHE stares at him strangely from some alien space SHE has never known before; frozen in cross-checked emotions)

CHERYL: Earl! . . .

(She grabs him so violently, so desperately—holding on as if for her very life—he is stunned, alarmed)

EARL: Cheryl, baby? . . . What is it? . . . What's wrong? . . .

(He looks down at her: Her arms locked around him, her face turned away, pressed to his chest. He puts his arms around her)

EARL: Cheryl? . . . Baby? . . .

(Lights slowly fade on them; come up on E. J. outside the house, DOWNSTAGE)

E. J.: *(To audience)* I'm waitin'. She ain't threw no money out in the yard, *yet.* Uh-huh. It's a trip what this stuff can do . . . *(Holds up a smaller roll of bill)* Yeah. This is the *real* drug. Got everybody hooked. Green Magic, Big John calls it. Yeah, makes big people little; and little people big. Just like the drugs do. Like, Big John has us hang out at the houses sometimes; so we can see what happens to chumps who start to dip into the rocks. And this one time this big-time lawyer dude comes in shinin' like gold, and sharp as a dragon's tooth. You know: Lookin' ready. Like he's on his way downtown to a big deal, and he just wanna get a little whiff to get ready, you know. Like he don't usually be in no place like this on this sidea' town, but it was on the way, you dig. And he didn't want to have to stop at the bank to get his usual stock-up buy. You know: Droppin' bullshit all the way. He was sure 'nough big time. I mean, I've seen his picture in the paper. Big. Big. Until he ran outta this . . . *(Holds up money)* And wanted some more of that . . . *(Mime smoking pipe)* . . . Then this Big Fella from the newspapers turned into a whinin' worm. I mean it was sickening. They say, "That's a nice watch, man" and, Boom, he's givin' it up. A damn Rolex. What size shoes are those, man? And he's kickin' 'em off. Fresh shoes. Then ol' dirty Joe started hintin' about—about sex. And you could see the dude considerin' until Big John told him to get the fuck out and find some money. Yeah, really make you crawl when you need it. Worse than this . . . *(Holds up money)* 'Cause everybody bad as a junkie when it comes to this. Everybody needs some of this. Watchin' that dude with his Rolex and fresh shoes, made me think of Dad. Strongest dude I ever knew. And they sayin', "Want your daughter to go to college, huh, Earl? . . . Well, crawl! . . . You also want to keep up the mortgage and the payments on that car, things like that, right—Crawl! . . . You can't work 'cause yo' back hurts? . . . Crawl, suckuh! . . ." Yeah, and my mama's standin' there watchin' this, so she's tryin' to grow big muscles overnight. Getting' all outta her rhythm. Uh-huh. And my sister's got to come home to join the circus. And, meanwhile, I got my hand out for lunch money? Naw. Uh-uh. I don't think so. I ain't with that. My folks been on the good foot forever. Doing things the right way. So we need it, I'm gonna go get it. And if I gotta get it then I wanna be the one callin' out the tricks: Crawl, jump, roll over, play dead . . . Yeah. Well, I'm waitin' . . . You really think she gon' throw that money out? . . .

(He smiles knowingly, shakes his head; looks across stage.

Lights up on Earl/Cheryl: He standing behind her now, one arm around her waist, the other at her shoulders; she holds on to the hand at her shoulder; he looks at her puzzled; she stares out, as if at E. J. out on the street with his back to the house. E. J. gestures, crosses to meet Eric also wearing new jacket. Bert enters, watching the two from Down Right. The two exit. Bert goes center; looks from the two to Earl/Cheryl still standing in light)

Earl: Everything all right, baby? You okay? . . .

(Lights to black)

ACT II

(Lights up on living room. Hip-hop/rap music blares, as E. J./Gail/Sherrie dance Center, in front of couch—while Downstage Left, Earl sits at telephone table, on phone)

Music: SAY, YO!! . . .

E. J./Gail/Sherrie: Yo!! . . .

(Music/cast repeats)

Earl: *(Putting finger to ear against music)* Huh?! . . . How come it's gonna cost so much?! . . . What else y'all got goin' in that joint? You bookin' Bingo and square dances and shit!! . . . What?! . . .

Music/Kids: YO! . . . YO!! . . .

(Eric comes in door, calling to E. J.)

Eric: E. J.!! . . . E. J.!! . . .

Earl: *(On phone)* What!? . . .

(E.J. looks to Eric, who, shielding actions from Earl, Downstage, indicates his beeper, makes motions of telephone call, then indicates car outside, holding up mobile phone. E. J. nods, exchanges looks with Gail then goes out past Eric, taking mobile phone and car keys)

Earl: *(On phone)* This is me, man, okay!? Earl Carter! Not some stranger!

(Gail now dances with Sherrie, avoiding Eric's persistent stare. Finally she looks up at him with irritation. Eric gives her a slow, knowing grin, akin to a wink, nods: They are now equal coconspirators, with "equal" being the significant term. He goes over to join her and Sherrie in the dance)

EARL: *(Continued)* . . . Man, the last time that place was full up, Sugar Ray Robinson was givin' an exhibition, and we all had to stand on milk crates to see! . . . That's how long it's been! . . . Yeah? Well, I think the money you askin' for that big ol' *empty* gym is funny too . . .

(Behind EARL, ERIC has now stepped between GAIL and SHERRIE: Dancing aggressively, suggestively at/with GAIL. Disgusted, embarrassed, SHE breaks off and sits on couch, picking up book. Laughing, ERIC now dances playfully, innocently with SHERRIE)

EARL: *(Continued) (Turning to them)* Turn that stuff down!—In fact: turn it off! . . . Throw it out in the alley, with the rest of the junk . . .

SHERRIE: *(Going to turn music down)* Aw, Dad, chill . . .

EARL: Aw, Dad, nothin'. I got your chill. That's where you should put that music: In the deep freeze . . . Hey, Eric. When you get here? . . . *(HE dials another call)*

ERIC: Hey, Mr. Carter. Just pulled up a minute ago.

EARL: Where's E. J.?

ERIC: *(Glancing to GAIL)* Uh, he just drove up to the store.

EARL: That's right: You got a car now.

ERIC: Well, really it's my brother's car.

EARL: Oh, I was wondering. What's wrong with you, Gail? You alright? . . . *(SHE has been glaring at ERIC. Now gets up gathering books)*

GAIL: Don't feel so good. Think I'll lay down for awhile. Before I get my things together to go back to school tonight.

EARL: That's right, you goin' back up tonight.

ERIC: Yeah, me and E. J. takin' her up.

GAIL: *(Sharply)* I'm riding with my brother—alone. We have things to talk about—privately.

ERIC: *(Holding arms out, shrugging)* Hey . . . *(Sits on couch)*

EARL: Well, just make sure we have our little pep talk 'fore you go . . .

GAIL: I will, Dad . . . *(SHE crosses down to kiss him on cheek. SHE crosses as jealous SHERRIE comes to take her daddy's hand)*

EARL: *(In phone)* Uh, yeah. Wanna talk to Mr. Jones . . . Earl Carter . . . Uh-huh *(Kisses SHERRIE)* . . . Hey, sugar. Where you get those new sneakers? Sharp, girl . . .

SHERRIE: Bad, ain't they . . .

EARL: Yeah, they're tough . . . *(On phone)* . . . Hello? . . . Alright. Naw, he's got the number . . . *(Hangs up)* Yeah, those are sharp, baby. Me and yo' mama was pricing some for you two, three weeks ago. Yo' shoes cost about much as mine, girl! . . . So yo' mama went on and got 'em for you, huh?

SHERRIE: Uh-uh. E. J. bought 'em for me. Got me two pair. Wanna see the other ones? . . .

EARL: Two pair? . . . E. J.?? . . . *(Looks questioningly at ERIC)*

ERIC: Uh, really it was me and E. J. . . . Yo, it was such a cheap deal we went on and got two.

EARL: Cheap? . . . Reeboks? . . . These shoes ain't hardly cheap.

ERIC: It was a deal, see: Me and E. J. was out to the mall, where we worked before, you know, lookin' for a job.

SHERRIE: They ain't cheap lookin', Daddy. Wanna see the other ones?

EARL: *(Watching squirming ERIC)* In a minute, baby . . . You say y'all was out to the mall, lookin' for work. Uh-huh. Then what? . . .

ERIC: Well, this white dude comes up, says he's got this big truck load'a shoes, and his help didn't show up. Say he give us ten dollars a hour—maybe twenty, thirty bucks apiece—to help him unload it at the shoe store . . .

EARL: Ten dollars an hour.

ERIC: Yeah. And that was a big ol' truck, Mr. Carter. Stacked up full. Even with both of us humpin', it took us almost three hours. The dude at the store didn't do nothin' but stack 'em after we got 'em inside.

EARL: The driver didn't have no dolly? . . .

ERIC: No, sir. Said his helper had borrowed it. The dude at the store used his hisself.

EARL: Ten dollars an hour. So y'all got thirty dollars apiece.

ERIC: Yeah. And it was a hard thirty, too. I couldn't hardly stand up straight.

EARL: Well, that ain't enough to pay for these shoes. Not two pair.

ERIC: Naw, see, Mr. C., it was a deal. There was a coupla' boxes, three or four, way in the back on the bottom, that got all busted up, tore open and everything. He couldn't leave 'em at the store. They was kids' shoes, so, thinkin' of Sherrie, E. J. asked the dude could we have a pair. Since we had worked so hard and everything . . .

EARL: So he just gave 'em to you, huh?

ERIC: *(About to nod, reconsiders)* Uh, naw. Think he was gon' hustle 'em anyway. Say he could let us have 'em for, you know, cost. Twenty dollars apiece, like that . . .

EARL: Twenty dollars . . .

SHERRIE: *(Apprehensive)* Daddy?! . . .

EARL: Hold it, baby. Twenty dollars . . .

ERIC: Yeah, twenty. But E. J. didn't go for it. Jacked him down to twelve-fifty apiece. Twenty-five for two. E. J. called Miss C. and got her okay on the size. I didn't have nobody that size to give 'em to—so I just went in for Sherrie too.

SHERRIE: What's wrong, Daddy? I got to take my shoes back to the store?! . . .

EARL: *(Looks at her for a beat)* Naw, baby. Go get the other ones; let Daddy see 'em.

SHERRIE: Okay . . .

(Runs out.

EARL turns to ERIC on the couch; begins to walk around couch as HE talks)

EARL: I don't know what you take me for, boy . . .

ERIC: *(Getting up)* What you mean, Mr. C? . . .

EARL: Mr. C., my ass. Sit back down.

ERIC: *(Overtly innocent)* Huh? What?! What's the matter? . . .

EARL: Just hush, boy. Now you gon' tell me that some dude comes along with a truckload of shoes, and you and E. . . .

ERIC: That's the way it went down, Mr. C! . . .

EARL: Eric, listen: Now you've been around here long enough to know I wasn't raised on no fairy tales. Grew up on Hastings Street, son . . .

ERIC: I don't know what the deal is, Mr. Carter. But I ain't tryin' to hype you. Swear: Went down just like I said—

(Sound of front door opening/closing)

E. J.: *(Offstage)* Yo! Eric! Let's hit it, man!! . . .

ERIC: *(Moving quickly to doorway)* Here he is! You can ask him yourself! . . . Yo! Jay! Tell him: We helped this dude! At the mall! Unload this big-ass truck'a shoes. And that's how we got Sherrie's shoes! . . .

(E. J. has entered)

ERIC: *(Continued)* . . . For twenty-five for two. Right? . . .

E. J.: *(Picking up)* Yeah. That was the deal. Right. Twenty-five. What's the deal wit' you, Pops? . . .

EARL: The deal is, far as I know, you haven't lied to me since you knocked over your mother's vase that time. So I don't want you to start tryin' to sell me no shit now . . .

E. J.: *(Quick glance to ERIC)* What you talkin' 'bout, Pops? . . .

EARL: You and your buddy here sit down a minute and I'll tell you . . .

E. J.: Hey, Pops, we gotta go pick up Eric's brother from work . . .

EARL: Won't take but a minute. Sit down.

(E. J./ERIC sit on couch, exchanging glances. EARL circles couch)

EARL: *(Continued)* My daddy used to tell me how during the depression him and his buddies would come outta the house in the mornings, headin' for school with their stomachs growlin' . . .

ERIC: Mr. Carter, we have to get my brother . . .

EARL: With their stomachs growlin' 'cause they didn't wanna embarrass their folks askin' for breakfast—'cause they knew there wasn't none. So they would have to hustle breakfast on the way to school . . .

E. J.: Dad, I heard all this.

EARL: Well, hear it again. He say they used to hit Eastern Market like a pack'a wild animals: Just runnin' and snatchin' whatever they could get. Fruit, carrots, whatever. And Lord help a milk wagon anywhere . . .

E. J.: Dad, like, what's the point here? We got the man's car, we got to go.

EARL: The point here is: A depression can turn a—a—Martin Luther King into a Bumpy Johnson . . .

ERIC: Who's Bumpy Johnson? . . .

EARL: He was a gangster. In New York.

E. J./ERIC: *(Looking at each other)* Gangster/Gangster?? . . .

EARL: Uh-huh. Washington can be cute and call it a recession, if they wanna, but what we're in is a damn depression.

E. J.: Gangsters? Depression? Dad, what's up with this?

EARL: I'm sayin' that I know things been kinda rough aroun' here lately. Not like what you've been used to. Now you ain't never been hungry. But I know you want all the latest name jeans and sneakers, and all that.

E. J.: It's cool, Pops. I'm cool . . .

EARL: And I know there ain't been much good time money flowing through here, lately. But I think we've gotten through the worst of it now, son. Your mother's been like . . . like that song: A bridge over troubled waters. And your sister—bless her heart—has pitched in like a true trooper. Poor thing, workin' two, three jobs up there to take up my slack with her school money . . .

(At this ERIC/E. J. look at each other: ERIC covering a grin with his hand)

EARL: *(Continued)* And you too, Junior. Through it all you ain't never whined or complained. In fact, you told me to straighten up my act. I appreciate all that.

E. J.: *(Getting up; motioning for ERIC to follow)* Think I know where you're comin' from now, Pops. It's cool . . .

EARL: I'm sayin' it would be a shame, after all we've been through, for you to blow it all for some Nikes or some blue jeans. Get shot, or locked up, for being in the back of somebody's truck—or store.

ERIC: *(Relieved; amused)* Aw, you can chill easy, Mr. C! We ain't been rippin' off nobody.

EARL: I'm glad to hear it, Eric. But I'm talkin' to my son.

E. J.: Pops, believe me: We ain't been stealin' no shoes, or nothin' else. It was just a one-time lucky stroke, like he said.

EARL: Uh-huh. But sometimes when luck happens, people start tryin' to *make* it happen again.

E. J.: Step off from the Columbo bit, Pops. We ain't out stealin' from nobody.

EARL: *(A beat; then grins)* Yo. I got your damn Columbo . . . boy, I bet I'll . . . Columbo, huh . . . *(Starts playfully punching him. Relieved, E. J. ducks, and cringes under the light blows)*

E. J.: Look out, Pops! . . . Hey, man . . . Watch it now!! . . .

EARL: Columbo, huh? . . . Got your Columbo! . . .

(As ERIC laughs with the TWO of them, THEY don't hear the front door. CHERYL comes to entrance)

CHERYL: What're you all doin'? . . . Cut that out! . . . E. J.? Whoever's car that is blockin' me in the driveway, get it out of my way. Now! . . .

E. J.: Sorry about that, Ma. Come on, Eric. Tell Gail we'll be right back, to take her up to school.

CHERYL: *(Holding out keys)* Park my car in the driveway.

(E. J. takes keys as HE goes past her; ERIC follows him)

ERIC: How you doin', Mrs. C?

CHERYL: *(A beat; on guard)* Fine, Eric. How are you? . . . *(SHE moves aside as HE slowly passes her)*

ERIC: Oh, I'm doin' fine.

E. J.: *(Offstage)* Man, will you come on!? . . .

ERIC: Yo! . . .

(HE crosses. CHERYL continues to couch; takes off shoes)

EARL: How you feelin', baby? . . .

CHERYL: Tired.

(EARL crosses behind her; begins massaging her shoulders)

EARL: Tell you what: You take one'a them bubble baths. And, when Sherrie goes to bed, I'll give you a little rubdown.

CHERYL: *(Eyes closed)* I take a hot bubble bath, I'm goin' straight to sleep.

EARL: Straight?

CHERYL: Straight.

EARL: Damn, girl, you ain't getting' tired. You getting' old.

CHERYL: It happens to everybody.

EARL: Well, that's grounds for a trade-in, you know. Get me a younger model.

CHERYL: Fine. I could use some help.

EARL: *(A take)* Damn . . .

(SHERRIE comes in with second pair of "fresh" multicolored sneakers)

SHERRIE: How do you like *these*, Dad? . . . *(Tosses them to him as SHE goes to hug CHERYL)* Hey, Mama . . . Daddy told E. J. not to buy me no more shoes off no truck. Buy 'em at the store, right, Daddy? . . . I'm goin' to help Gail pack! . . .

(SHE runs out. CHERYL watches EARL as HE puts shoes on table)

EARL: I don't know what he told you, but him and Eric gave me some jive about helpin' this dude unload a truck at the mall. I know they doin' some lightweight hustling out there. Calling hisself helpin' out, you know. Just checkin' him before he get carried away. People see two young bushy tails out there lookin' hungry, subject to feed 'em anything. Run into all kinds of propositions out there. Have to watch 'em, keep a tight leash on 'em, nowadays . . .

CHERYL: *(Covering herself)* I know. By the time I saw the shoes, Sherrie already had 'em on, and was in love with 'em. And when he said he had—had worked for 'em, I . . . I mean, I didn't have any reason to—to doubt him. I mean, he's never gone around *lying* to us, or anything . . .

EARL: He said he called you to get the size.

CHERYL: What? . . . Well, maybe he did. I can't remember everything that happens around here. What are you insinuating? . . .

EARL: Hey, baby, whoa, whoa. I ain't puttin' nothin' on *you*. I know how you mothers are about your kids. Hell, mine was the same way about me.

CHERYL: Now what the hell does that mean? . . . What kind of—of male-ass, chauvinistic-ass statement, is that?

EARL: What? . . . Chauvinistic? . . .

CHERYL: Don't hand me that, I-know-how-you-mothers-are mess! I am just as aware and concerned about these kids as you are!! . . .

EARL: Whoa, sugar . . .

CHERYL: Whatever they are, I've had just as much—just as much . . . Oh, damn . . . Shit . . .

(SHE tries to compose herself as SHE has started to cry)

EARL: *(Going to her)* Baby, what? . . . What's the matter, Cheryl? . . . Listen, I ain't tryin' to put nothin' off on you, baby . . . Cheryl, listen . . . Baby? . . .

(HE tries to take her hands from her face; turn her to him. SHE pulls away, turns her back)

CHERYL: Leave me alone . . . Just . . . I'm alright . . . I'm okay. Just let me alone . . .

(The phone has started ringing)

EARL: Cheryl, baby, listen: I know we've all been under a lotta pressure. But it's gonna be alright now. I can feel it . . .

CHERYL: I'm alright now, Earl. I'm okay . . .

GAIL: *(Offstage)* Dad?! . . . Telephone!! . . .

EARL: Who is it!? . . . Tell 'em I'll call 'em back!! . . . Cheryl, baby, it's gonna be cool. We're through this thing now. You'll see . . .

(SHE gets up and moves UPSTAGE of couch, her back half-turned to him and audience)

CHERYL: I'll be okay, Earl. Just . . . give me a minute . . .

(GAIL peeps in)

GAIL: Dad? It's Mr. Jones. He says he's at work, can't get any calls where he is today . . .

EARL: Damn, I'm . . . Alright, I'll get it. Damn . . .

(GAIL crosses)

EARL: *(Continued) (Coming down to phone)* Just relax, baby. This is Jones about our Golden Oldies dances. This is what's gon' pull us outta this. Just watch . . . *(On phone)* . . . Hey, Jones! Look. You gotta help me with Wheeler, over at that center . . .

(CHERYL remains UPSTAGE of couch)

EARL: *(Continued)* . . . How come he won't?! . . . Listen. I've got all that. Everything he asked for. Figures, perspective, all of it. Got it right here! Yeah . . . Hold on, I'll read it to you! . . . Naw, jus' hold on!! . . . Jones, you hang up this phone, I'll come down there and shame you in fronta yo' coworkers . . . Hold on. Just, wait . . . *(Puts phone down; turns to CHERYL)* Baby? Can you hang this up for me when I get on the other phone? Gotta get this straight, right now! . . .

(SHE nods; HE crosses out. SHE comes DOWN FRONT, picks up phone; holds it to ear a beat or two)

CHERYL: Got it? . . . Hello Clyde. Fine . . . You too. Tell the family hello for me . . . *(SHE hangs up phone. SHE moves DOWN FRONT into isolation spot. To audience)* You ever been coming upstairs in the dark, and you think there's one more step up, *know* there's one more step—and there isn't? . . . You take that step up and there's nothing there. You half-fall, half-stumble, back down, hard, to the *real* last step. And for a second you're—shocked, and, disoriented. Even frightened. Yes: frightened. Because, in that second, you've lost confidence in yourself. In what you think you know. What is *so*. Is *real*. All the many times you have come up those stairs. How could you not know where the last step is? Well, it's like I've been frozen into that moment of—doubt. Doubt of—myself. And my son. *(Wry chuckle)* I've known us both since birth. How could I have not known that there was another level to him? A step deeper down? Darker? And that I would—agree?—to step in and—and, join—him there? It is utterly incredible to me: That last step that isn't there—but, *is*. It's like I've stepped through a wall that was always solid and real—into a . . . a—twilight zone; that must have always been there behind the false wall. Waiting for me. I am a whole new person, in a whole new space. It's like I've been born again. Yes, like they sing in church: I looked at my hands and they were new. Looked at my feet, and they were too . . . Yes, I looked at my son, and he was new. Looked at myself and I was, too. And, Gail, my oldest, she is too. But in reverse of the church, the song: Instead of being born into a new light—we're all three new behind some shadowy wall. Standing there naked. And Earl and Sherrie can't see us through the wall. Because they've never taken that step—past what is assumed, accepted. They don't need to be able to see in the dark. But we are shamefully naked to each other. And to those who know, like that boy, Eric. I can't stand his eyes knowing me like they do. God. I swear, if somebody were telling me this, I would say it was the thoughts of a crazy woman. But it is going on right here, everyday: Absolutely, utterly, incredible, but—now, just as normal as pie. It seemed so—expedient, so temporary at the time. It was supposed to be temporary. E. J. kept telling me he was quitting. And at first, I made myself believe him. But then Gail will receive a check. Or, like the sneakers, Sherrie will get a great gift. Or he comes to me, always at some crisis time, with: "Here, Ma, why don't you slide somea' this to Pop. You know, if you see he needs something. You know, pay a bill. Or keep it—just in case." Was he always this—clever? I don't know. It was all about Earl; about the family. About saving, protecting him from all the pressures for a short while. As he had protected us for so long. That' s all. But it all turned on us: Now he's on the other side of the wall, the shadow. And I wear gloves and a false face with him now. I don't dare touch him with this. Yes, it's awful: Now I have to protect him from—us. Hmmph. Sometimes I wonder if it was about Earl at all. I can't be sure of anything I did, or do, anymore. My motives. My self . . . *(Wry chuckle)* . . . I watch gangster movies now. Especially all the Godfather stuff? But it's not the gangsters themselves I watch. It's the wives, the mothers. I try to see how they do it? Live it? It—isn't easy . . .

(Lights come back up as SHE *crosses out past* EARL *entering with a cordless phone.* SHE *gives him a brief, tender kiss, then crosses past him)*

EARL: Cheryl? . . . What you say, Jones? . . .

(Loud hip-hop music comes up as SHERRIE *runs on to entertainment center, turning on tape.* ERIC *comes on to dance with her,* UPSTAGE, *as* EARL *continues on phone,* DOWNSTAGE*)*

EARL: *(In intermittent lowering of music)* Can't make no money over there!?? . . . Jones, you been around fools so long, you startin' to think like one! You heard me! . . . Yeah!! . . .

(Music goes back up, as E. J. dances out with two large suitcases; hands them to ERIC, *pointing for him to take them out to car.* ERIC *dances off. E. J. dances awhile with little* SHERRIE*)*

EARL: *(Continued) (With lowered music)* . . . You better move back down here with us!! Them folks out there got you thinkin' like them! . . . That we inner city folks can't do nothin' successful!! That's what!! What?! . . .

(Music goes up again as GAIL *walks on carrying another bag; hands it to E. J. who has just returned from last trip.* ERIC *exits again. Music lowers as* GAIL *talks to E. J.)*

GAIL: I don't want him riding' up to my school with us.

E. J.: Hey, Gail, come on. It's a long-ass boring ride back down here. Plus, he's got my back. Need that all the time: somebody lookin' out behind you. Know what I mean?

*(*GAIL *turns from him in frustration and disgust as* CHERYL *comes out in robe)*

EARL: . . . Just think about it!! IF you can still think for yourself!! . . . *(*HE *puts phone down and crosses up to join* CHERYL. *To* SHERRIE*)* Turn that hiccup music off! . . .

*(*SHE *does and then crosses to join him and* CHERYL. *Isolation lights pick up* EARL/CHERYL/SHERRIE UP RIGHT, GAIL/E. J. DOWN LEFT, *in a kind of family portrait: Parents seeing their daughter off to school—with, in this case, charged undercurrents.* GAIL *and* CHERYL *break the picture by rushing to each other for a tearful embrace. E. J. understands the undercurrent, turns away)*

EARL: *(Continued)* Lord, women! . . . Come on, Cheryl, she's just goin' off to school—not off to war.

(At this, the TWO WOMEN *look from each other to E. J. who shrugs, turns to cross out, meeting* ERIC *on his way back in, turning him around again)*

E. J.: We'll be out in the car. Don't take all night.

*(*THEY *exit)*

CHERYL: *(To* GAIL *intently, with tears)* You be good up there, baby. You hear? You be good.

(Gail nods, turns to run and hug Earl; then runs off. Cheryl, wiping eyes, hurries off Right)

Earl: *(Arms raised; shaking head)* Lord. Women! . . .

Sherrie: *(Taking his hand)* Yes, women . . . Come on, Dad, let's get us some ice cream . . . *(Leading him toward kitchen)*

Earl: Uh-huh, women. And you one of 'em. All y'all just work ol' dad like a yo-yo. Huh? . . . Huh? . . .

(Picks her up, tickling her.

Lights fade as they go off, laughing.

Nighttime lights up on Bert outside the Carter home. He carries a six-pack of beer; starts up steps; stops, sits on steps, pops cap on can of beer, drinks)

Bert: Naw . . . Ain't gon' bother him tonight. Even though he's one of the few who knows. Who understands . . . *(Drinks)* . . . Myrna would say I'm just doing some more crazy cop stuff. Yeah, crazy cop stuff. Like, I got this habit, see. Whatever part of town I'm in, I'll go by the house of onea' the old neighborhood folks. Don't necessarily stop in. Just: Drive by. You know, checkin'. Makin' sure everything is cool. Safe. You know? . . . Myrna says it's "neurotic, crazy cop stuff" . . . *(Starts to drink again; then chuckles)* . . . She had us goin' to this—an-a-lyst. When we was supposed to be tryin' to—"preserve" our marriage. He said I was a cop because it was—how'd he put it?—"because it was a socially acceptable" way for me to articulate my feelings of—outrage. My heightened sense of—injustice. Might've said—justice. Yeah. Somethin' about a code of justice. Shit, I don't know. Maybe . . . just a habit: Checkin' on my people. Yeah, habits are somethin'. Know a dude's habits you can set your traps. He can change cities, his face. His damn fingerprints, even. But he gon' get the same cigarettes, hold 'em and put 'em out in the ashtray, the same way. Uh-huh. Gon' have a short, bow-legged big-ass woman. Or, a tall one with her box sittin' up like it's on a shelf. Yeah. Some things he ain't gon' change. *Can't* change . . . *(Drinks; stands)* . . . Hell, a man sposed to check his neighborhood. Protect it. Preserve it. And they ain't killed the neighborhood 'cause they done put in a damn expressway. Tore down the houses, the stores, and moved the people out with this—urban renewal. Ain't done nothin'. 'Cause it wasn't the street, the houses. It was the people building their lives together. The feelin', the connection between 'em. They can't do nothin' with that, Jim. Ain't done shit but scattered the neighborhood around—stretched it out further. Yeah, now we's out in mansions in the suburbs. And over around in here. And, yeah, some still living' in housin' projects, or whatever they callin' 'em now. But it's all the same neighborhood. 'Cause it's the same people: Some growin', some standin' still. But all still together, still tied some kinda' deep down way. Shit, our crowd have a reunion in a minute! Two, three times a year! Myrna don't understand that. 'Cause out there where she lived everybody was just tryin' to get the hell out. Didn't wanna take nothin' or nobody wit' 'em, either! Scramblin' to be the first one out. First one livin' somewhere else. Move or get trampled! . . . *(Laughs, drinks)* . . . Maybe they was already livin' in the future while we was growin' up in the past. Yeah, guess the future's here now. These kids done dropped the neighbor part of neighborhood now. Just call it: *The Hood.* Don't even sound like where people live. Sound like a battlefield—war zone. Callin' each other: Dog! . . . *(Drinks)* . . . Guess they *have* to call the girls, "bitches." That's what female dogs are, right? Bitches? . . . *The Hood.* That damned dope. Turned the neighborhood into: *The Hood!* How you gon' open yo' doors to your neighbors—when you got to close 'em on your nephews and nieces? . . . Hell, *your own kids?* . . . See what I mean? Ain't the houses, the streets—it's the people. Not urban renewal, but the damn dope, that tore everything down. We survived all the rest of the bullshit they put on us. Couldn't kill us with all that, so they got real slick. Saw how they could get us to kill ourselves: Hook us on dope wrapped in money. Understand? . . . Whether you reach for the money or the high—you caught up in the killin'. That's the game they got goin' now. From the White House—check Noriega—to pistol Pete's house, same game: Dealin' poison. And everytime I get my hands on one of 'em dumpin' it around my folks—I try to stomp his brains out. Uh-huh, that's why I can't get no more promotions. Got as many violations as citations, almost. Say I don't show good judgement; can't control my emotions. I judge real good; and it ain't me I'm trying to put some control on. Uh-huh, been *shot* three times. Yeah, but I been shootin' back too. And some of the sonsofbitches ain't walkin' round here no more. Uh-huh. Sonofabitches! *(Looks around, drinks)* Used to be you wouldn't be cussin' out in fronta' certain people's houses. You'd wait till you got down on the corner. But now, these kids? . . . Shhh, who am I talking to? . . . Don't nobody care about this shit but me . . . *(Gets up with six-pack)* Yeah, but I care. Some things, some people, you gotta try to protect—Naw, preserve. Yeah, preserve. 'Fore the shit rise up and flood everything . . . Like my man Earl here, and his Cheryl. They're the neighborhood. Stickin' together, and startin' new roots; growin' something, building somethin'. Buildin' . . . Fuck! . . . How the hell am I supposed to go in there and tell him his son is one of 'em!? Huh? One of the wild little monkeys jumpin' up and down with automatic weapons? Slingin' poison everywhere for money! Huh?! How am I supposed to tell them that? . . . Earl? Cheryl? . . . Naw, shit, naw. Not tonight. Got to do it, but not tonight. Naw . . . *(Starts off)* . . . Maybe I'll just shake up the little fucker myself . . . Yeah, grab him up 'fore somebody else do. Somebody who don't give a damn . . .

(Bert goes offstage.

Earl comes out onto porch area as we hear Bert's car door opening and closing)

Earl: Bert??! . . . Thought that was you. What are you doin' out here drinkin' in fronta my house, boy? . . . Call the cops on yo' ass! . . . Hey?! Where you goin'? You alright!? Bring yo' crazy ass on in the house and give me onea' them beers! . . .

(Sound of car starting)

Earl: *(Continued)* You don't give me onea' them beers, I'm gon' call Myrna, tell her you out here drinkin' again! Embarrassin' me in fronta my neighbors! . . . *(Grins. Engine starts; sound of screeching tires)*

Earl: *(Continued)* Hey, fool! Don't be backin' over my grass! This ain't Hastings Street! We have laws out here! . . .

(Car horn; then car going off with the sound of a siren. Earl stands, shaking his head; his smile fades and a look of concern replaces it. Fade, as Earl goes around to back of house.

Lights up on living room area. Afternoon. Gail/Eric enter; Gail carrying small bag, Eric large suitcase)

Gail: Ma!? . . . Dad!? . . .

Eric: Don't think they're here. Didn't see no cars.

Gail: Guess not. You can put that down there. And—thank you.

Eric: Put the bag down there. And you can go now, flunky. Right? . . .

Gail: You picked me up and delivered me home. Mission accomplished. You've done my brother's bidding.

Eric: You can squash that bidding shit. Don't do nobody's bidding but my own.

Gail: Oh, really? I thought you were, like, E. J.'s—lieutenant.

Eric: Ain't hearing that. We're like—partners. Yeah, partners. So that means I'm in with that money he be layin' on you to keep you in school. All them fresh college girl clothes, and all that. I'm in with all that.

Gail: Really?

Eric: Yeah. Check that. So you can step off from lookin' down yo' nose at me an' shit.

Gail: Is that what I do? Look down at you?

Eric: From day one. But check it: Not so much now.

Gail: Oh? . . .

ERIC: Yeah. You jus' like the rest of the wanna-be bitches . . .

GAIL: Excuse me? . . .

ERIC: Yeah. Y'all switch up on yo' attitudes real quick—once the cash and the flash start poppin'. *(Displays his flashy rings, gold neck chains; pulls at the collar of his expensive leather baseball jacket)*

GAIL: That's all it takes, huh?

ERIC: You got it. I dug you checkin' me out on the way up in the ride. Sittin' up front now.

GAIL: You insisted that I ride in front.

ERIC: Damn right. I ain't no fuckin' chauffeur. I dug you: Yo' knees all up on the seat; all cute and sexy. Pretendin' like you readin', goin' to sleep, and shit . . .

GAIL: *(A beat; then smiles, moves away)* Yes, I was checkin' you. But not really you: Checking the stereotype.

ERIC: The what? . . .

GAIL: Stereotype. Someone who—umm—typifies a—a pattern of behavior. That's how it's defined in our social psychology class.

ERIC: Behavior, shit, huh. Well, whatever me and E. J.'s behavior is, you all up in it too.

GAIL: I see. Well, you and E. J. are a very often discussed stereotype: The economically depressed ghetto male trying to overcome hardships by criminal activity. Historical. Typical. Only E. J. is no longer of the ghetto, while you never left.

ERIC: Shit. Y'all ain't left nothin'. Y'all just moved. Ghetto came right with you.

GAIL: Yes: As when E. J. brought you along.

(ERIC springs to grab her by the front of her coat; back of her head)

ERIC: You losin' it, bitch! But I know where you at. Diss this! *(HE forces her into a kiss. At first SHE struggles, then goes passive, blank. HE releases her, stepping back with a quizzical look)*

GAIL: Kissing the princess does not automatically transform the frog into a prince. He must be loved. *(SHE laughs)*

ERIC: Princess my ass. You wack, bitch.

GAIL: *(Laughing)* E. J. is becoming a powerful ghetto prince. But the likes of you can only aspire to squire! Or, at best, lieutenant . . .

ERIC: Fuck you, bitch. You outta yo' fuckin' mind . . .

GAIL: You just don't understand my references . . . *(Laughing)* Not even the fairy tales! . . .

ERIC: *(Grabbing testicles)* Reference this! . . .

GAIL: Easy: The last resort for status. Or, if you will: power.

ERIC: Fuck you, bitch.

GAIL: No thank you.

(Sound of car parking; its door opening/closing—makes them release their glares, relax their stances. E. J. enters, immediately recognizes the charged air between them)

E. J.: Y'all still actin' wack? . . .

GAIL: *(Curtsies)* Hail! The young Prince of Drugdom! All hail! *(SHE turns, and goes off, flourishing her hands regally)*

ERIC: What's up with that? She's wack! Losin' it! You pickin' her up from now on. I'm outta here. *(Starts for door; E. J. follows, chuckling)*

E. J.: Hey, I'm with you . . . We got business! . . .

(THEY cross.

Lights up on GAIL in off area; drinking down a glass of water in one long swallow)

GAIL: *(To audience)* Maybe I am comin' a loose. Losing it . . . I know where all that prince talk is coming from. From Machiavelli, not fairy tales. We're studying his *Prince* in class. I relate to him, the things he says: "The way men live is so far removed from the way they ought to live, that anyone who abandons what is for what should be, pursues his downfall rather than his preservation." That sounds real to me. I sit in class hearing how shocked all the nice little pink coeds are at his premises. How wicked, and awful, and wrong they say he was—is. And I feel that they are lying. That in their heart of hearts they understand him perfectly. Some of their daddies are probably princes. Princes of industry! Da-da-da-dow! They see it on TV, in the newspapers. Politicians, TV evangelists, government officials. They're all saying one thing, and living another. That's the way it is: You say what you oughta, and do what you have to. That's the *real* truth! The way life makes you be. Machiavelli said it: "The prince must stick to the good as long as he can but, *being compelled by necessity,* must be ready to take the way of—evil!" . . . The way of evil. Ugly. Awful. And Eric is right: I'm in it right along with him and E. J. . . . And, oh God, Mama. Mama too. Aw, E. J.! All I wanted to do was stay in school! . . . E. J. . . . E. J. . . . What are you doin' to us?! . . . E. J. . . . E. J. . . . E. J. . . .

(Lights go down on her, shaking her head, crying softly, as SHE intones his name.

Lights up on outside area. E. J./ERIC)

E. J.: A new market area? Where? . . .

ERIC: Up there where Gail's goin' to school. Cut into a dude up there, wants to be down with us. Got a little game, a little heart. Wants to get paid. Told him we'd try him with some marijuana. Slide a few pills and things on him. Then drop the crack in. Boom! Brand new money! Be phat, man!

E. J.: Naw. Uh-uh. Skip that.

ERIC: What's up? Why not? . . .

E. J.: 'Cause that's where she goes to school. That's how come. Ain't no shit connected to me, to her family, gone be where she at. Understand?

ERIC: Naw. I don't. Look: Lotsa money up there wit' them square-ass college chumps. Black *and white* chumps! Hey. You don't have to show in the deal. I'll handle it all.

(E. J. grabs him in his collar)

E. J.: Look, nigguh: You came up there with me. I came with her. So you out. The whole shit is out! Understand?!

ERIC: Yeah. Chill, E. J. . . .

E. J.: *(Releasing him)* Serious business. Long as me and you together—nothing's happening where she is. Serious. Very serious. Understand?

ERIC: I been understanding you, without you grabbin' on me and shit.

E. J.: We together on this?

ERIC: *(A beat)* Yeah. We together.

(An uncomfortable moment passes between them)

E. J.: Damn! Can't believe you come with that.

ERIC: Hey. It's all about the money, man. Just business.

E. J.: Naw. It ain't all about the money. It's about family too! About the money doin' somethin' for the family. Not getting' the family all tied up in it. Maybe it ain't like that with you and your family. But that's how it is with me and mine.

ERIC: To me: they takin' money they tied already.

E. J.: That's you. Not me.

ERIC: Uh-huh. And how come it's got to be different with my family? . . .

E. J.: Hey. Don't even try that. You got your little brother dealin'. Had to get a room somewhere to hide the stuff from yo' mother and uncle, 'fore they use it up. That's how it's layin' over there. But it ain't like that over here. And it ain't gon' get like that. Okay? . . . So cancel all that, and let's get back on what is—and go get paid.

(THEY start off. Headlights hitting them along with the sound of car screeching to a stop—stops them. THEY take a couple unconscious steps backward, as DET. BERT comes on, confronting them)

E. J.: *(Continued) (Recovering)* Hey, Uncle Bert . . .

BERT: Uh-huh. I usta' be your uncle. Now I'm just a cop who's a good friend of your old man . . .

E. J.: Yo. Why you havin' it like that, Uncle Bert? . . .

ERIC: Uh, I'm steppin' up outta here. You comin', E. J.?

BERT: Naw. He ain't comin': He's talkin' to me.

ERIC: *(To E. J.)* Want me to chill in the car? . . .

BERT: Hell, naw. I don't want you at my back. That McDonald's round the corner? You wait for him there.

(ERIC looks to E. J.)

E. J.: I don't like how you comin', Unc—Bert. Lieutenant Childs. So me and him both steppin' up outta here . . .

(THEY start past him. BERT pushes E. J. back, hard; then spins to ERIC, turning him to grip him in a stranglehold, forcing him to his knees)

E. J.: *(Continued)* What's wrong wit' you, man?! . . .

BERT: This is called a stranglehold, boy. You struggle against it—you strangle yourself. Understand? Just cool out . . .

E. J.: What's up with you? . . .

BERT: *(To gasping ERIC)* I'm gon' let you breathe now. Stay cool . . .

E. J.: Man, you can't . . .

(BERT takes an automatic pistol from back of ERIC's waistband, under his jacket)

BERT: Looka here what I found: concealed and unregistered weapon!

E. J.: *(Lowering voice, looking back at house)* Man, what you doin'?! . . . Out in fronta the house? What's up with this?! . . .

BERT: Why don't you call your old man out here? So I can tell him what's up? Huh? Why don't you? . . . *(HE pulls ERIC to feet, holds gun up near his face)* You busted. Could put your maggot-ass away from him for awhile. But, if I do, I might have to bust his jive-ass to his old man. Don't know if I'm ready to do that, just yet. Understand? So, you run on up to McDonald's. I'll get you in my sights again. Next time I go rat hunting. *(Pushes him away)*

ERIC: *(Holding throat; barely audible)* Fuck you, cop . . .

BERT: You a slow learner, ain't you, boy? Get on round to McDonald's. And don't even think about getting' in that car—or I'll light yo' ass up, and lay this gun in your hand . . . Oughta check the car out. See what other toys you two got in there . . .

(ERIC looks to E. J.)

E. J.: I'll pick you up around there in a minute.

BERT: Maybe. If he ain't there in fifteen, twenty minutes, catch a cab, 'cause he ain't comin' . . .

(Eric moves off, cussing under breath, still holding his throat)

Bert: *(Continued)* Now, you. Move over here, outta sight of the house.

(They move into an area of street light)

E. J.: Ain't nobody home, but Gail. But my folks might be drivin' up any minute, man.

Bert: So you better listen fast, right? . . . First, tell me somethin'. How'd you grow up under two lions? And end up runnin' with snakes? *Being* one?

E. J.: Look, man, this is tired. Out here jumpin' on people; dissin' people. This all you got to do? . . .

Bert: *(Grabs him in collar)* Shut your mouth and save your ass! Understand? Huh? . . . *(Pushes him away)* Alright. Now I don't know if I really care much for savin' yo' little ass anymore. But savin' yo' folks from knowin' how all their workin' and plannin' has gone to shit—that I'm willing to do. For old times sake. So here it is. I'm gonna tell yo' dad you got to switch schools and all. 'Cause . . .

E. J.: Aw, man, where you at with this?? . . .

Bert: *(Holding up finger)* Shut up and listen. That's twice now, no more warnings. Gotta switch schools, I'm gonna say, 'cause through that little nigguh there, you getting' crowded into maybe doin' the wrong things. Even been nibblin' at it a little . . .

E. J.: Hey, man, look . . .

(Bert gives him warning look; E. J. chills)

Bert: Listen good, little fuckup. Then me and yo' daddy gon' call you in to talk. And you gonna admit that I'm right. That you probably *do* need a change. Know your grades gotta be slippin', 'cause friends at your school tell me your attendance ain't worth a damn. So that' ll be our proof . . .

E. J.: You talked to people at my school?

Bert: Old friends. Called 'em up at home. So. You'll cut all ties with this shit out here, before it's too late. That's it. You'll have a chance. Especially with me hangin' off yo' ass all the time. Them other little dogs will go real wide around you. Might wanna hurt you you try to involve them in something. That's it. The deal. Or, I bust your little ass. And put some heavy pain on my best friend.

E. J.: *(Looks away a beat)* So, you the sheriff, huh? Gon' ride in with yo' badge and gun, and straighten out everything, huh? . . .

Bert: Whatever.

E. J.: *(Pulls thick roll from his pocket)* Well, how much'a this you got, man? Huh? Right now? In yo' pocket? Huh? . . .

Bert: Boy, don't go there with me . . .

E. J.: Why not? It's the only place to go—with everybody! To the *bank*, baby! This is where it's at! Uh-huh. You gon' pay to keep my sister in college! . . .

BERT: Don't try it. How all these other people go to school without dope money, huh?

E. J.: Yeah. Uh-huh. And when the—the—mortgage. And—and—taxes . . . And all the other . . . Whatchacallit? . . . Middle-class! Yeah! All the other middle-class stuff, they been tryin' to pump all these years. All comes due. All the bullshit notes. You gon' slide some paper on my mother, *then*? So he don't be drinkin' and cryin'! Goin' to pieces! You gon' stop him from goin' all the way out this time? Out to where maybe he can't never get back? Back up to where he was? Where he spose to be? You gon' do that? Huh, Sheriff? . . .

BERT: *(Taken aback)* What? . . . Hold it . . . Back up. Your mother? Cheryl? She knows? . . .

E. J.: *(Sarcastic chuckle)* Aw, wow, man. You just as fulla bullshit as all the rest. If *you* know from across the street—don't you think people in the house with me gotta know?! Yeah, they know. Mama! Gail! They know about this! *(Hold up roll)* 'Cause you gotta have somea' this! Or be damn homeless, or somethin'. Damn right they know . . .

BERT: But Earl . . . Earl don't know . . . Am I right?

E. J.: Sometimes I wonder . . . Naw, hell, I know what it is: He don't know, 'cause he don't wanna know! He can't—afford to know! Yeah, that's it: He can't afford it, so he—avoids—it. Yeah, sometimes I think, that's what it is.

(Struck by his thoughts, BERT stares at him, stunned)

E. J.: *(Continued)* Uh-huh. Now you work with that. Do what *you* know. I got to get on my thing . . . *(HE starts off)*

BERT: *(Warningly)* E. J.!? . . . Hey, boy! Hold it! . . .

E. J.: *(Stops; turns)* What? You want me to make your day, *Clint*? This ain't no movie, man. This is real. Like, Big John says: This is America! Land a' the rich! I'm just trying to get it on with the country, man! . . .

(HE laughs as HE leaves. Leaving BERT stunned and shaken. HE pulls out the automatic, aims it at E. J.; then whirls and points it at the house; lowers it; goes a few steps toward house; then turns and leaves stage.

Sound of Duke Ellington [more specifically, Johnny Hodges] as lights come up on living room area. EARL sits in easy chair, sipping a drink. CHERYL puts clothing packages on coffee table; turns to him expectantly, hopefully)

EARL: Far as I'm concerned you can take all that right on back. Can't afford it nohow.

CHERYL: Oh, Earl. We haven't missed a reunion, yet. Our 33rd year . . .

EARL: I know how many there's been. Too damn many. And I ain't goin' this year.

CHERYL: *(Sits on couch)* Earl, why? Just tell me, why?

EARL: You know why . . . Them jive-asses just come to show off how good they doin'. All they bought this year. The trips they took. Tryin' to outdo each other. Puttin' on a show . . .

CHERYL: Aw you be right there wit' 'em. The loudest one.

EARL: I know. That's why I ain't goin' this year. I don't have nothin' to be loud about. And they all know it, too.

CHERYL: Earl, everybody's catchin' it hard this year. They all know that too.

EARL: Not everybody. You remember what happened last year.

CHERYL: No. What? . . .

EARL: You remember, I'm sittin' there actin' like I'm sharp in that old-ass suit . . .

CHERYL: That crème-colored suit? That's a beautiful suit.

EARL: Beautiful and old. Old-ass cut to it. And that damned Mobley cracked on me. You remember: "That's a nice looking suit, Earl. But I think I told you that before. Didn't I?" Didn't I? Sonofabitch . . . With his country-dressin' ass.

CHERYL: Well, that was pretty jive. But you and him always on each other. Remember how you talked about his little boat, after you and Jones got that new fishing boat? Kept callin' him Andy. Tug Boat Andy.

EARL: *(Pouring a fresh drink)* We was leasin' that damn boat. Lost it. Lost my sense of humor too. He was to come crackin' on me bout what I was wearin' this year, I'm subject to do somethin' bad to him. Break up the whole damned reunion.

CHERYL: He won't be able to crack about *this* tux outfit. Won't you at least look at it? . . .

EARL: For what? Told you: I ain't goin'.

CHERYL: *(Coming to sit on arm of chair)* Earl. Please, baby. They callin' it DÉJÀ VU: Blast From The Past. All the songs and everything from our prom time. I got us the same kind of outfits we had then. Remember?

EARL: White tux jacket, with black pants? . . .

CHERYL: Uh-huh. And The ______'s Blue Velvet was hot then—so that's what I wore.

EARL: I damn sure remember that dress. Yeah, you was the best-lookin' thing there in that dress.

CHERYL: *(Chuckles)* It sure got a *rise* outta you: you were tryin' to get me outta there ten minutes after we got there . . .

EARL: Yeah, baby: Damn dancing. That blue velvet was in the way.

CHERYL: Aw we had a ball that night.

EARL: Yeah. Our first really nice hotel room. Let me see that dress.

CHERYL: Uh-uh. Not till we get ready to go. Tell you what: Let's go and do *everything* just like we did that night.

EARL: We do things better now. Tell you what: You go and when you get back . . . We'll do everything like we did that night.

CHERYL: Won't be the same . . . *(Gets up)* Well, I'm gonna go, with or without you. I'm gonna get my hair done . . . oh wow, what time is it? Oh Gawd, I almost forgot my hair appointment! . . . Noooo! This was the only spot she had open! . . . I gotta go. *(Picks up wallet and car keys; gives him a quick kiss)*

CHERYL: Will you please think about it?

EARL: I've stopped thinking about it, ain't goin' . . .

(SHE goes out the door. HE sips his drink. Sound of car door closing/then opening. SHE comes walking back in, picks up garment bag from couch, starts off to bedroom with it)

CHERYL: Forgot to put this coat up . . . *(Exits)*

EARL: Why? You think I'm gonna steal it!? . . .

(HE picks up magazine, flips through it. SHE comes rushing back in)

EARL: *(Continued)* What you need with a coat in this weather? . . .

CHERYL: Not really a coat-coat. Kind of a little thing I couldn't get back there. Bye . . . *(SHE exits again)*

EARL: *(Calling after her)* You rented a coat, warm as it is? . . .

(HE goes to the window to look out; sound of car starting, pulling off. EARL comes from window, muttering)

EARL: *(Continued)* A coat . . . as warm as it is . . . They go crazy with this damn reunion shit . . . Everybody showing off . . . *(Comes to pick up drink, sips)* Sure would like to hear Duke, Johnny Hodge, play "Blue Velvet" . . . Yeah, that would be something . . . *(Sips. Goes to couch, takes sequined dress from plain, unmarked box, holds it up, puts it down, hesitates, then takes tux jacket from box; does a double take at the elegant, luxurious look of it . . . quickly opens coat to see label)* Armani? . . . *(Looks quickly at dress again, looking for label)* The label cut off? . . . *(Stands a moment, then drapes dress on couch; goes—still carrying tux jacket; to bedroom area. HE returns with stunned look, carrying mink jacket; goes to CHERYL's purse on table, sits in armchair, going through purse. Pulls out sales receipts, looks at them incredulously as light fades on him. In dark we hear)*

EARL: *(Continued)* Ain't none of this shit rented . . .

(Lights up on EARL, standing CENTER, holding receipts and mink stole out to CHERYL who has just entered front door)

EARL: Armani's? Saks Fifth Avenue? All cash? . . . How you doin' this, Cheryl?

(CHERYL moving from the door)

CHERYL: I told 'em to take the labels off . . .

EARL: Damn labels. I got the receipts. How you doin' this, Cheryl? I can't buy for you like this no more, who is buying for you now, Cheryl? Huh?!

CHERYL: Oh Earl, please . . .

EARL: Oh, Earl, my ass! Who's doing this for you, Cheryl? Huh? . . . Who is he, what's the bastard's name? Who is he?

CHERYL: *(Topping his tirade)* Your son!! . . . Our son!! . . . E. J.!! . . . E. J.!! . . . E. J.!!

EARL: *(After stunned pause)* E. J. What you mean? Where he get money like this? What you mean? Don't try to put E. J. up in your shit!

CHERYL: Yes, E. J.! E. J.! . . . The mink! The Armani! Saks! all of it is E. J.! E. J.'s money.

EARL: I don't believe you trying to put our son up in this . . .

CHERYL: Earl . . . wake up. All the new clothes, the cars. You really believe it is all Eric's or Eric's brothers? He's out there in the street, dealing. E. J. is a dealer, a drug dealer. Your son, our son . . .

(EARL is in stunned limbo for a moment; then advances on her)

EARL: Dealing? Drugs . . . and you knew?! You knew?! *(HE grips her shoulders)*

CHERYL: Yes! Yes! I knew!! Yes, and you did too. Didn't you? Didn't you?!

(THEY are face to face. EARL staring in dazed wonder. Lights go black . . . "Blue Velvet" plays.

Lights upon ERIC in isolated spot, on mobile phone)

ERIC: Hey, Big John, I ain't sayin' nothin' but how it's layin' . . . He cancelled getting' busy up there where his jive time sister is goin' to school. Then he steps off with that cop, that Detective Bert. Yeah, that's the one, you know him? Well, like he's a friend of E. J.'s old man . . . Check that! Uh-huh. Yeah, the cop told me to step off, so him and E. J. could talk by themselves. I don't know. I ain't sayin' he's turning. I'm just telling you what's happening . . . Huh? Put a test on him? What kinda test? What you mean "thee" test? What test is that? . . . Huh? . . .

(Lights up on living room. EARL sits in armchair, staring blankly. CHERYL sits on arm of couch, staring at him)

EARL: Naw, uh, uh. You can talk all that subconscious bullshit you want. I didn't know. You did . . . And Gail! . . . Did she know where all her school money was coming from? . . . Did she? . . .

CHERYL: Yes, Earl. Gail knew . . .

EARL: Ain't this a bitch?! . . . And Sherrie? My baby? . . . *(HE stands up)*

CHERYL: No, Earl, the baby doesn't know. She . . . I don't think she has any idea of what's going on here . . .

EARL: You don't *think* . . . ?? *(HE takes a step toward hallway)*

CHERYL: Earl, you know she's not here. She's with her grandmother.

(EARL leans hands against frame of doorway, then turns to look at her)

EARL: I thought we was doin' a good job with him, Cheryl? With all of 'em. How'd . . . how'd he get away from us like this!!! How'd we . . . lose . . . lose him . . . *(HE turns his face as a sob bursts out)*

CHERYL: *(Starting to him)* Earl, don't . . .

EARL: *(Moving away from her)* Yeah, yeah, you're right, my damn crying . . . Probably what turned him around. Seeing me crying around here . . .

CHERYL: Earl, don't blame yourself, E. J. made that decision on his own. He knew exactly what he was doing. Knew how we felt about that kind of thing.

EARL: Yeah? . . . What does he think about how you feel about it, now? Huh, Cheryl, with your mink coat, and shit, huh? . . . *(HE grabs the clothes from the table, crunching and throwing them into the hall/against the wall)* What you think he thinks about his mother now, Cheryl? Huh, what?! . . .

CHERYL: *(Moves to sit on couch)* Earl, I don't know how, what to tell you . . . What to tell myself . . . I feel like . . . like my own son bought me . . . *Prostituted* me. Can you imagine how that feels? . . . Can you?

(EARL turns away from the pain in her look)

CHERYL: I just . . . just accepted that first money, to get us over the hump . . . I couldn't stand what was happening to you, to us. So, it was there, on the table, all we needed. And I took it. Just for that once, and he was lying to me. He wasn't really into the dealing. Just making deliveries, packing it. He was quitting. Lies. Then another bad situation would come up and there he was with . . . more money, or he'd give it to Gail, in case we needed something . . . Then I just gave in . . . I just . . . just . . .

EARL: Got hooked. Like a damn junkie! . . .

CHERYL: Yes. Exactly. But I wanna just ask you one thing, Earl. If the situations were reversed, and I had always been the strong one, the one holding everything up . . . the pillar. And you saw me coming apart, maybe, about to break. What would you have done when E. J. came with the money? Huh. Earl? If you loved me and saw this house about to fall on me, what would you have done? If he offered you a . . . a . . . a pole to hold it up for awhile? Huh? Earl? . . .

EARL: *(After a long rest)* No, uh-uh. Can't run that one on me. If I'd stopped to think about it . . . I'd have missed the play just like you did, Cheryl. Shouldn't have to think about it. When you're in a game and a play come up, if you have to think about it . . . you're lost. It's supposed to be already *in* you what to do. You've practiced it, and practiced it, until it's in you what to do. It's in me! And I thought it was in you. And in our kids! Don't have . . . shit to do with no drugs. No drug money, drug cars, drug clothes . . . If it takes drug money to keep this house up . . . let the sonofabitch fall! If Gail's got to have drug money to get through college . . . then let her work at McDonald's for the rest of her life! Just say fucking no to drugs! That's it. That's all . . . Y'all just got weak for that money! That's all . . .

(CHERYL sits a beat, then gets up, getting her purse, etc. Starts out)

CHERYL: I guess you're right, Earl. I probably deserve everything you're saying. I did get caught up in the money. I mean, even after that first time it was like you being a little bit pregnant. You're either in it . . . or not . . . *(Steps before hallway)* . . . But my first weakness was for you . . .

EARL: What you trying to say now? . . .

CHERYL: I didn't want to lose faith in my "God." I saw you about to fall, and I couldn't take it. But then I don't think God cries in his sleep. *(SHE goes off. EARL goes to hallway)*

EARL: Hey, don't try to put it back on me!! . . . I cry but I don't quit!! I don't quit!! . . . You're the one let that shit come in here!! Not me!! You . . . quit! Gave up! . . .

(HE slams door and goes to stand outside of house.

Lights fade on CHERYL, up on EARL sitting on porch steps. HE looks up at sound of car pulling up; door opening/closing)

E. J.: *(Offstage)* Catch you tomorrow, man . . .

(Sound of car pulling off. EARL stands, comes down steps. E. J. enters)

E. J.: Hey, Pops, what you doin' out here this time night?

EARL: Waiting for my dope dealin' son . . .

E. J.: Who told you? Ma, or . . . Ma told you? Or Detective Bert?

EARL: Oh, Bert knows too? Guess I'm the only one didn't know, huh? Me and little Sherrie. So, if Bert knew how come he didn't arrest yo' little ass?

E. J.: Because of you and Ma, I guess. So? You out here for what? What you doin'?

EARL: Waiting to see you. Wondering what to say. How to talk to you.

E. J.: Talk like you always do, Pops. Straight.

EARL: Uh-uh. You left outta here one day as my son, E. J. The one I raised. But you come back as somebody I don't know. And ever since then I been talking to a . . . a stranger, like he's my son. But you do things somebody I raised wouldn't do. I don't know you, boy. How am I supposed to talk to you? What am I supposed to do? Huh? How am I supposed to let you come back up in my house, when I don't know what you might be bringing with you? What you might do next? Huh? Tell me why? Where you come from? Who the hell are you?

E. J.: Pops . . . man, you don't . . . why you? . . . Okay, you know. And I guess you don't want me in yo' house. Hey, no thing. It ain't all that. Like I was just trying to hold on here till I finish school. 'Cause it's like I promised to do that: finish. But, hey, I was really helping y'all out. I got a place to stay. Real cool place. A place *I* paid for. Like, I don't have to be here. Like, let me come in, make a call, and get a ride . . . alright?

EARL: How you do this, E. J.? How you turn everything around on me? Your mother? Your sister?

E. J.: Pops. Look, just . . . okay . . . just let me make a call, alright? . . . And I'll be outta here . . .

EARL: That's right. You got a place of your own now, right? What else you got, E. J.? A gun? . . . You got a gun, E. J.? . . .

E. J.: Pops, hey, look . . . I . . .

EARL: I thought about that sitting out here. I told myself I was going to back you down when you came up here. But then I thought if I did I might have to kill you out here, 'cause you might try to pull a gun on me. And just like I gave you life, I'd have to take it. You got a gun, E. J.?

E. J.: Dad . . . look, just let me call . . .

EARL: Crack, E. J.!? . . . Crack!? . . . That shit got women sellin' they babies . . . Men on they knees, wit' they mouths open for other men? That shit done turned us into a bunch of wild rats eating at each other? That what you doin', E. J.? . . . You? My son?

E. J.: *(Fighting tears)* Couldn't just stand around and watch what was happenin' to you, Mr. Help Everybody. Had to do something! What you want me to do?

EARL: Work! Like we did. Fight the bullshit, and make yo' way out! It's a fight, E. J. Gotta work your way off the ropes!

E. J.: Yeah, you fight, forty years. Then one slip and they got you in the food stamp line, on the ropes. Yeah, I ain't with that. Ain't no fair fight. Not no more. Gotta have a gun, and some money. Else they punk you, man . . . punk you!

EARL: *(Grabbing him by the shoulders)* The fight ain't never been fair for us, E. J.! Never! Okay, you got a gun and some money. Now what you give up for it? Your family? Your mother? Your sister? Me? . . . How you feel, E. J.? Huh? . . . Look at me. How you feel now that you done tore down our house? How you feel, E. J.? Huh? . . . How you feel? . . .

E. J.: Come on, Pops . . . Let me go, man. Let me go . . .

EARL: That what you want, E. J.? Want me to let you go? Let you go back out there in the jungle with no family? That what you want? . . .

(Little SHERRIE comes out on the porch in pajamas)

SHERRIE: Daddy . . . you mad at E. J.? He stay out too late? You gonna whip him out here where everybody can see? Tell him you sorry, E. J.

(CHERYL comes out)

CHERYL: Sherrie? . . . what're you doin' out here? . . .

SHERRIE: *(Going to her)* Daddy goin' whip E. J., Mommie. Out here in fronta the neighbors.

CHERYL: *(Concerned)* Earl? . . . E. J.?

EARL: He's alright, baby. It's okay . . . Go 'head. Take Sherrie back inside . . . Go 'head, it's alright . . .

(CHERYL starts in with SHERRIE)

SHERRIE: You come inside too, E.J . . . Come on . . .

E. J.: I'll come in later, Sherrie. Go 'head . . .

(CHERYL takes SHERRIE inside . . . E. J. turns away, takes deep breath, lowers head, puts hand to his eyes to squelch the tears)

EARL: Sometimes tears can help, can clean you. And you goin' to have to be clean, to come back in this house. I didn't know what you were doing before. Now I know. I can't act like I don't . . . You got to tell me now you're gonna cut all that stuff loose . . . Eric and all the rest of them out there. Just cut it loose and come on back with us. And we'll work this out. Get you back on track in school. Work it out.

E. J.: It ain't easy like that, Pops. People's money hangin'. Got to make it cool . I gotta think about it.

EARL: Naw, when you gotta *think* about it—you don't *know*. You gotta *know*! E. J. You gotta know what's right. What you will do and what you want! . . .

E. J.: It ain't easy like that, Pops. What I'm supposed to do? Come back and be asking you for lunch money? . . . I don't know if I can be like that again, Pops. I don't know, man! . . . Gotta make a call . . .

(HE runs off)

EARL: *(Shouting off)* You gotta know!! . . . You supposed to know! I'm supposed to taught you to know!! Boy, you supposed to know!!

(CHERYL comes out to porch)

CHERYL: Earl? . . . Earl? . . .

EARL: *(Glares at her)* He supposed to know!! . . . You all supposed to know!! . . . It ain't that hard . . . ain't that hard.

CHERYL: Earl, come in please . . .

EARL: *(Waving her off; sits on steps)* It ain't that hard . . . ain't that hard . . .

(SHE goes in. HE sits there. Lights change to mist like early morning. Like shadows in his mind, CHERYL and SHERRIE come from house dressed for work/school)

CHERYL/SHERRIE: We're going now, Earl . . . You been out here all night, Daddy? . . . Get some rest, Earl, eat something . . .

(HE doesn't acknowledge them. THEY exit off; and to car, starting, etc . . . Lights go down.

Lights up on EARL/BERT DOWNSTAGE)

BERT: Maybe he ain't too far gone, yet. Maybe together we can pull him back in. Get him clean . . .

EARL: *(Back to him)* How could I not know, Bert? How could he have been out there and I not know? . . . See him every day and not know?

BERT: Sometimes we don't see what we don't wanna see . . . Lots of 'em like him. Got it all worked out: be off the streets at night; do they homework; go to church. Hell, even go to college, spread the shit up there. Slick as grease, and just as slimy . . . Sorry . . .

EARL: Hell, you tellin' the truth . . . But the clothes, the cars. Say he even got a place of his own. How he do all that, and I don't see it? Huh? . . .

BERT: Hell, Earl, if the baby's slick, what you think the daddies, the bosses are like? Hell, that Big John got a interest in the stores they buy the clothes from. Them kids too young to buy them cars in their own name. That John buy 'em for 'em, through his set-ups; his company's got crooked lawyers, bankers, working with him. Them kids be payin' the notes to *him* every month. Might not ever pay off what they owe. And if they do, you can bet he gonna be making a profit.

EARL: John Martin? The same one from the neighborhood came along in the class after us?

BERT: Same one.

EARL: Well, maybe he what we should be dealing with. Lay for his ass.

BERT: Don't you think I thought about that? . . . Could see the whole set-up. Bam-bam. Just another rat killed in the alley. But then what that make me? How am I any different than him? Right is right. Wrong, wrong. Gotta bust him right. In the line of duty. Then tear his ass to pieces! . . . Best thing we can do now, is like with E. J., take the kids from them sonofabitches. Cut 'em off.

EARL: E. J. . . . How'd I miss him, Bert? What did I do wrong?

BERT: Man, them drugs, that junk money, done bought damn near whole cities, whole countries. The truth be told, drugs broke up the mafia! What you think it'll do to E.J!, Cheryl?, Gail? . . .

EARL: But he is mine. Raised in my house. He's suppose to learn better, be better than that, man. Now . . .

BERT: Looka here, man, it's hard on 'em nowadays. On one hand the world treating 'em like they ain't worth paper. And, in the other hand, with the TV and all, teaching them they'll be something if they have hundred dollar Italian shoes and five- hundred-dollar jackets. Used to be the whole neighborhood will show you right from wrong. Yo' folks didn't go to church every Sunday, but the folks down the street call you up on the porch and tell you about God, right and wrong. You didn't have no daddy, go over to the playground. Mr. Finney and Mr. Sanders straighten you out. Use baseball and basketball to show you *how to be*. Now, the dope man standing on the sidelines. Man, hell, you lucky if your kids *make it* to the playground. Ain't no neighbors hardly. Just scared people with bars on their doors. Come to the windows with guns, you start up on their porches.

EARL: *(Sits)* I don't understand what happened, man. Not just E. J., all of it.

BERT: Look, too late for all that. It's like we'd be down two runs in the bottom of the ninth, but, hell, look here, we get somebody on, Earl'll be up. Hell, we can pull this thing out. That's how we felt about you, man. You was special. You, the way you lived, your marriage, your family. We looked to you, man. So, you got to get on up . . . *(Pulls him to feet)* . . . *And show us again* how to pull off a comeback. Damn, what you did, what Cheryl did, Gail. *Just get your family together* . . . First though, wash your hands and make me some coffee. And some eggs too. Cheryl got me up over here to check on you before God got up this morning. Feed me, sucker! . . .

(THEY move to door)

EARL: Church . . . Maybe that's it. Cheryl used to go, take the kids. But I talked about those jive preachers so bad . . .

BERT: Don't care what the preachers doin'. If baseball works, churches ought be some use. We need everything we can get . . . And right now I need some food. And some damn eggs too. Open the door, we look like two drunks coming in late.

EARL: *(As lights fade)* Don't be pushin' me, boy . . .

(As lights fade on them, lights come up on E. J./ERIC, entering DOWNSTAGE. ERIC unwraps cloth, removing two automatic pistols.)

ERIC: Big John says we use these on him. Fresh virgins, just come in the country. Can leave 'em laying there with 'em . . .

E. J.: I don't think I'm with this, man. These dudes ain't even down with us. They don't owe us.

ERIC: They owe Big John. But they know him. He wants us to go, 'cause they don't know us like that. We'll be just two more dudes coming to buy some shit . . .

E. J.: I don't think I'm into this . . . Fuck this! He got his enforcers for this shit. How come he wants us to go? . . .

ERIC: He says it's a test, man. See if we really down with him. A test, like in school, man, we'll be graduating. Be really big after this . . .

E. J.: Be in some really big shit! That's what we'll be. And how come all of a sudden he's talking to you . . . and I can't talk to him? Huh? . . . What's up with that? . . .

ERIC: I don't know how to figure it, you're the man round here. So it's mainly yo' test. Yo' graduation. I'm like the Western Union. You know how he is, like if somethin' go wrong, you ain't heard nothin' from him, just me.

E. J.: What's up with that? What makes him think I'll be saying who I talked to? . . .

ERIC: I don't know, E. J. . . . He asked me a lotta questions about you, man.

E. J.: Yeah? What kinda damn questions?

ERIC: Like, well, man, like, he hears everything, you know.

E. J.: Like what?

ERIC: Like he heard that Detective Bert been watchin' you, askin' about you. Tellin' people to step off from you.

E. J.: Oh; where he hear *that* from, Eric? Huh? . . .

ERIC: Hey, don't crowd me, man. He ask me about it. Ask me if the cop came down on you, on us. I told him the dude came down. But he didn't talk to me, he talked to you. Tried to run some soft family shit on you. You told him fuck him. Ain't that what you told me? I ain't goin' be lyin' on you, man. He already knew bout that cop. Let's just do this, man. He's got it set up with the two bitches. When they come to do business and get down, it be curtains . . . we be already waiting. We do it, split, that's it.

E. J.: All set up, huh? . . . How you know we ain't the ones being set up? Huh? . . . Yeah, check *that*. I didn't get into this game for this kinda shit. You tell him I ain't getting with this until I talk to him myself.

(Starts off. Eric blocks him)

Eric: It's a test, E. J., understand? Give the wrong answer, you don't pass, man. You . . . out!

E. J.: Maybe it's time to be out. You oughta think about that, Eric. Maybe it's time for us to step off. Think about it, man. We got in about the money. Money ain't even come up in this, man. What's this about? Huh? . . .

Eric: It's about the money, E. J. It's always about the money.

E. J.: Is it? You sure? I ain't. Feels like it's about something else to me . . . He's gonna have to talk to me himself. Tell me what this is. I ain't with it . . .

(He starts across stage. Eric pulls automatic out)

Eric: It's my test, too, E. J. . . .

(He clicks the cartridge into the gun. At click E. J. starts to turn, pulling gun from back of his waistband. Eric moves on him, holding gun sideways, fires. E. J. is hit, spins, goes down on stomach, turned away from Eric)

Eric: *(Continued) (Coming to him)* Yeah, E. J., you can run on back to your nice little family. I can't get it like that. This is it for me. Understand? This is it . . .

(He moves toward E. J. prepared to administer the coup de grace, to the head. E. J. suddenly rolls over to fire one, two, three shots; sending Eric hurtling backward, falling dead. E. J. struggles toward him on knees, gun ready; collapses, dead.

In dim light, Bert/Others come to kneel over bodies; take them away. Bert turns to look toward house where lights come up. He crosses)

(Earl/Remaining family come from house dressed in funeral outfits. Little Sherrie walks in front of others carrying flower arrangement. They come down front, make spaced semicircle. They stand waiting, each in their own spoken thoughts, not hearing the others.)

Earl: Like we know where they come from, but can't see where they're going . . .

Cheryl: It's about getting' through the stone and the steel . . .

Earl: My grandfather was talkin' to my father about ridin' mules while my dad was lookin' at cars . . .

Cheryl: My grandmother told my parents to send us kids down south to them. "Get those kids outta' those cities" . . .

Earl: And then my daddy was talkin' to me about cars and I was lookin' up for jet planes . . .

CHERYL: She said, "Cities is for sellin' thangs. Not growin' thangs." . . .

GAIL: I never knew how much I depended on E. J. . . .

EARL: E. J. was seein' spaceships! Computers! All of that new stuff . . .

GAIL: Not for money. But for a necessary sense of . . . of daring . . .

SHERRIE: I see them all the time in my mind, together: E. J. and Eric; Eric and E. J. . . .

GAIL: You dare more when you know—the world knows—there is a strong man somewhere, tied to you by blood. You—dare more . . .

CHERYL: Have to plow down deep to take root in steel and concrete . . .

GAIL: You reach higher . . .

CHERYL: Or these hard winds cutting around these sharp corners just blow you away . . . like, loose blossoms . . .

SHERRIE: E. J. and Eric . . . Eric and E. J. . . . Homies . . .

CHERYL: Blowing loose in the air. Landing everywhere. Anywhere. Becoming all these things. Identified by all these things. Cars, houses. Things. Forgetting how few things it really takes: Rules and rituals, coming out of love and respect. Values. Not things at all. But the reasons for the things. The reasons . . .

EARL: *(Breaking down)* Naw! Don't have to see where they' goin'! Naw! Just have to know who you're sending out! What you're making out of 'em! . . . *(HE pulls away, STAGE RIGHT. Though none can hear the others' thoughts/words, the others see him slumping, breaking, and rush to him. HE waves them off, struggling for composure.)*

EARL: It was all right there in front of me: Cars, clothes, money. How come I didn't see? Was I scared to see? Shamed? Shamed of one more thing I let get away? Like my job. My strength. Gail's education. Oh, God, I shoulda' seen. Seen him going and just grabbed him. Grabbed him and told him we already had everything we needed. Everything we needed . . .

(During the last of these lines, HE has rushed across to first hug SHERRIE then reach out pulling close CHERYL, then GAIL)

SHERRIE: Daddy! You holdin' me too tight. I can't breathe . . .

(HE releases her to allow her to bend to place a wreathe on the grave.)

SHERRIE: *(Looking up at him)* Daddy? Mommy? E. J. and Eric were friends. You think I should have friends? . . .

(THEY all move to touch her. Lights fade. Lights up for bows as BERT comes out to join them in a final ritualistic funeral step forward. Lights fade. END.)

Jazz-Set

CHARACTERS

Tenor: The leader. A la John Coltrane, reaching for a spiritual plateau, a unity.

Alto: Believes only in the individual: contest and conquest.

Pianist: Wife of the Tenor, finds it difficult to match his spirituality. Is a spiritual fulcrum between Tenor and Alto.

Trumpet: Older carrier of southern black experience.

Drummer: Older stabilizing force.

Bassist: Younger version of the drummer. Muted ego/ambition.

TIME

The present

PLACE

U.S.A.

SET

The set consists of three areas. Primary is the BANDSTAND *area which dominates the* CENTRAL STAGE *area, and might even be inclined, or "raked." Framing, or fronting the bandstand area is the* CLUB *area, merely an indication with the traditional small round tables with the candle-bottles centering them—maybe four tables, two* STAGE LEFT, *two* STAGE RIGHT. *And* STAGE RIGHT *is a small* DRESSING ROOM *area used by all the musicians. Or this can be* CENTER-LOWER, *with a raised bandstand.*

The bandstand should have two levels: the top level contains—with performing space on each side—frames of a drum set, stool, chasis for snares, cymbals, etc., but no real drums (perhaps see-through wire frames).

Centering the lower, main level is the wire frame for a bass, but only a top and bottom—no middle, no strings. Right of the bass is the wire frame for the piano, no keys, strings, etc., just a real stool for the pianist.

DOWN LEFT *is a stand for holding horns, but there are no horns, only the tops, mouthpieces, that can be worn around neck as identifying necklaces for the horn men. Near each instrument is a duffel bag for both symbolic and functional value: as each musician plays out of his/her own "bag," and from the bags come the needed props and costume changes.*

Alternative to all this is simply: UPSTAGE, *forming a semi-circle, are the traditional band music stand structures, traditionally curved structures bearing the band insignia/logo. These can shield all of each members' props, costume pieces, etc.: leaving an open* Downstage *playing area. (Actually in the past this effect has been preferred over the original suggestion.)*

ACT I

(Bassist/Drummer, then Tenor and Pianist, come through audience to dressing room area. Calling out and waving to audience members: "How you doin?" "Glad you can make it!" etc. They take seats around dressing area)

Drummer: *(Checking watch)* Tenor, Abe and Aaron here yet? I sure hope the brothers hit on time.

Bassist: Gotta give the man his money's worth.

Drummer: Haw, it ain't about the money. It's about time. Time can't be wasted. You either do something with it or it does something to you. *(To Tenor)* You dig?

Tenor: Yes-sur . . .

Pianist: *(Irritated with the waiting; undertone)* After that interview this morning, we'd probably be better off if Aaron didn't show at all . . .

Tenor: *(To Pianist)* Negative thoughts come out your mouth because they're in your mind. Keep 'em . . .

Drummer/Bassist: *(Reciting playfully to Pianist)* Keep 'em in your mind, and they get into your music!

Pianist: *(Joining the two for this last line)* Into your life!

(They laugh)

Tenor: *(Nods, smiling)* That's right. You better lift your mind, "sister."

Pianist: Lift *his*, "brother." 'Cause that's all he is: one long negative drag. Trying to pull everybody down to his level.

Tenor: *(Less jovial)* Keep on you'll catch fleas.

Pianist: Better than a monkey . . . *(As Tenor and others look at her)* That's right, I don't think he's clean. He's still usin'. That's why won't nobody hire him but you.

Tenor: *(After beat)* Have you seen him using, Aisha?

Pianist: No, but I've . . .

Tenor: But nothing. That's a hard thing to be blowin' on somebody when you don't know for sure.

Drummer: The brother is a beautiful horn.

Pianist: That's a matter of opinion.

BASSIST: No, it's a matter of perspective. All beauty is.

(PIANIST looks at him; they exchange facetious but jovial nods)

PIANIST: Thank you, Professor Ray.

BASSIST: *(Bowing)* You're welcome, dear.

DRUMMER: There's no doubt about it, Aaron can play that horn.

TENOR: Yeah. And it's a long journey back from *that* hell. I know. You don't come all the way by yourself. Somebody has to help you back. *(He gives pointed look to his wife)*

PIANIST: So you help him and he spits on you. Like at that interview.

BASSIST: Yeah, he was really doing a ham trip on us, I mean, I didn't know it was such a privilege for the rest of us to assist him every night.

TENOR: He didn't actually name any names. He just contrasted styles and concepts.

PIANIST: Lifting his and putting yours down.

BASSIST: Speaking of lifting, dig, Joe. After we do our opening theme? And come in on "Popsicles"? I'm gonna' toss you a thing . . . *(Important: He reaches into his bag and pulls out two baseball caps, and tosses one to the drummer. Putting the caps on backwards they each take identical little boy attitudes and stances they are to take later in the actual 'tune' . . .)* And you come with me on that little 'walk.' Like just a beat, a step, behind me, dig?

DRUMMER: *(Affecting dumb kid act)* Like: Duh—uh—yeah-duh—yeah . . .

BASSIST: *(Chuckling)* Not that far behind. But a off-beat or so. I figure since the tune is kind of a Monk-like nursery rhyme kind of thing—until its gets down heavy into the adult thing—I figure, like, rarely is one kid out there 'playing' by himself, dig? . . .

DRUMMER: Cool. I'm like your buddy grooving along with you, right? *(He tosses the cap back to the bassist)*

BASSIST: Right.

PIANIST: *(To BASSIST)* Yeah, I can hear that, Ray. That's nice. Now if our Alto can just pick up on it and ride with it, instead of against it, we'll be cool . . .

(TENOR gives her a look)

DRUMMER: Speaking of Aaron, sounds like him coming now . . . Yeah, here he is . . .

(LOU, THE ALTO, ENTERS STAGE LEFT. He waves at someone in the audience, then stops still, looking across at the MUSICIANS, the TENOR. There is in his person, his dress, his manner, the air of something at once insular and dramatic. Added now is a sardonic gleam of humor as he is obviously poised on a delicate drug high. He stands for a moment, his hands in his dark raincoat pockets

(he being the only one wearing a coat), then comes over to the group with a sly grin. He stops before the Tenor, *ignoring the others, and smiles at him, looking steadily into his eyes, defying him to comment on his lateness, yes, but also studying him, as if looking for some opening, some vulnerability)*

Alto: And there before the heavenly hosts they did meet and do war. *(Chuckles wryly)*

Bassist: What?

Tenor: We try to hit on time, Aaron.

Alto: Cool. I'm here. That's all the people wanna hear. So what're we waitin' for?

Pianist: Ain't this a . . .

Tenor: Abe is late, too.

Alto: *(Sitting)* Oh, wow. You really serious about playin' with that old-fashioned clown? That country-playing alky?

Pianist: Look who's talking . . .

Alto: *(Laid back)* So what's that supposed to mean?

Pianist: It means make sure that's not your hand flying through the air when you're throwing dirt . . .

Tenor: Irene.

Bassist: *(To* Drummer*)* Irene?

Alto: *(Focusing now)* And what's *that* supposed to mean?

Pianist: All right: it means there's worse things to play with than alkys.

Alto: *(Up straight now)* Such as? Wives who play piano!

Pianist: Naw! Such as smartass junk—

Tenor: *(Touching her shoulder)* Lift it. Both 'a you!

Drummer: Yeah. If civility is too tough—try silence.

(Leaves dressing area. Waving at someone in the audience, Drummer *goes up to bandstand, starts to arrange "drums," tightening screws, etc., checking out his bag)*

Tenor: Now, listen: the only way we gon' have harmony up there is to have it down here.

Bassist: Right. We can't find each other up there, if we don't feel for each other down here.

(He goes to join Drummer *on stand. Gets his "instrument," his bag, ready)*

Alto: *(To* Tenor*)* Yeah, you know all the sweet things to say, don't you leader-man. Why don't you admit that your wife jus' comes out an' says what you *wanna* say. Huh? Admit it, leader-man.

Tenor: *(After beat)* I say exactly what I wanna say, brother. Nobody else's trip takes me off it, either. Nobody's.

(He and his wife exchange a look and she goes up to bandstand, to her instrument, her bag. Tenor *and* Alto *hold each other's eyes for a moment) (Relaxing)*

Tenor: *(Continuing)* Say, brother, lift it, man. You don't have to come from there with me. I've been there too, remember?

Alto: *(Deep resentment triggered)* Naw, I don't remember shit about you being there. Just me. You dig? When you were there, I was somewhere else. And when I got here, you were over there. Understand?—Yeah. That's your problem, right there—

Tenor: Brother, we don't need this right now—

Alto: I need it. Yeah, that's the problem. You think that in life and in music, nobody can go nowhere, or play nothing, that you ain't already been, or already played. Ain't that right now, *brother*, huh?

Tenor: Hey, brother, look. We all still *tryin'* to say it, play it. Nobody ever gets on top of it all.

Alto: You can keep your carmel corn, "brother." Yeah, that's what you think. But, maybe tonight I'm gonna send you out further than you're prepared to go.

(He laughs as he walks up to the bandstand, puts his horn piece around his neck, prepares his bag.

Trumpet comes rushing in, waving to people in audience as he Crosses to Tenor)

Trumpet: *(To audience)* Hey, man! Hey, baby! How you been? . . . Good! . . . Good! . . . *(To Tenor)* Man, I ran into some people and before I knew it the time done flown and gone. Tempus fugited a jet, baby! *(Laughs)*

(The Tenor has to smile in spite of himself, leads him to bandstand to join the others; they both put on their "horn pieces." Leader/Tenor comes to (false) mike to speak to the audience, bows as they are evidently applauding)

Tenor: Thank you. Come on, good evening, brothers and sisters. And peace. Welcome to the music. This is our Pianist . . . *(She bows)* My wife. The Drummer . . . *(Bows)* Our Bass . . . Trumpet . . . Alto . . . and I'm the Tenor. Thank you. We pray that through our music our spirits and yours will come together in harmony. Thank you for being one with us tonight. Thank you . . .

(He moves back from mike to join the Alto and the Trumpet: they make room for the rhythm section as the lights change and the rhythm section comes down front with the start of the music. Everyone begins walking, criss-crossing, searching the stage. Pianist, Bassist and Drummer are Downstage.

Lights change. The Rhythm section comes down front starting the music. Bassist and Drummer are slowly softly walking in place)

HORNS: *(In B.G.)* They're walking and talking. Talking and walking, UP on the music . . .

BASSIST: You see . . .

DRUMMER: You see . . .

BASSIST: The music! . . .

DRUMMER: The music! . . .

(The two circle the others who are giving quick flashes (visual riffs) of things to come; flashing masks, props, etc, quickly coming out of each flash)

BASSIST: Is a blending! . . .

DRUMMER: A blending . . .

BASSIST: Of harmony and reality.

DRUMMER: Harmony . . .

PIANIST: And reality . . .

BASSIST: A blending . . .

PIANIST: A blending . . .

BASSIST: Of melody and memory . . .

DRUMMER: Memory . . .

PIANIST: Melody.

BASSIST: Because the mu-zi-shuns! . . .

OTHERS: *(In WAVES)* The mu-zi-shins! The mu-zi-shuns! The mu-zi-shuns! . . . are Ac-tors! Ac-tors! Ac-tors! . . .

BASSIST: And the music is our lives!

OTHERS: The music . . . is our lives!
The music . . . is our lives! . . .

(Repeat low under following lines)

TRUMPET: *(Coming down front)* Yes! The music is our lives. Like, say, I want to talk, through my horn, about my ex-wife, well, then Aisha, may take a note from me, and play my wife . . . *(PIANIST comes and takes his handkerchief and makes it a hair bandana)* In a melody from my life . . .

DRUMMER: *(Joining PIANIST as TRUMPET fades)* Or she might grab my beat . . . And play my woman, Mae . . . On one of our sweet dayyys . . .

(He takes bandana from her head; makes it a shawl, as the dance—romantically)

ALL: Because . . . The music is our lives! *(Three repeats)* Hey! Harmony . . . Reality . . . Reality . . . Harmony . . . Melody . . . Memory . . . Memories . . . Memories . . . *(As ALL whirl leaving BASSIST and DRUMMER center stage:)* POP-SICLE MEMORIES!! . . .

(Bassist nods to Drummer; tosses baseball cap to him. They put them on backwards, come down front. Bassist "walking," Drummer "skipping")

Bassist: *(To audience)* Me an' Jason was about ten-twelve years old an' we'd be hustlin' our way downtown to the show, you dig?

(All the musicians become people on the street, as the ten-twelve-year-old Bassist and Drummer cat along animatedly, Bassist leading the way)

Drummer: Man? What we walkin' all the way downtown to the show for? We don't have no money?

Bassist: We'll have some 'fore we get there. We always get it, don't we?

Drummer: Well, almost. I mean, most of the time we do.

Bassist: And if we don't get it, we have fun anyway, right?

Drummer: Yep. See things we don't see stayin' home in the neighborhood.

Bassist: Right. Gotta move out. Jus' keep yo' eyes open. We get it . . . *(Stops)* Dig! . . . Dig . . . White man. White man . . .

(He points across stage to where Alto stands with white mask on. Bassist and Drummer start to move toward him, Drummer following Bassist's lead of looking around on the ground as though for something lost, sniffling back tears, wiping eyes)

Alto: *(As white man)* Uh? Is there something wrong?

Bassist: *(Bursting out tearfully)* See, mister—we—we los'—los'—los' our—los' our carfare! *(Cries)*

Drummer: *(Crying)* An' now we cain't get hooomme!!

Alto: *(As white man)* What? What is it? You lost your carfare?

Bassist: Yeah, an' now we, we cain't get home!

Drummer: *Botha* us!

(They cry into each other's faces, holding onto each other)

Alto: *(After beat, totally sincere)* Oh? That's awful . . . Oh, here. Here's a policeman. Maybe he can help you get home.

Drummer/Bassist: The Poo-leece!?

(The two immediately straighten up, drying their eyes; quickly take a couple steps away from "white man," talk to him furtively over shoulders)

Bassist: *(Indignant, petulant)* What, man? The Poo-leece?

Drummer: You know how they do when they see us!

Bassist: Yeah. Think we lyin' all the time!

Drummer/Bassist: You gonna give up the damn carfare, or not?

Bassist: Yeah, come on, man. Later for him.

(They walk in place, indignantly, as Alto *(white man) backs out of light, stunned)*

Bassist: Mosta them suckuhs give up the money right away, damn . . .

Drummer: Yeah. This hard-hearted joker gon' wave for the Poo-leece . . .

Bassist: Yeah. Dumb chump, don't know the game . . .

Drummer: Yeah. Rather spend his money calling up lost and found . . .

Bassist: Hold it . . . The flower cart, man. The flower cart!

Drummer: Yeah . . . Come on . . .

*(*Trumpet *has donned white mask and apron; acts out man arranging flower cart.* Bassist *runs up, jumps in air, waving arms, pumping legs, giving Tarzan shout, etc. He snatches imaginary bouquet of flowers, making cart man chase him in circles, as* Drummer *rushes in unseen and snatches bouquet, puts it under his shirt and hurries off.* Bassist *tosses flowers back to angry cart man, waves, and goes off to join* Drummer. Pianist *crosses stage, acts out lady waiting on corner for her date,* Tenor, *who comes strolling up, peacocking.* Bassist *and* Drummer *point, get heads together on their act; go across,* Drummer *with flowers extended,* Bassist *whipping out handkerchief from pocket)*

Drummer: *(Handing them to her)* Pretty flowers for the pretty lady!

Bassist: *(Bending down to shoes)* And a fine shine for some fine shoes!

(He "shines" the shoes, as Pianist *and* Tenor *pass a look; she nods)*

Tenor: All right. How much, little hustlers?

Bassist: Uh, fifty cents . . .

Drummer: *(Cutting in, with reproving look for* Bassist*)* For the flowers. An' fifty cents for the shine.

*(*Tenor *gives them dollar and he and* Pianist *stroll on across stage into darkness)*

Bassist: Hot dog! Y'all sho' look good now, Miss.

Drummer: Yeah! A pretty lady wit' pretty flowers!

Bassist: And fine shoes wit' a fine shine!

(They slap palms, link arms, and stride in place, facing audience)

Bassist: Hustling through the sun and the rain . . .

Drummer: Carfare, showfare!

Bassist: Through the dangerous jungle . . .

Drummer: . . . Of the adolescent psychic terrain!

Bassist: Anywhere fare!

Drummer: Bet we get there!

Bassist: Little black kids practicin' . . .

Drummer: Practicin' . . .

BASSIST/DRUMMER: Practicin'—getting' there!

BASSIST: *(To audience)* You get that, Jack?

DRUMMER: We be . . .

BOTH: *(Stomping out two beats in tune to last words)* Right back!! *(Tipping caps.*

They bow, once, twice, again, as they back out of the center, as ALTO *comes* DOWN FRONT, *clapping sarcastically)*

ALTO: Yay-yay. Rah-rah. Ooo, that's cute. Yeah, me an' Clay was buddies, too, yeah . . .

(Looks across at TENOR, *tosses him one of two "apple caps" in his hand. They put them on, becoming teenagers.* TENOR *comes forward, slowly, angrily.* ALTO *cowers, as though ducking punches, being hit, trying feebly to get his hands up to block)*

TENOR: Fight 'em back! Goddamnit! I said fight 'em back!

ALTO: *(Ducking, cowering)* But I don't wanna fight, Clay! It don't make no sense!

TENOR: If you don't they gon' be punkin' you off everyday! Everywhere you go! They gon' *keep* a foot in yo' ass!

ALTO: *(Tearfully)* I don't care what they do . . . I jus' wanna be left alone . . .

TENOR: They'll never leave you alone if it don't cost 'em nothin' to fuck wit' you!! Either you gon' fight them, or me! You understand!! Fight, punk, fight!

(It is stylized this "fighting." First it is the TENOR *whipping the* ALTO *like a punishing parent)*

ALTO: All right, Clay! All right!—Humph-humph—come on, fuckers—humph-humph — come on, bastards — humph-humph — come on — humph-humph!

TENOR: *(Rocking in rhythmical empathy)* Get him, get him—yeah, yeah, yeah, that's right—kick him, kick him, uh-huh—What?! Naw, it ain't gon' be like that! 'Cause I said so! All right! Come on then, black bastards! Humph! Humph! Humph!

(And now the two are back to back, fighting off gang; their punches and their grunts being synchronized, rhythmical accents, as they punch the chumps out—disperse them)

ALTO: We beat 'em, Clay! We beat 'em! We beat 'em, man!

TENOR: *(Putting an arm around his shoulder)* Right, damn right! Told you you could . . .

(They stand grinning as LIGHTS PICK UP PIANIST STAGE RIGHT, *with kerchief tied around her head. She is now* ALTO*'s mother. When she calls his name she extends sound to make it a warning fire/police siren)*

PIANIST: Aaron?! Aaron?! You stay away from that Clay! You hear me? He ain't nothin' but a ol' hoodlum! You hear me?! Stay away from him!

ALTO: *(Arm around TENOR's shoulder as they still grin at each other)* Aw, Mama, he's my friend. He's my buddy . . .

PIANIST: *(Calling out)* Aaron! . . . Aaron! . . . *(Extending it siren-like)*

(LIGHTS DIE on her.

TENOR pulls away from ALTO, putting finger to his lips in traditional high sign)

ALTO: *(Whispering)* What, Clay? What, man? What we come round here for?

(TENOR reaches into his bag and pulls out pistol)

ALTO: A gun? Say, man, hey, listen, naw, man, I don't want no part of this shit . . . I'm gon' man . . .

(TENOR pulls him back around, gripping his collar)

TENOR: Don't punk out on me, man. All you gotta do is watch out for me . . .

ALTO: Say, man, let me go, goddamnit . . .

TENOR: Look. We ain't kids no more. We got to have money. And they got it all. An' the only way to get some is take some!

ALTO: Man, we can make money wit' my music. Get us a band . . .

TENOR: That takes money, too! An' I can't play no music. Sing, or dance! Dig? Look, nigguh, don't I always help you out? Anytime? No matter what? *(ALTO nods)* Well, can't you help me this once? Help me get somethin' for both of us? Huh? All you got to do is watch my back . . .

(ALTO nods. TENOR creeps OFFSTAGE, gun ready. ALTO is left alone in alley looking around nervously)

PIANIST: *(With RISING, FALLING LIGHT ON her)* Aaron!! Aaron!! . . .

(Silence. Then gunshots, one, two. TENOR COMES FROM WINGS firing another shot into wings)

TENOR: Move, man!

(They simulate running)

ALTO: Clay? You *shot* him, man??!

TENOR: Naw! The fuckuh hit me an' ran! Missed him! Didn't even intend to use it!

(They both freeze, staring out, then around, as other MUSICIANS approach with police caps with white masks dangling from the bills, they grip one wrist as if holding a pistol. TENOR puts gun down, they both raise hands as "police" close in. SIRENS are heard, accompanied by Aaron's mother screaming his name. Police sit them down facing the audience with their caps on their knees)

PIANIST: *(As mother, shrieking, angrily flailing fists up and down)* I told you! I told you!

DRUMMER/BASSIST: Told you! Told you! Told you! . . .

(TRUMPET has moved up to high rear level, as judge)

TRUMPET: *(Pointing to ALTO)* Three-to-seven years!

(ALTO stands up and turns back to audience)

TRUMPET: *(Pointing to TENOR)* Five-to-ten years!

(TENOR stands and turns back to audience)

PIANIST: *(Shouting to both)* Go to hell!

(LIGHTS OFF on everyone else, as CIRCLE OF LIGHT is on ALTO and TENOR, FRONT CENTER)

(There is shrieking, hyena-like laughter from the other MUSICIANS, eerie in the darkness. ALTO collapses to knees, covering ears, moaning)

TENOR: Pull yourself together, baby. Hold on.

ALTO: *(Desperate)* I can't take it in here, Clay! These dudes are like animals! Dogs! I can't make it, man! Head's screamin'. Stomach goin' to pieces. I feel like I'm shittin' on myself all the time, man. All the time.

OTHERS: (Laughing)

Time . . .
Time . . .
Time . . .

TENOR: *(Wryly)* You definitely gon' have to keep yo' shit together my man. 'Specially since we sharin' this cell together.

(He chuckles as ALTO looks up him. ALTO beings to smile/chuckle also, stands up)

TENOR: Yeah, it's a bitch in here. But, dig, it's jus' like outside . . . They can't punk you off if you don't let 'em. Remember? You gotta fight 'em! Fight 'em! Fight 'em!

(He throws mock punches at ALTO who throws a few back. Then they turn back to back, not touching, crouched as they throw punches at the invisible marauders)

ALTO: Yeah. Yeah. Ummph, ummph . . .

TENOR: *(Punching also)* Long as we stick together! . . .

ALTO: Yeah, yeah. Ummph. Ummph . . .

TENOR: We can beat this shit! . . .

ALTO: Right! Together! Right!

TENOR: *(Weaving, bobbing)* I know 'bout this jail shit!

ALTO: *(Ducking, feinting)* Right, yeah, uh-huh . . .

TENOR: I'll get us through!

ALTO: Right, yeah, uh-uh.

TENOR: We get us some weapons!

ALTO: Right, yeah. Uh-huh.

TENOR: Then we let 'em know that we together! We're one! . . .

ALTO: Right! . . . Together! . . . One! . . .

TENOR: Right! . . . You watch my back . . .

ALTO: I watch yo' back . . .

TENOR: An' I watch yours . . .

ALTO: An' you watch mine . . .

(They repeat the "watch/back" lines as they crouch, back to back, not touching, punching in a circle. They straighten up, back to back, back of fists against back of fists. And now TENOR's hand moves over to grip ALTO's fist as his tone changes to a new intimacy)

TENOR: You watch my back and I'll watch yours . . .

(ALTO slowly turns to look at TENOR's hands covering his)

ALTO: *(Haltingly)* Clay! . . . Man? . . .

TENOR: *(Hand and tone caressing)* I know 'bout this jail shit, Aaron. We got to be as one . . . as one . . .

ALTO: *(Squirming)* Clay . . . Man? . . .

TENOR: We have to be each other's everything . . .

(Now TENOR's hands grip ALTO's thighs, drawing him closer, still back to back)

ALTO: *(Breathing heavily, frightened)* Clay, man, listen, naw, man, let me go, man . . .

TENOR: *(Labored breathing)* If we gon' make it we have to be each other's father, mother, brother—lover . . .

ALTO: *(Struggling)* Hey, man, naw. Let me go, man! Let me go! . . .

(TENOR turns quickly and bear hugs him from the rear, pulling his head back roughly by the hair)

TENOR: Listen! I been through this shit! Ain't no women here! No women for years! Now we gon' have to do somethin' in all this time! . . .

ALTO: *(Shouting)* Let me go, goddamnit!

(Laughter from the darkness)

OTHERS: Time . . . Time . . . Time . . .

PIANIST: *(As mother)* Aaron!! *(Siren)*

TENOR: You get to messin' wit' one a them punks out there they'll turn you aroun' or somebody'll kill yo' little ass over one. But me an' you can take care a each other an' come out cool. Cool . . .

ALTO: *(Screaming)* Let me goooo! . . .

(And now, still from behind him, Tenor is forcing him to floor—all this action, though it must suggest rape, and is pointedly erotic, yet must in the end have a poetic, ballet effect)

Tenor: *(Tightening grip)* Listen?! You want my protection! Huh?! Huh?!

Alto: Yeah, Clay, yeah! But . . .

Tenor: But nothin'! Listen, this way we come out, cool, 'cause we both be men, we both play women. I do you, an' you do me. All fair . . .

Alto: Clay . . . Man . . . *(Tenor forces him down, straddles him)* Clay, Clay, Clay, Clay!! Naw!! Naww!!! . . . *(Laughter rises from the darkness)* Clayyy!!! *(Lights pick up Alto's hand reaching back to pull at Tenor's hair. See it move down to touch, resignedly, gently, Tenor's face)*

Alto: *(Tearfully, but with acceptance and a new intimacy now)* Clayy!! . . . Clay . . .

(And now they change positions as Lights fade)

Both: You do me—and I do you—And we both be cool . . .

Pianist: *(Siren)* Aaron!

(As Lights dim on them, Pianist comes Down front right, as Alto's wife. Waits as Lights come up center where Alto takes from his bag a jacket and puts it on, stands facing Tenor who straightens his collar gruffly)

Tenor: Like night an' day, man. What's a dream in here is a nightmare out there. You wake up outside the walls and you forget it. Go on like it never happened, man. Never happened . . .

(They solemnly shake hands. Alto crosses to his wife—on the way he becomes a high scratching junkie)

Alto: *(Touching her face)* Mama? . . . Mama?? That you? . . . Where you been, Mama?

Pianist: *(Sighing at this oft-repeated scene)* No, baby, I'm your wife. Your mother died when you were in jail, remember?

Alto: *(Going on to wings)* Right, right. Wow, funny shit in my head . . .

Pianist: *(Calling after him)* Clay's comin' home today, remember? Your friend's comin' home today!

(Alto turns to her with a look of apprehension, backs Offstage shaking his head. Tenor comes down center, is greeted warmly by Alto's wife [in pantomime]. Offered seat, meal. Then she brings him imaginary baby in her arms. They make over him, laughing.

Alto approaches them slowly. He snatches wife to feet, grabs baby, pushes it into her arms, points for her to leave. She does, wondering. Alto takes wife's seat, taking dope-shooting paraphernalia from his pocket, as Tenor rubs hands and arms eagerly, rolls up sleeve)

TENOR: You salty 'bout somethin', man?

ALTO: Naw, man, jus' wanted to get right to it. Got it all ready for you. Ticket here to the outersphere! You can use my rocket . . . *(Gives him needle)*

TENOR: *(Getting arm ready)* Remember when I first got out an' you was trying to turn me on an' I didn't wanna have nothin' to do wit' it?

ALTO: Yeah, well, I figured you gon' be sharin' the music, you might as well share the rest of it. The music is my life, dig?

TENOR: I don't know, man. You think I'm hooked?

ALTO: Well, I don't know. Did Duke Ellington have a band?

TENOR: *(Chuckles)* You know, man, I think you on your way. Yo' music getting' recognition now . . . *(Shooting up)* You know, I dig it better when you make up the works. Seem like it's better, stronger, faster when you— Yeah—

(Suddenly, his eyes go wide. He grips stomach, falls to floor with O.D. spasms jerking through him intermittently, like a headless chicken in the last feeble throes of death. ALTO *sits back in chair watching calmly, lights cigarette, chuckles)*

ALTO: *(Chuckles, takes a snort)* I don't want you to get the wrong idea, my man, my buddy—like I appreciate what you did for me. And it's not because of what you did *to* me. Naw, it's not that you insulted me, up there in that jail. Violated me. Naw. It's because then I realized that you were trying to climb all up inside me. Be one with me. Use my mind, my music, for your own salvation, your survival, yeah. I don't even know if you completely realized it yourself, man. Probably called it love, or friendship, or brotherhood, some shit like that. But I realized it, and that ain't what I called it. Naw, I called it invasion. Forced occupation of my mind and soul. You miserable ass-parasite! Fuckin' leach. Shit! *(Growing agitated)* You did it to yourself! Yeah! See you shoulda went on somewhere else! But naw, you attached yourself. And you stunted my growth! Yeah, I couldn't grow past you! Every time I look up there you are, reminding me of where I've been! What I was! Every time I'm ready to stretch, grow, evolve, there you are blocking, reminding, pulling me back to some old tired photograph. Got me draggin' 'round a dinosaur! Tied to some old twisted tree! Eternal milestone! Fuckin' fossil! Miserable-ass relic! I'm the one suited for survival, not your old creaking ass. Understand? A jungle isn't about fighting! It's about killing! Dig, ol' antique ass? Dig the difference? Mine is an absolute fight for an absolute freedom! Understand, huh?! Fool-ass nigguh, let somebody else make up your works, for you. *(Picking up the needle, tie "works")* And you gon' share my wings! My flight? Shit! The atmosphere up here would scare you to death, fucker, you wouldn't be able to breathe, fucker.

Cut me loose! Go to hell! Fool ass. Long lump of nothing. Nigguh! Ptuie! *(Spits on him and kicks him; looks up to see "wife" staring at him wide-eyed)*

PIANIST: *(Terrified whisper)* You killed him. You *killed him.*

ALTO: *(With half-hearted innocence, almost laughing)* Hey, baby, what can I tell you? The dude O.D.'d. He O.D.'d! What can I do? Wow . . . I gotta dump his ass somewhere. Know what I mean? . . . Wow! *(Laughs)* Wow. *(Laughs)* Wow. *(Laughs)*

(WIFE looks away, terror-stricken, as ALTO laughs and is joined by others in the hyena laughter heard earlier in jail scene.

DRUMMER and BASSIST COME DOWN FRONT as ALTO and PIANIST back off)

BASSIST: Hustling through the sun and rain . . .

DRUMMER: Carfare, showfare! . . .

BASSIST: Through the dangerous jungle . . . Of the adolescent psychic terrain! . . .

DRUMMER: Anywhere fare! . . .

BASSIST: Bet we get there! . . .

DRUMMER: Little black kids practicin' . . .

BASSIST/DRUMMER: Practicin' . . . Practicin'—getting' there!

BASSIST: Somewhere!

DRUMMER: Anywhere! . . .

BASSIST: *(To audience)* You get that, Jack? . . .

DRUMMER: We be . . .

BOTH: Right back!

(They stomp out two beats in time to the last two words.

ALL COME DOWN FRONT to bow as TENOR takes mike)

TENOR: Thank you! Thank you! The Drummer! *(Bows)* The Bass! The Trumpet! The Alto! The Piano! And yours truly, the Tenor! Thank you. And now looking for the spirit . . .

(Everyone begins walking, CRISS-CROSSING, searching the stage. PIANIST, BASSIST, and DRUMMER are DOWNSTAGE)

DRUMMER: *(Walking in place: talking, not singing or chanting)* Walking, walking, walking always walking.

DRUMMER: Looking, looking, looking for the spirit, for the spirit . . . for the spirit.

PIANIST: You can't be runnin' an' funnin' 'cause you might run right by it.

BASSIST: 'Fore you spy it. You got to walk up on it.

DRUMMER: If you want it. Got to walk and talk up on it! . . .

PIANIST: *(Giving five to DRUMMER, BASSIST)* If you want it!

(Rhythm section MOVES UPSTAGE *as horns come circling* DOWNSTAGE*)*

TENOR: Uh-huh. That's true. But where to? . . .

ALL: Well, you can't be flyin' by it, if you want to spy it! . . .

TRUMPET: But where to? I mean, what's the flight? Where's the spirit, tonight?!

DRUMMER/BASSIST: What, what, what? Where, where, where? . . .

*(*TENOR *and* ALTO *circle each other down front on* LOWER LEVEL*)*

ALL: Is the spirit, is the spirit, is the spirit? . . .

(As the other HORNS *and* RHYTHM PIECES *go back into some of their earlier question lines, working their way back to the above lines, the* TRUMPET *and* PIANIST *have stepped outside the searching and questioning, digging each other, as* PIANIST *reaches into her bag and takes out apron and scarf, makes shorter skirt of her long one, ties apron over it, tightening the whole effect of her bodice—pushes hair straight back, a la pony tail, ties scarf on head as a ribbon—becomes demure, sensual, naïve, country girl waitress, stares over as* TRUMPET *takes out huge handkerchief, wipes face, then tucks handkerchief into his collar making it a bib; steps to edge of bandstand and lifts up small table and chair from club area; carries them* CENTER, *stands watching her as others finish up chant-questioning)*

OTHERS: To-night!

(On that beat sound, "To-night!" TRUMPET *puts the table down,* CENTER, *and claps his hands for silence)*

TRUMPET: Down at Bud's damned steakhouse! That's where the spirit's at tonight!

ALTO: *(Waving disgustedly)* Aw, please. Spare us tonight, all right?

TRUMPET: Right there at ol' Bud's steakhouse . . .

(He sits at table with fists up on it as if holding knife and fork, staring across at her as PIANIST CROSSES *to him with provocative walk as waitress)*

TRUMPET: *(Continuing)* Been goin' in there for awhile now. Everything looked the same till I sees her.

PIANIST: You're a musician, ain't you? I know you are by your bag. I like musicians. I mean, what little I know of them.

(Other MUSICIANS *assume roles of attention-envious customers)*

DRUMMER: Service! Service over here!

BASSIST: Yeah, we customers, too, baby!

DRUMMER: Right! Spread yourself aroun', girl!

PIANIST: Y'all hush! They make me sick.

TRUMPET: Me, too, dawlin'. Now speak to me 'bout how you like musicians. Older, more mature musicians.

PIANIST: Aw, when I used to sing in church, ol' Reverend Thomas used to jus' cry.

TRUMPET: I bet he did. Wishing he still has all his teeth. The old buzzard.

PIANIST: Well, anyhow, the reason I wanted to talk to you is . . .

TRUMPET: Soon as I saw you I wanted to talk to you, too, dawlin'. I could jus' smell yo' greens an' yo' cornbread, way ovah here . . .

PIANIST: Well, you don't seem like these others aroun' here. You look like you come from down-home.

TRUMPET: *(Laughs)* Honey, if my home hadda been any further down, we'da lived undergroun'!

PIANIST: I thought so. Well, see, I don't know whether to be a nurse . . .

TRUMPET: *(Near slobbering, rubbing her arm)* Aw, sweet flutes played by sensual saints, sugar! You'd look delicious in white: an angel's food cake.

PIANIST: Uh, thank you. But then I thought maybe I'd be one a these secretaries . . .

TRUMPET: Whatever you want, dawlin'.

PIANIST: But you have to study so to be a nurse. And I would like to work in one a those pretty buildings . . .

TRUMPET: You's a pretty building, yourself . . .

OTHERS: *(Sing)* SHE'S A BRICK HOUSE!

PIANIST: *(After rolling eyes at other customers)* . . . In one a them pretty buildings, with all that glass everywhere. But that's just it, I don't seem to fit. I look at them girls, black and white, and it's like . . . like them big ol' glass offices is like . . . What you call it, you put flowers in? . . .

TRUMPET: Vases? . . . *(Says it like "faces")*

PIANIST: Yes, it's like them girls is like these flowers you buy up here in the department stores? Plastic flowers? They're pretty, and they's jus' right for those vases. But they ain't from the fields. Ain't from the earth, like me. You know? You think you have to be born in the city to be one a them secretaries?

TRUMPET: Honey, them women is just like them flowers; they ain't born, they's made. Made by the men who's made by these cities. You see, these cities is what you call marketplaces. Now if you in the marketplace and you's young and pretty, and you ain't got nothin' to sell, then you best stay out the way. 'Cause if they don't see you with nothin' in yo' hands to sell, well, then they think you sellin' what they can see . . . You understand? And, well, you got to eat. So you go on to school, hear? Get somethin' in yo' head that'll put somethin' in yo' hands to sell. So you won't have to sell yo' hands. Understand?

PIANIST: *(Touched, sits, touching his hand gratefully)* See? I knew you'd tell me right. Talk to me jus' like my daddy. Bet you and him would get along too. Bet y'all about the same age too . . .

TRUMPET: Well, now, me an' him might get to be friends. But I don't think we're the same age now, little girl.

PIANIST: *(Coyly)* Lookin' at you up close, I guess you're right about that.

TRUMPET: *(Covering her hand with both of his)* Uh-huh. You say you get off about three?

(She nods. They sit there in DIMMING LIGHT *as* ALTO *starts sneering laugh)*

ALTO: Shee-it! *(Extended as he crosses)* One year. One damned year. Jus' watch the Jitterbug-Waltz. Yeah . . .

(Going to her and extending his hand like the "cats," the "cool ones" do in asking for a dance.

She comes away from table and TRUMPET. *He puts table back on club floor at edge of bandstand and sits in chair with back to them just out of the light's focus. She moves toward the* ALTO *as if in sex-daze fever, fluffing her hair, leaning her head back as he raps)*

OTHERS: *(Sing)*

PUT YOUR LITTLE FOOT
PUT YOUR LITTLE FOOT
PUT YOUR LITTLE FOOT RIGHT IN! . . .

ALTO: *(Continuing)* Sing. Yeah, sing. Your whole body is a song. Honey and fire. Liquid flame. Come on, girl.

(He turns her around slowly, slowly, caressingly)

ALTO: *(Through singing)* One year. Scorch her damned soul. Burn my initials in her forever!

PIANIST: Yes . . . Yes . . .

ALTO: Fly, baby, fly . . .

PIANIST: I'm trying . . . I'm trying . . .

ALTO: You can do it, baby. You can fly.

PIANIST: Yes . . . Yes

(He twirls her slowly, moving her in and out and around in a slow, hip, fertility dance of seduction)

ALTO: Spread your wings, baby. Spread your wings . . .

PIANIST: Spreading, flying . . .

ALTO: Liquid. Liquid song. Spreading, flowing . . .

PIANIST: Singing all *around* me! All *through* me!

ALTO: A thousand watts lighting your veins! A river of lights! A river of fire!

PIANIST: Oh, baby, bay-bee!

DRUMMER: Peter-Peter-Pumpkin-eater . . .

BASSIST: Had a wife and couldn't keep her . . .

ALTO: *(Chuckling)* He put her in a pumpkin shell . . .

BASSIST: And there/then he kept her . . .

ALTO: *(Laughs, accents)* Very well! *(To her)* Don't you feel it spreading, baby, flowin', growin'?

PIANIST: Ooo, baby. Concentric involutions moving to a flaming spire!

ALTO: *(Laughing at her)* Spire?!

PIANIST: Spire! Spy-err! . . . Oooo, baby, baby, baby . . .

(She slumps to floor, holding his legs)

DRUMMER: Uh-huh. Uh-huh.

BASSIST: Why not? Why not?

ALTO: Uh-huh. Why not? Of course. And now you're ready to really fly . . .

PIANIST: *(Looks up, backs away on knees)* What? Aw, naw, honey, you know I don't wanna fool wit' that stuff. Wish *you* would leave it alone . . .

ALTO: What? Don't you want to really fly, baby? So high over all this shit that even the odor can't reach you?

PIANIST: Please, baby, don't do it no more. Leave it alone. Please. Do it for me.

ALTO: *(Bending to her, preparing arm for fix)* Shee-it. This is greater than any need I might have for you. Or your need for me . . . *(Shoots up)* Awww, yeah. Like that weird poet, Countee Cullen said, I wrap my dreams in a silken cloth, An' lay them away in a box of gold—*(Nodding)* A box of—Fuck you, then, don't care if you don't—*(Nods out)*

PIANIST: *(Slowly, resignedly, takes needle)* Yes, I want to know what this is that takes you so far from me. And keeps you there. That closes your eyes, and makes you so content. So content . . . *(Pushes needle into arm)* Oooo, baby. Oooo . . . bay-bee . . . *(Goes out)*

(ALTO wakes, sees her with needle, chuckles, takes needle and starts to shoot again. She wakes and reaches for needle. He pulls her to her feet, laughing)

ALTO: Oh, so now you want it, huh? Well, that means you're in the jungle now, baby. And out here in the bush all the predators must hunt on their own. Got to feed your own monkey. Understand?

(LIGHTS UP on TRUMPET, sitting forlornly in chair, back to them. ALTO points PIANIST to him. She goes to him as he sits drinking)

BASSIST: She's pregnant!

DRUMMER: Her rent is due.

BASSIST: She wants to go to school!

BASSIST: She's pregnant!

DRUMMER: Her rent is due.

BASSIST: She wants to go to school!

(They do this sequence of lines twice with resigned cynical attitudes as they slap each other five, shaking heads)

PIANIST: *(Nervous, agitated)* I can't have a baby right now. I realize my mistake messin' with him now. That's why I need the money for the abortion. So I can go back to school. Don't want him anymore. Want to stay with you. Are you gonna give me the money?

(TENOR, ALTO, RHYTHM PIECES chant of rent is due, pregnant, etc., as TRUMPET hesitates, shakes head no. She loses cool, drops sweet act, grabbing his face, putting her foot on his knee)

PIANIST: What the fuck else can you give me? Huh, ol' man?! What else but money? Want to take me aroun' yo' friends. Showin' off yo' sweet young thing that's so crazy 'bout you! Want to lay up with this young heat? Well you pay for it! Hear me, ol' man?! You want me to stay, you pay!

(ALTO laughs)

BASSIST: The rent is due.

DRUMMER: Baby done got grown.

BASSIST: Already been to school.

(TRUMPET hands her money, buries his face in her leg as her foot is still planted triumphantly on his knee; she takes money and hands it back to ALTO who has come over to grip her hair from behind. The three of them form a tableau of transferred power and corruption)

ALTO: *(Laughing)* One year! One damned year! . . .

(The tableau is frozen in strange INDIGO LIGHT. The TENOR reaches into his bag and takes out and puts on over his shirt a white Dashiki trimmed in gold; goes toward the three of them, as ALTO releases her and backs away into darkness)

TENOR: Remember? . . . How your soul rose, full and bright? Remember?

(TRUMPET gets up and moves away, staring at TENOR. PIANIST stands with lowered head)

PIANIST: No, no.

TENOR: Yes, you remember. A lily. A lily of the field . . . *(Leading her into brighter light)*

DRUMMER: *(Striking "sanctified" pose)* The A-men corner moanin' Lord Gawd! O' my Gawd! . . .

TRUMPET: Dear sweet Jesus!

TENOR: Remember!

BASSIST: Fat ol' sisters rockin' like trees in a hail storm!

TRUMPET: Stormin', deep down in their souls!

BASSIST: Soul-stormin'!

TENOR: Remember?

PIANIST: No! No! . . . Please! . . .

TENOR: And you trembled there all in white . . .

PIANIST: But I was dirty! Dirty! . . .

ALTO: *(Cynically)* Yeah!

TENOR: And for the first time!

TRUMPET: Lawd!

TENOR: You heard your true name spoken.

PIANIST: *(Shirking away)* No! No, please . . .

DRUMMER: Spoken in tongues!

BASSIST: Ancient mystic tongues!

ALTO: *(Cynical, sing-song)*
Wade in the bullshit,
Wade in the bullshit, children.

PIANIST: *(Frantically looking from ALTO to TENOR)* Yes! Yes . . .

(TENOR holds her hands as LIGHTS put them in GREEN and GOLD GLOW)

TENOR: And there was a stairway leading from your soul to the universe. And you *saw—saw* your soul ascend . . .

PIANIST: But my eyes were dirty. Dirty . . .

ALTO: Right. And so was all the rest of 'em's eyes . . .

(TENOR has taken her DOWN CENTER where TRUMPET has spread picnic blanket)

TRUMPET: *(Like a country preacher making a happy announcement)* And when they'd all been baptised . . .

DRUMMER: Yes-suh!

BASSIST: Speak suh!

TRUMPET: Why, we had us a nice little picnic. With fried chicken . . .

DRUMMER: *(As deacon)* And potato salad . . .

BASSIST: And barbecue . . .

ALTO: You mean he rushed her right to the grass, with the snake throbbin', like always . . .

(TENOR is now shy country boy, touching her hand as they sit at picnic blanket. PIANIST stares him intently in his eyes as she shakes her head no)

TENOR: Lilly, I'm gonna be askin' you to have—have me for your husband. And I'm hopin'—hopin' you'll say you will . . .

PIANIST: And with the baptismal water still dryin' on my hot skin, and the Holy Spirit still risin' inside me, I sat there tremblin' with shame an' fear. Ashamed and scared 'cause I wanted to jus' grab him . . . *(Grabs and straddles him)* . . . and thrust him between my thighs . . .

ALTO: Hallelujah!

PIANIST: And drown us both in the flood of my body. And then . . . then swallow him whole and devour him . . .

(She gets off him and pushes him away)

TENOR: *(As country boy)* Why won't you have me, Lil?

PIANIST: *(Getting up, moving away)* 'Cause all that he was plannin' to put me in was too small, an' too too clean. That lil' ol' country!

ALTO: *(Sarcastic)* A-man!

PIANIST: —Little ol' house—

ALTO: A-man, sister!

PIANIST: —Lil' ol' church!—

ALTO: Sang for us, sister, sang for the church!

PIANIST: Yes, I would close my eyes and sing about—Heaven!

ALTO: Memphis!

PIANIST: *(Ecstatic)* Heaven—

ALTO: New Orleans!

PIANIST: Heaven!

ALTO: Chicago!

PIANIST: Yes! Yes!!

ALTO: *(Holding out arms)* New York City . . .

PIANIST: *(Moving to him)* Yes—So I left—

ALTO: *(Gripping her hair again)* An' brought yo' fine funky self where you belong. With yo' own kind.

PIANIST: *(Lowering her head)* Yes . . .

TENOR: *(Jumping to feet, going to her)* You never forgot! You always remembered!

(Takes her up across his forearms, turns her around to BASSIST, DRUMMER, and TRUMPET, as if she is an offering in a ceremony)

BASSIST: *(Shaking chain of bells, seashells, taken from his bag)* The way! The will! The memory!

DRUMMER: *(Whirling with bright cloth, then spreading it before the TENOR)* Is never forgotten!

TRUMPET: Never!

BASSIST/DRUMMER: Is always remembered!

TRUMPET: Always!

(TENOR sets PIANIST down on bright cloth and leaves her)

PIANIST: But I was dirty! I am dirty!

BASSIST/DRUMMER: *(Into her face)* Is always remembered!

TRUMPET: Always!

(TENOR has moved to higher level, takes off Dashiki and throws it, hitting her)

TENOR: Aw, shut up, woman! Your ignorance is dripping like blood from an unattended wound! Don't you remember *me*?

(He takes off shirt and stands with bare chest. Moves as at once a pacing warrior/Baptist preacher/hip black platform speaker)

TENOR: *(Continuing)* I ran. I ran. Up hills and down valleys, I ran—

TRUMPET: Run it, brother, run it! Tell her 'bout it! Run it!

TENOR: *(Running in place)* Yes! Ten, fifteen, twenty miles, I ran!

TRUMPET: Yes sir, yes sir . . .

TENOR: Ran with hot, dry stones in my mouth!

TRUMPET: Runnin' an' a burnin'! Ho! The Almighty knows! Jus' listen to this man!

(TRUMPET and DRUMMER give each other five)

TENOR: *(Coming back down to LOWER LEVEL)* And when I ran back into the tribal circle—to the elders— *(Moves into semi-circle of TRUMPET, BASSIST and DRUMMER)* those stones were still dry . . . *(Reaches to mouth as if taking out stones, holds out open palm)*

TRUMPET: Dry! Proving! To the fathers! The mothers!

TENOR: That I had not stopped for water—

TRUMPET: Proving!

TENOR: That I had not once removed the stones from my mouth as I ran—

TRUMPET: Proving!

TENOR: To you! That I was a man who would do what he had to do!

TRUMPET: When he had to do it! How he had to do it!

TENOR: *(Going to PIANIST)* Provin' an' being, for you too. Provin' that I was strong enough to bring strong life—from this! *(Draws her to him, hips to hips, loins to loins)*

PIANIST: *(As if remembering dream)* And they took me to the water—The stream—The stream that had washed and fed our ancestors for centuries—The women took me in secrecy to the stream—All of us who were of age. They washed all of us—

(TRUMPET, BASSIST, and DRUMMER cover her in white cloth, taken from DRUMMER'S bag)

PIANIST: *(Continuing; touching her groin)* And they anointed me there to make a way for you—

TENOR: And your blood ran, purifying you—*(Nodding like old deacon)* Cleansing. Purifying you as the gods do every new moon—

PIANIST: So long ago—

TENOR: It always was, always will be—then and now, the same moment. It's the same old rhythms—

TRUMPET: Yeah! James Brown ain't nothin' but uh ol' time witch doctor!

DRUMMER: Say it loud!

TRUMPET/DRUMMER: James Brown ain't nothin' but a ol' time witch doctor!

(As the others make an aisle, TENOR leads PIANIST up to higher level)

TENOR: And you understood the old-time religion—The primal religion! That everything livin' on earth is holy—The trees, the water—The fish, the fowl—A-man, and A-woman.

(BASSIST, DRUMMER, and TRUMPET kneel beneath the two. ALTO stands aside in dark)

TENOR: *(Touching her face)* Coming together in consummation.

TRUMPET: *(Defiant declaration)* And there ain't nothin' dirty about it!

TENOR: What you felt was the desire to be whole. Wholly involved with the holiness of life—

PIANIST: *(Softly as she begins embrace)* A-man—

TENOR: A-woman—

BASSIST: A-woman—A-man . . .

DRUMMER: Coming together—

BASSIST: To be born again—

(Covering the two of them with the bright cloth, as LIGHTS DIM, CHANGE, COME BACK BRIGHTER on the two—she in gold dress, he in golden Dashiki. He lifts her and she slides legs around his waist, as the other sit cross-legged beneath them)

TENOR/PIANIST: To make new life.

(A freeze as the lights highlight the two)

ALTO: Wade in the Bullshit. Wade in the bullshit, children! . . .

(LIGHTS UP QUICKLY on bowing MUSICIANS, all—except ALTO—coming DOWN FRONT to applause)

TENOR: Thank you! Thank you! *(Starts song)* "We did it, we did it, we really did it, yeah!" *(Repeats three times)* The Drummer! *(Bows)* The Bass! The Trumpet! The Alto! The Piano! And yours truly, the Tenor! Thank you. We're gonna take a short break now, an' then we'll be back with more music—more mind and soul food for you. Thank you.

(He leaves mike; others are stuffing their bags, etc.)

ALTO: *(Blowing)* I did it! I did it! I really did it, Yeahhh! *(Repeats two times)* . . . Wade in the bullshit, y'all! . . .

(He bows.

Block)

ACT II

(LIGHTS UP on all the MUSICIANS, except ALTO, in the dressing room area. DRUMMER and BASSIST are both stripped down to the waist with towels around their necks. TRUMPET takes swig from pint bottle. PIANIST sits at table talking to TENOR, who stands with hands in pockets, in shirtsleeves)

PIANIST: *(Heatedly)* You wanna know why we can't *lift* it? Stay up there when we get up there? I'll tell you! It's him! That's what it is. He's always standin' outside the—the flow.

BASSIST: Messin' wit' the rhythm.

PIANIST: No matter what we're playin', tryin' to create. He stays outside it. And every chance he gets to blow he just Bogarts everything on off into whatever he feels like blowin'.

BASSIST: Well you know the horns, the stars, they fight it out up there in the heavens—while we mere mortals watch and keep score down here on the ground.

PIANIST: And it was the same thing with that interview today. I'm getting' sick of that bull myself!

DRUMMER: You seemed to flow into his thing pretty good out there Sounded all right to me.

PIANIST: *(Having to give up smile in spite of it all)* Well, I'm a musician. He brings me some music, I've gotta do the best I can with it, I mean, you know . . .

(She and DRUMMER laugh as TRUMPET slaps her palm)

BASSIST: Yeah. But that interview today *was* kinda uncalled for . . .

(ALTO has come back ON STAGE LEFT, and waving coolly to his fans, CROSSES to dressing room, waits outside, listening)

TRUMPET: Now that's the truth.

DRUMMER: Yeah, now, we're either a team playin' in harmony or we're not.

BASSIST: Yeah, and where he took it definitely wasn't for the team.

TENOR: Hold it. Listen. One more time. If anything or anybody in life or in music is pulling you down, all you got to do is think high and lift it. That's all, jus' lift it . . .

(ALTO goes into room, stands giving TENOR glazed grin—obviously high)

ALTO: *(Chuckling)* Lift it. Lift it. Shit. Why don't you rent a hydraulic jack or somethin', man? For all this liftin' you always talkin' about.

PIANIST: It would take a hydraulic jack to lift what we were talkin' about.

ALTO: Oh, yeah, Mrs. Tenor-Player? And what was that?

PIANIST: Six feet of bullshit.

(DRUMMER, BASSIST and TRUMPET are amused)

TENOR: Irene . . .

ALTO: *(Slowly smiles after beat)* I'm gonna tell Harold Arnold on you.

(PIANIST just stares at him with cold loathing. DRUMMER and BASSIST pass glances)

TENOR: *(With careful control)* What is that about, brother?

ALTO: *(Grins)* Nothin'. Ran into good brother Harold. He asked me if the good sister still had her wicked tongue. Gonna have to tell him, yeah, when I see him . . . *(Grins at her)*

(DRUMMER and BASSIST look at each other, nod, and go out into club area)

TRUMPET: *(Taking swig)* Think I'll get me some air, too.

PIANIST: Me, too. It's kinda foul in here . . .

(She storms out after TRUMPET, continuing on OFF STAGE LEFT as he joins DRUMMER and BASSIST near bandstand STAGE RIGHT. BASSIST sitting on the stand, DRUMMER at the table. They pantomime conversation with each other and the "audience." They are unlit shadows. ALTO and TENOR are left alone in dressing area. A beat, as they stare)

ALTO: Like man, the brother . . .

TENOR: *(Raising hand, stopping him)* Listen carefully, man, I made a vow to myself to live high: to react as a man, not an animal. Unless I am attacked by animals.

ALTO: Attacked, man? The brother merely commented about . . .

TENOR: *(Stopping him again)* When you attack that woman, you attack me.

ALTO: *(Moving back a step, putting hand in pocket)* Hey. The brother just asked me . . .

TENOR: Aaron, I know about Harold Arnold and my wife. She told me. So I don't need no one else to tell me. Now if you mention it again, you just might meet my animal. Understand.

ALTO: *(Hand in pocket, steps back, grin fading)* Shit, bring him on.

(There is a rigid moment between them when, unnoticed by Tenor, *Alto half raises his hand from his pocket.* Tenor *finally controls himself, perhaps gripping a chair (kicking it?). Turns away)*

Tenor: *(Releasing tension)* Naw, I'm not gonna let you take me there, Aaron. Now the group feels that you took the interview off on an unnecessary trip this afternoon.

Alto: Oh they do? And what about you? What do you *feel* about it?

Tenor: *(Growing peeved)* I said the group. I'm part of the group. Yeah, I feel it was unnecessary, too.

Alto: Yeah, well I'm gonna tell you what I think. I think you're drugged because I took over your little interview the same way I take over your little bandstand.

Tenor: *(Shaking head, chuckling)* We shoulda stopped when it jus' ridiculous. Now it's absurd!

Alto: Yo' ass! That bitch sharpened her pencil and listened to me! To somethin' real! Somethin' she an' everybody else knows is true: funky, fucked-up and beautiful life! Blood and piss! Not them wish-it-were-so-hymns you tryin' to get everybody to play!

Tenor: The blood and piss is assumed, brother. Like oxygen. You don't talk about it. You do somethin' with it.

Alto: Yeah, uh-huh, you real slick. That's a neat trick you comin' outta yo' new music bag with, too, ain't it, good brother? Get everybody to copyin' you and naturally *you* gon' be the best you aroun'. So everybody else got to come up under you. Shiit!

Tenor: *(Stung)* I don't tell nobody to play like me! Understand? I'm jus'—jus' explorin' a direction! Understand? A direction for me! And my music! Understand?

Alto: Yeah, I'm hip. A direction right up under you. Well, I ain't goin' for it! I play like me, see? And those farmers comin' for those interviews, and these people comin' into the clubs? They're all startin' to listen to *me*. Understand?—Me! You dig the last *Down Beat* poll? I'm moving in mister . . .

Tenor: *(Has to laugh)* Poll? Aw, come on. What do those polls mean?

Alto: They mean somebody's hearin'! That's what they mean. Yeah, and you still on top. And that's where I want to be—on top! So, startin' tonight, you got to go! *(Starts for door)*

Tenor: And what does that mean, brother?

Alto: *(At door)* That means that startin' tonight I'm gon' blow you offa every bandstand we get on together. And do it every night until you admit it an' fire me. Or I get tired and quit. Get my own shit. *(Opens door)*

TENOR: *(Shouts)* Music is not war!

ALTO: *(Pauses)* Life is . . .

TENOR: *(Going towards him)* It shouldn't be! And music is one of the things that oughta show how it could be!

(ALTO goes into club area, standing apart from other MUSICIANS. TENOR waits a couple beats, then goes out, joins others near bandstand. LIGHTS DIM in dressing room area, BRIGHTEN in club)

DRUMMER: *(To TENOR)* Everything cool?

TENOR: *(Nods)* I'm all right. Just need to meditate awhile . . .

PIANIST: *(Concerned)* You sure? . . .

(ALTO snorts coke, then comes over to them)

ALTO: *(To TENOR)* Well? Let's get it on . . .

(He goes up on bandstand, begins athletic warm-ups as he prepares his bag for playing. Others look from him to TENOR)

TRUMPET: Awfully short break . . .

TENOR: *(Watching ALTO)* Let's go on up . . .

PIANIST: What?

(DRUMMER and BASSIST shrug, go up. TENOR starts after them. PIANIST catches up to him)

PIANIST: Since when did he get to be the leader?

TENOR: The point is, we came in together, we gon' play together, and go out together. That's what the music's about. Findin' each other and stayin' with each other. I'm not gon' let him break that . . .

(He leads her up to bandstand. As OTHERS get their "bags" together, TENOR goes to mike)

TENOR:Welcome to the second set, brothers and sisters . . . I think we'll start with . . .

ALTO: Uh, y'all? Uh, he's gonna tell y'all the names and things of the different tunes he's gonna say that we're gonna be playin'. But the truth is that no matter what they call it, or how they dress it up, everybody only plays one tune, and the real title of it is—Themselves. Dig it? Themselves. That's the only tune anybody can play . . .

(Gives false comic bow to the audience and to the sardonic applause of the BASSIST, DRUMMER, and TRUMPET. TENOR bows to ALTO)

TENOR: *(To audience)* On that honest note I think it's catharsis time. I think we ought to do a little soul cleaning. As in house cleaning. Start way down in the basement and clean ourselves *up* as we work ourselves *up* . . . With those old spirituals called The Blues . . .

(He turns his back as if preparing his horn. BASSIST "cat-walks" DOWN FRONT and on around front area)

BASSIST: Yeah, let's take a nice, long, loose, blues walk!

DRUMMER: *(Strutting with cane)* Awww, tip-tip-tip . . . Heyyy, tap-tap-tap . . .

ALTO: *(Stopping them)* Naw! No more walking, some easy talking. A floating blues. A glowing blues . . . A Harold-Arnold-smoking-a-joint blues . . . Alllllll blues . . .

(Starts everyone to swaying from side to side in their places)

BASSIST: *(Whispery effect, swaying)* What kind of blues? What mind of blues?

OTHERS: Allll blues . . .

TRUMPET: A sitting-in-the-rocking-chair-with-nothing-else-to-lose blues.

OTHERS: Allll blues . . .

ALTO: A floating blues. A glowing blues . . .

TENOR: *(CROSSING to ALTO)* A clear-your-groove, scrape-away-the-dirt-and-let-your-soul-loose blues.

ALTO: *(CROSSING AWAY from TENOR)* A cocaine-clear-kiss-my-ass blues.

ALL: Alll blues . . . Allll blues . . . Allll blues . . .

(They stand in place, swaying from side to side. ALTO CROSSES to PIANIST as others weave, wave, whispering "Allll blues")

ALTO: *(To PIANIST)* Harold Arnold, smoking-a-joint-blues. Harold Arnold, stroking-a-breast blues—

(She moves away from him to CENTER)

OTHERS: *(Intoning softly)* All blues . . . All blues . . . All blues . . . *(A la Miles)*

PIANIST: Yeah, all blues, well, here's the blues I choose! All night long! Y'all been projectin' on me. Makin' me be, play, say what you all want me to be, say, play. Yeah, an' that's all right. But that's all in the one hand. *(Raising, stretching right hand)* The tickling, tingling, treble hand. The prettifying, pleasing hand. The hands that lends, and bends to his, *(indicates TENOR)* and your, *(to OTHERS)* fantasies. What y'all would have me be, and play. And that's sweet, nice. Has its place. But on the other hand, the bass hand, there's another level of being. And that's me basically—the root-me. The over-me. And it don't have nothin' to do with anybody else's view. Nothin' about a slave or a queen. Just me, the woman—Irene!

(She goes through the motions of packing)

TRUMPET: *(As her father)* Irene!

PIANIST: *(Smiling tolerantly, fondly)* Yes, Daddy . . .

TRUMPET: Girl, are you crazy?! You gon' be a jazz-musician?!

PIANIST: *(Finished packing, ready to go)* Gotta have that music, Daddy. Got to make some of it. *Be* some of it.

TRUMPET: That ain't no world for no young girl!

(PIANIST, grinning, goes through fast, eager, traveling motions, waving back to father)

DRUMMER/BASSIST/PIANIST: *(Traveling motions)* Fast, fast, eighteen-year-old sass! Out to do it! Out to go! . . .

TRUMPET: That ain't no world for no young girl!

DRUMMER/BASSIST/PIANIST: Fast, fast, eighteen-year-old sass. Out to do it! Out to go! . . .

TRUMPET: Girl! Ain't nothin' but men in that world!

PIANIST: I'll win 'em, Daddy! Win 'em wit' my music!

(MEN applaud, but laugh leeringly.

MEN give her room as she confronts them, hands on her hips)

TENOR: Uh, pick up the sheet music, Irene . . .

BASSIST: And stop by the grocery sto' . . .

DRUMMER: Yeah, and see if my shirts are ready . . .

ALTO: Uh, I don't have no piano but come on up to my room, an' let's see what you can do . . .

DRUMMER: Yeah, sing a few bars and dance, girl. Show a little leg . . .

(OTHERS behind her continue softly "All blues . . . All blues . . .)

PIANIST: I'm not out here to be no part-time, laundry-girl, go-fer, and whore! . . . Uh-uh, I'm here to play piano. Not dab sixteen cute bars and grin. Lay out in the middle and bump a chord or two. I got full rich deep tunes I got to play. A whole essence about which you can only guess. Can't say it for me. Got to listen to me tell you about it. Like sometimes men ain't no more to me than objects, and obstacles. So, if you want a man piano, let him come up here and outsay, outplay me, for the same pay. And then hire him. Otherwise what you got is a woman who plays piano. Nothing more. Nothin' less.

(BASSIST takes hat and lunchpail from bag, goes to table, putting hat and pail on the table, stares forlornly as PIANIST comes slowly, sadly over to him)

BASSIST: But, this nightlife, this musician's life, ain't fair to the baby, Rene, ain't fair to me . . .

PIANIST: Bobby—listen, maybe soon I won't have to do so many night gigs. Be able to just record, and maybe teach, an' jus' do a gig now an' then. Maybe . . .

BASSIST: *(Stands, not looking at her)* We tried that, Rene. Rene, I need a woman, a wife, not a musician. The baby needs a mother—not a piano player . . .

PIANIST: Bobby—don't say that, Bobby. You can't divide me like that, Bobby.

The music is me, I am the music. You can't love me in pieces like that, Bobby, please.

BASSIST: *(Putting hat on, starting out)* I guess not, Rene. I'm sorry. I can't make it—I got to go. Good-bye, Rene. *(Pauses as he enters darkness)* Rene? I love you, baby . . . *(Goes on)*

PIANIST: *(Desperately)* Bobby!! Bobby!? . . .

(He looks back. She hesitates, resigns herself)

PIANIST: Liar. You don't love me. You don't even know me.

(He CROSSES)

PIANIST: I'm keepin' my baby! You hear me, Bobby!? I'm keepin' my baby!! *(Defiantly, but tearfully)*

(TRUMPET'S "Mamie Theme" starts. PIANIST moves angrily over to her bag to tie on bandana as TRUMPET "blows."

ALTO laughs, puts on white-man mask. CROSSES to PIANIST with a bandana)

ALTO: Yeah, what about some of that old-time down-home shit. Uh, boy? Yeah, boy, yeah.

TRUMPET: Whewww. *(Laughing)* Shee-it. Mamie, Mamie, Mamie. I know you jokin' wit' me! *(Laughing till tears)* Goddamn girl! I know that what's happenin' ain't what I see! Cain't be! I mean he's workin' me for seventy-five cents an hour. Seven dollars and fifty cents for ten years a day in that sun. And I come up the road an' hear you moanin' and groanin'? Come in the house an' see him zippin' up his pants?! *(Sits down, chuckling, wiping face)* Mamie, naw, shit, naw, goddamn baby, naw. Tell me anything. Tell me you done sold the kids to gypsies! Tell me Mama done come back from the grave and said ol' Jim wasn't my daddy. Tell me anything you think I can stand! But don't tell me you got to lay wit' *that white man!*

DRUMMER: *(Solemnly, after beat)* All the gods fell dead!

BASSIST: *(In Lord, Lord, Lord tone)* Charred coals for breakfast and ashes for dinner.

TRUMPET: Mamie, aw, baby, naw. You ticklin' me wit' a razor!

BASSIST: James Baldwin said it . . .

DRUMMER: Said it in a play!

TRUMPET: *(Covering his ears)* Mamie! Naw! I don't wanna hear it!

BASSIST: Had this woman in the play . . .

DRUMMER: Had her say . . .

BASSIST: Had her say on the witness stand—

DRUMMER: Say she had to stop her man . . .

BASSIST: From *being* a man . . .

DRUMMER: Stop him, she say . . .

BASSIST: Because . . .

TRUMPET: *(Shouts)* Mamie!!

(PIANIST has moved near TRUMPET, strikes hands-on-hips pose)

PIANIST: *(In sudden silence)* If you was a man youda been dead by now!

DRUMMER: If you was a man by now youda killed one a them . . .

PIANIST: And you'd be dead by now!

BASSIST: That's what this Baldwin woman said.

TRUMPET: *(Holding ears)* Mamie! Naww!!! Gawd!! Naawww!!!

DRUMMER: *(Suddenly rips shirt off, flings it)* Nawww! . . . It never stops! Goddamn! Ol' meee an' Uncle Sam—It never stops. Goddamn! *(Repeats, making it rhythmical chant)* Ol' meee and—Uncle Sam.

BASSIST: *(Repeats, softly)* Never stops—God-damn . . .

OTHERS: *(Moving to leave DRUMMER, CENTER STAGE)* Ol' mee an' Uncle Sam . . . Ol' mee an' Uncle Sam . . .

DRUMMER: *(Jumping, dodging bullets CENTER STAGE as he makes machine-gun sounds)* Bah-da-da-da-dow! *(Jumps)* Bah-da-da-da-dow!! *(Begins running, shooting pantomime)* And I'm runnin' and duckin' and shootin'—Bah-da-da-da-dow!! . . .

(BASSIST repeats firing sound as others do sound of whistling explosives, LIGHTS CHANGING as he runs, jumps, shoots)

DRUMMER: And I'm killin' them Chinamen . . . *(With BASSIST)* Bah-da-da-da-dow! *(DRUMMER alone)* Killin' them Kor-reans!! *(With BASSIST)* Bah-da-da-da-dow! *(DRUMMER) alone)* An' we runnin' and a shootin'. An' Jones fell! An' Jenkins fell! Lord! An' Jackson fell! Oh, Lordy, he ain't got no head! Jackson ain't got no head!—Mama! There's blood on meee! There's blood on—meee! *(Runs to audience, points, stalks)* What am I doin' out here, fightin' for you?! . . . Huh? . . . What am I out here for, Uncle Sam?! . . . We suppose to be supplies! Drivin' the trucks an' bringin' the stuff up! We ain't suppose to get caught up in no full-fire shit like this! . . . But I'm gon' get back, you hear me?! . . . I'm not gon' die out here! You can bet on that! I ain't dyin' out here! *(Starts running, shooting actions again with BASSIST, as others do whistling, bombing sounds)* Bah-da-da-da-dow!! . . . I fought my way to a truck. Turned it around an' . . . *(Here he goes into a hesitant conversational tone)* . . . Now you gotta understand. See you—you had to—to go back through this—this pass. Like a railroad tunnel.

BASSIST: *(Moving slightly UPSTAGE of DRUMMER)* Our engineers had cut and built it so we wouldn't have to go around, or over that hill . . .

DRUMMER: Anyway, it was narrow. Single file. Only one truck could get in there at a time!

BASSIST: One at a time . . .

DRUMMER: *(Becoming animated and disturbed again)* Bah-da-da-da-dow ! One at a time! And them Koreans, they was shelling up over the opening of that tunnel—*(Sound of bombs exploding by the others)* Bah-da-da-da-dow! Forcing rocks and dirt down! . . .

BASSIST: Closing it off! . . .

DRUMMER: *(Shout for help)* Uncle Sam! Soon it would be closed! Nobody'd get through!

BASSIST: Nobody . . .

DRUMMER: I gunned that truck for all it was worth! Rrrrooom . . .

BASSIST: Bah-da-da-da-dow! . . .

DRUMMER: And it was getting' closed up! And I was almost to it! Uncle Sam! . . .

BASSIST: Bah-da-da-da-dow! . . .

DRUMMER: And then I see Perry coming up on the side! Lord! He done got a truck! . . .

BASSIST: *(Driving)* Rrrrooom! . . .

DRUMMER: And he's got the angle on me! He gon' get there first. Lord, we shoulda been in the same truck! Only one can get through!

BASSIST: *(Driving)* Only one! Rrrrooom! . . .

DRUMMER: Uncle Sam! I'll be damn he gon' beat me! Leave me here to die! I didn't look at Perry. Perry didn't look at me. I cut him off! *(A pained remembrance of guilt)* I sideswiped him! Took him. Just went a little off the road! Just a little—He straightened up an' come on! And just as I went into the tunnel, I saw him coming in my mirror. But the shell hit! And the dirt an' rocks fell! Closing him off! . . . Trapping him . . . Leaving him there *(BASS falls aside out of the light; rolls over—away)* . . . Uncle Sam . . . Mama . . . Mama, there's blood on me! . . . There's blood on me . . .

(He sinks to knees, whimpering the line over and over, looking at his trembling, bloody hands. Others rise to come to him)

PIANIST: *(As nurse administering shot)* It's all right, soldier, it's all right . . .

TRUMPET: *(Giving Catholic signs of last rites; singing lines in manner of last taps)*

A sold-ier fell!
A sold-ier fell!
Open Wii-de the gates of hell!
A sol-dier fell! . . .

(They all freeze now as ALTO moves forward, laughing)

ALTO: Yes ho! I know exactly how to keep you niggers confused, locked in that old-timey blues. I got ya'lls' keys and can open the doors anytime I choose.

TENOR: Naw! Lift it! Lift it! Past blues! Past space! Past words and events! Into true meanings! Images! Visions! Spontaneous truths! This is a command! Understand?

TENOR: *(Taking over, hard Sonny Rollins-like harmonic riff, or Amiri Baraka blowing his '60s rhythms)* Negative thoughts and fears begat negative thoughts and fears! Wars and killings begat just that! Let's lift it! Lift it! Lift it to harmony and rhythm and peace! Create artifacts of joy! Artifacts of spiritual release! Fruition! Completion! . . .

(PIANIST cuts him off, coming DOWN FRONT with LIGHTS CHANGING, stretching her body everywhere like a cat in heat, almost dancing with it)

ALTO: *(Starts, gathering cast)* PUT YOUR LITTLE FOOT . . .

PIANIST: Awww, I don't want to hear it! All I want to do is dance, an' prance, an' make regal rotundas! *(Chuckles)* Ro-tundas of the soul. Of the inner body. Know what I mean? Castinets and shit clickin' inside you with Christmas tree lights goin' off an' on . . .

TRUMPET: Aw, turn off the lights an' call the law!

PIANIST: *(Moving to him, sliding around him, against him)* Yeah . . . You know what I mean?

TRUMPET: Damn right, I do. Scalding, scalding inside.

PIANIST: *(Looking at TENOR)* Yes, yes. Not way out. But way in. Way in . . .

(She turns away from TENOR, moving with herself)

BASSIST: Do tell. Do tell . . .

DRUMMER: Twirl the world! An' make the rivers run!

TRUMPET: It's good. And it's holy! It's holy. And it's good!

PIANIST: Yess, it's like soul bathing. You know, like sunbathing but it's soul-bathing. Like makin' love to yourself. I mean, it's open. Your man can come in if he wants to. But he doesn't have to. 'Cause you're filled up with yourself. Jus' rich inside yourself.

(Like A-Man chorus)

TRUMPET: Rich inside yourself!

DRUMMER: Can come in if he wants to . . .

BASSIST: But he don't have to—

(TENOR starts toward her, reaching into his bag. ALTO pulls him back and steps up to her imaginary door, stopping the flow by stomping on the floor three times as if knocking on the door. PIANIST assumes flustered aspect, checking hair, etc., before going to the "door")

BASSIST: He don't have to . . .

DRUMMER: But he can, if he wants to—

ALTO: Who taught you that, baby? Harold Arnold? Can I come in?

(TENOR moves to PIANIST who is again going through packing motions as:)

BASSIST/DRUMMER/TRUMPET: *(Sadly, slowly)* Fast, fast, twenty-eight-year-old sass.

TENOR: Harold Arnold?? . . .

(She nods, continues packing)

TENOR: Is he worth all this, Aisha? . . .

PIANIST: Irene! My name is Irene. You gave me Aisha. I'm giving that back, too!

TENOR: You chose that name.

PIANIST: Chose it because you—! Never mind. No, it's not about Harold Arnold. He was just somebody there. Someplace I could play a funky note with . . .

TENOR: That you couldn't play with me? . . .

PIANIST: Not comfortably, no!

TENOR: Well, you don't think we should deal with that? Don't you think it's the easy way out to just leave? . . .

PIANIST: Not as easy as you accepted it all when I told you! Like a damned saint. Some spirit! A man would've done more than just break a damned chair! A man would've—would've—

TENOR: *(Gripping her shoulders)* Done what, Aisha! Broke what—*Irene*!? Huh?! I used to break lots of things! When I was that junkie animal with my first wife!

PIANIST: Dope?!—You? You?? . . . Dope?!

OTHERS: *(Plaintive chant of sorrowful woman)* Baby, why don't you come on home an' leave all that junk alone? *(Repeat)*

(She backs away. He follows her ACROSS STAGE, simulating slapping)

TENOR: Give me that money!

PIANIST: That's the kids' money, no, please . . .

TENOR: Give it to me now! *(He wrenches the money from her)*

PIANIST: Ani-mull!!

OTHERS: *(As chanting children)*
Daddy, Daddy, Daddy
Why you treat us so mean?
You the meanest ol' daddy
We done ever seen!

PIANIST: *(Freeing self, moving away)* Leave us alone!! Get out! Get out!

(DRUMMER, as junkie, comes to and pantomimes conversation with TENOR)

OTHERS: YEAH, MAN! COOL, MAN! I CAN COP, MAN! *(Repeat)*

(DRUMMER takes money from TENOR and CROSSES, laughing)

TENOR: *(As junkie)* I gave him that most obscene of all money—and waited—and waited—and waited . . .

OTHERS: *(Laughing)* YEAH, MAN! COOL, MAN! I CAN COP, MAN! *(Repeat)*

TENOR: He never showed—I had taken the money from her, from the kids . . .

OTHERS:

DADDY, DADDY, DADDY,
Why you treat us so mean . . .

TENOR: *(Continuing)* And he had taken it from me.

OTHERS:

You're the meanest old daddy
We done ever see.

TENOR: *(Continuing)* It was one and the same thing . . . Junkies . . . junkies . . . junkies . . .

(TENOR stoops to pick up "pipe," suddenly runs to nodding DRUMMER, knocks him to floor, chokes, beats him with pipe)

TENOR: *(Beating, shouting)* Junkie! Junkie! Junkie!! . . .

OTHERS: *(Building shrieking agony)* LIKE, MAN! HEY, MAN!! I'M SORRY, MAN!! *(Repeat)*

(TENOR staggers DOWN FRONT as others roll DRUMMER away)

TENOR: I killed us both in that alley. Two junkies. No one cared—just another street scavenger gone. No one cared but me. I have carried him in my head ever since . . .

ALTO: *(Mock-singing)*

GUILT SO HIGH CAN'T GET OVER IT!
GUILT SO LOW CAN'T GET UNDER IT!

(Sudden accusation, laughing)

So you're a killer too!

TENOR: I left two junkies dead in that alley. Ran back to my music. Twelve—fourteen hours a day, I practiced, and practiced! And it saved me. Led me away from the drugs! Gave me some frail justification for leaving her and the kids, saved me and now . . . Is that what you want me to return to, Aisha? Huh? . . .

PIANIST: *(Getting up)* Irene! I'm not talkin' 'bout no junkie! I'm talkin' 'bout a man! A man wouldn't have to ask me nothin'! A man . . .

(TENOR suddenly grabs her and lifts her over his head)

TENOR: Enough! . . .

(He lowers her slowly with his next lines. Her mouth is open in a silent scream)

TENOR: How can you tell me how to be a man? Have you ever struggled to be one in this Caucasian zoo?

ALTO: *(Laughing)* Lift her! Lift her! . . .

OTHERS: Shhh!

TENOR: Shut-up! *(His hand covers her silently screaming mouth. The ALTO shuts up. TENOR removes hand)* My hands are very strong, aren't they, Aisha? Uh-huh, I could kill you and Harold Arnold with very little effort. Simply let the pain mix with the passion and the anger, and manifest itself.

(He gives her his hands and brings her gently to her feet)

ALTO: Oh—He's lifting again!

OTHERS: Hush fool!

TENOR: But, baby, I ain't got time for that. We got too much to do!

(DRUMMER, BASSIST, TRUMPET COME BACK ON STAGE proper, taking seats, arms around legs, at the periphery of the scene)

DRUMMER/BASSIST/TRUMPET: *(Coming on)* Pleny-pleny-pleny—to do! . . .

TENOR: We can't be refascinating and reconquering each other every other day.

DRUMMER: Run it brother, run it!

BASSIST: Spit out the stones! Spit out the stones! . . .

TENOR: You can't be wallowing in every little whim that floats in . . .

TRUMPET: Speak—sur!

TENOR: And I can't be constantly defending my crown in here with you, too!

ALTO: Well what can you do . . . *(Sarcastically)* Warrior!? . . .

TENOR: We got all these splintered pieces to put back together.

TRUMPET: Yes Lord!

PIANIST: What baby? . . .

TENOR: Restore and rebuild a people out of ruins . . . Aisha! Our fathers, oh Lord, our fathers . . .

TRUMPET: Every year . . .

DRUMMER: First day of school . . .

BASSIST: Fill out the papers . . .

TENOR: Address of fathers unknown—and state of the mothers—

PIANIST: Unnatural . . .

TENOR: Unnatural. The pyramid of a tribe, a race, a people begins with the triangle of you, me, family . . .

PIANIST: A new base—I can feel it, baby.

TENOR: A spiritual base . . . a sure foundation.

PIANIST: I can hear it, baby, I can play it.

TENOR: A cornerstone in the pyramid, you and me.

BOTH: Coming together to move new on the world, move new on the world, move new on the world.

(Others joining them for last two repeats)

ALTO: *(Moves them* DOWN FRONT, *continues on the other side of* STAGE*)* That's real sweet. Cute. But that ain't the way Harold Arnold runs it down. No, that ain't the way he runs it down . . .

OTHERS: Already enough fighting to do.

TENOR: *(Going to face* ALTO*)* Yeah, that too. The old battle royal, with them applauding our bloodletting . . . *(Indicates others who hold white masks before their faces)*

DRUMMER: *(Cracking voice)* I'll bet on the big buck! *(Tosses coin on stage)*

BASSIST: ALL RIGHT! I'll take the little nigger!

TRUMPET: Crabs in a barrel! Yes sir! Crabs in a barrel!

*(*TENOR *crosses to* ALTO*)*

TENOR: Just as you see me now, in your primitive state of mind, I saw him then in mine. He was number one in their polls. The audience was giving him their applause, their affirmation. So, like the John Wayne switchblader I was, I set out to get him. Like you, I was a cannibal, wanted to devour his heart and liver. So that all his strength would be mine. A cutting session. Yeah . . .

*(*ALTO/TENOR *circle each other)*

TRUMPET: My horn is longer than yours!

BASSIST/DRUMMER: I can peeee faster and harder than youuuuu . . .

TENOR: Yeah, I studied his ways, his sound, ohh, his songs, so well that I knew his way of doing and being better than he did!

(He and ALTO *are now like mirrors of each other with each move the* ALTO *makes being made by the* TENOR*)*

TENOR: *(Continuing)* Soon, I had him listening to his echo. Hearing his own reflection. And then I saw his weakness. I had him beneath me! Beneath *meee*! *(Raises foot as if to stomp down on cowering* ALTO, *lowers foot, helps him up)* But defeating him in the ego arena didn't free me. Naw, it isn't about super-hip sisters aching to get my horn between their legs, or slick dudes aping my barroom attitude. Naw, it was about my life, my music. Having real worth. Being some rallying sound-point for growth and peace in this poisonous war we call living. I ran to the holy books, and soon there was the light. A great light. Flooding me with the illumination of the holy trinity of the soul, the mind and the body! . . .

OTHERS: Father-Son-Holy Ghost!

TENOR: Electron-Proton-Neutron! Three energized points of a positive triangle! And I heard the bell ring! Ring—vibrating positiveness throughout the universe! Enfolding everything within one great eternal hum—yes—the bell of love! The bell of joy!

OTHERS: Bells of love! Bells of joy!

TENOR: The bell of peace!

(As he starts bell chant, the OTHERS, *excepting the* ALTO, *form a semicircle around him and as they sway one way, he sways the other. They being the sides of the bell, he the gonging tongue)*

TENOR: All is one! One is all! Hear the bells! Calling for all to lift and love, lift and love. *(Repeating as* OTHERS *come in)*

OTHERS: *(Singing together)* LIFT AND LOVE! LIFT AND LOVE! *(Repeat)*

TENOR: Hear the bells! Hear the bells! Hear the bells! . . . Be resplendent colors! Be joyful sounds! Glorious flowers of life!

OTHERS: LIFT AND LOVE . . .

TENOR: HEAR THE BELLS . . .

OTHERS: LIFT AND LOVE . . .

TENOR: HEAR THE BELLS . . .

(All singing together in a growing swaying, hypnotic wave of sound and motion. Until the OTHERS *have connected invisible wires to the* TENOR'S *back and as they chant—with him leading—he actually rises in the air above their heads . . .)*

ALTO: Nigguh—Please!

*(*LIGHTS GO OUT. COME IMMEDIATELY BACK UP, *marking end of song/set.* ALL *come forward to bow to applauding audience.* TENOR *taking two bows alone,* ALTO *eyeing him*

Group repeats: "We did it . . . really did it . . . Yeahhh!" riff)

ACT III

(Lights come up after intermission on musicians in dressing room area. All are there except Alto)

Pianist: Aaron had us doing his little dance for a while but oooo, I'm still up there with that last tune. That was a beautiful flight, baby.

Tenor: We were all on it together.

Drummer: Yeah, you called *all* the faithful to prayer that time. Took Aaron's blues right on up.

Bassist: I heard your bells that time, mister. Sure was nice.

Trumpet: Sho' was. Made me wish I was young again. I heard some things, had some notions, when y'all was flyin' up there, that I sho' would like to speak on myself. But well, the chops—I can't just jump on out all loud and brassy-like like I used to.

Drummer: It's not the volume. It's the intensity. You were right there, pops. Right there.

Tenor: Right. Everybody goes their own way, pops. I love your colors, beautiful earth tones. It's a pleasure playing with you.

Drummer: Right.

Bassist: Dig it.

Pianist: *(Pointedly to Tenor)* And I love your colors. And it's a pleasure playing with you. C'mere.

(He moves to her, bending over to receive a short kiss, and then some whispered words. He straightens up slightly embarrassed)

Tenor: And soon there'll probably be two more little people aroun' the house.

Pianist: Maybe three.

Trumpet: *(Starts for door)* Old man like me shouldn't be listenin' to that kind of talk. Think I got time for one more little nip?

Tenor: Do you really have to?

Trumpet: *(Shrugs)* Afraid so. Heard of *Deep Throat*? Well meet the original . . .

(Trumpet goes out and across stage left off. Alto comes on right, snorts coke, looks across after Trumpet, then comes slowly, purposely to dressing room area)

Drummer: Hey, man, dig. Want you to look at this piece I'm doin'. African thing. Six-eights time.

(Tenor goes over to look at music sheets which Drummer takes from his bag. Alto comes in, hand in his suit coat pocket. Grins strangely around at everyone for a long beat)

Alto: *(To Tenor)* That was a real nice hymn, or prayer, or whatever that was. Nice. Even had me up there for a minute. Uh-huh. But I still—still stick to my *guns*. Yeah. *(Chuckles)* My guns. Yeah. 'Cause that shit ain't real. The people all jump up clappin', givin' you two dips an' shit. 'Cause you help 'em wish. Wish it could, would, be like that pretty shit you playin'. Yeah, Hollywood. Technicolor wit' garbage cans dancin' an' shit . . .

Pianist: Aww, wow, please . . .

(She goes over to table and starts getting her bag ready disgustedly)

Bassist: *(Chuckling)* Garbage cans dancin' . . .

Drummer: *(Wryly, slapping five with Bassist) And* shit . . .

Alto: Yeah, you know, wishin' it was really like that. But who was it? Doris Day? Debbie Reynolds? Somebody like that said wishin' won't make it so. You dig? . . .

Pianist: *(Hefting bag)* When y'all get tired a listenin' to the junkie's preamble, I'll be out front . . .

(She gives Tenor a kiss, starts for the door. Alto moves to block the door)

Alto: Uh-uh, I want everybody in here for this . . .

Pianist: *(Starting again)* Will you please get outa my way?

Alto: Uh-uh. Get back over there.

(Almost casually, he takes hand from coat pocket, revealing pistol. Everyone is startled, moves away from him. Pianist backs to the Tenor)

Drummer: What is this, man?

Bassist: Don't point that shit at me!

Pianist: He's crazy! Crazy! . . .

Tenor: *(Trying to keep atmosphere calm)* Where you goin' now, brother, huh?

Alto: Yeah. Now see the difference? See how everybody jumps to attention, right away? Huh? Yeah. 'Cause this . . . *(Holding up gun)* . . . ain't no wish. No dream. This is real! Yeah. See?

Tenor: Where you headin', brother?

Alto: *(Sudden loud change of tone)* Shut up! An' listen to *me*! Dig? An' you'll find out . . . Yeah, so you can play real. You know? Like Bird said, "If you don't live it, it won't come outta yo' horn." Right.

Tenor: Right. And what do you want to come outta yours, brother?

Alto: *(Very calmly)* Hey? I'm doin' the talkin' 'cause I'm the one with the reality in my hand. Dig? A gun is so real you can't deny it, you know. Bang-bang. Death. Final. Absolute. Eternal. Yeah, you up there getting' double bows for your damn wishes! But to be real you got to be willin' to go all the way! Look down the barrel! Face death! Then you can blow the truth! That's what's wrong wit' nigguhs. They always tryin' to dream an' wish their way. Ain't willin' to go for it all. Stare down the fuckin' tube. Yeah, now other folks know 'bout this shit. Like the Russians. Now they was real. Real musicians. Come up with this roulette. Russian roulette. See, like . . . *(Opens bullet chamber)* There's six chambers. But only one bullet. And no one knows where the bullet is, only this time I'm using three. *(Closes and spins the chamber)*

(OTHERS spread out apprehensively, angrily)

BASSIST: Say, man, this ain't funny, goddamnit . . .

DRUMMER: Cool this shit, man . . .

PIANIST: *(Crowding into TENOR)* Baby, what's he gon' do?!

TENOR: Brother, listen! Hold it, now!

ALTO: *(Pointing at his face)* Shut up, goddamnit! Shut up! We all gon' stare down the barrel tonight! Face the truth! See who's got the guts to be a real musician! The leader!

BASSIST: Who made you God, huh?

ALTO: Me, I'm making myself God.

(TRUMPET player turns corner and COMES IN the door)

TRUMPET: Y'all ready?

(ALTO whirls and fires at him, clicking hammer on empty chamber. OTHERS jump him; as OTHERS punch and kick, the TENOR takes the gun from him)

BASSIST: *(Punching)* Muthuh-fuckuh!!

DRUMMER: *(Kicking at him)* Sonofabitch!

PIANIST: *(Swinging at him)* Crazy bastard!

ALTO: *(Screaming from the floor)* Ain't no bullets in the gun! Ain't no bullets in it!

TRUMPET: Lawd! . . .

(He slumps against door, wiping face with handkerchief)

TENOR: *(Examining gun)* Hold it! Hold it! He's right!

(ALL look at him)

PIANIST: What?!

TENOR: There's no bullets in the gun. See . . .

(ALL look, hold a beat)

DRUMMER: So damn what? We should still—

BASSIST: Waste his monkey-ass.

(ALTO squirms free, sits up touching nose, jaw)

ALTO: I jus' wanted to see where everybody was at! Make everybody face the real!

BASSIST: The real?

DRUMMER: Muthuh—

(They both start for him again. TENOR grabs them)

PIANIST: *(Incredulous)* He's insane! Absolutely insane!

TRUMPET: An' he done scared me outta *my* mind . . .

TENOR: *(Holding back DRUMMER, BASSIST; listening)* Hold it! They're clappin' for us out there, we gotta go!

DRUMMER: What about him?

BASSIST: Can't let him get away with this shit!

ALTO: *(On feet)* Wasn't no bullets! I was jus'—jus' conducting an experiment. Come on, le's go blow . . .

BASSIST: Blow? Suckuh, if you evuh come anywhere near me, you goin' *need* a gun and some bullets. Understand?

DRUMMER: If you still here when the set is over, we gon' get down to the real, all right. Me an' you . . .

TENOR: Come on. The people are callin' for us. That's what we're here for: the music. That's what's important, not him. Come on . . .

(He ushers them all out the door; then turns to ALTO, putting the gun in his coat pocket)

TENOR: You need to find yourself a woodshed, man. One with some mirrors in it . . . *(Starts out)* And an echo chamber . . .

ALTO: Hey, man. It was jus' a thing. All right, so y'all wasn't ready. I'm still playin', right? I'm finishin' the set? Right? . . .

TENOR: No, brother. Not with us. Not tonight . . .

(He joins the OTHERS waiting outside the door. ALTO runs over and opens door)

ALTO: What's the matter? You scared to play wit' me?

TRUMPET: You right about that. You crazy sonofabitch!

DRUMMER: Flipped-out fool!

(TENOR turns them around and they start for bandstand)

PIANIST: You goin' to make an announcement about him?

BASSIST: Yeah. Tell 'em *he is ill.*

TENOR: Nope, we'll jus' play the music on over him. On past him.

(ALTO snatches up his bag and leaves dressing room area, watches them as they go up to bandstand, acknowledging audience's applause with short bows. They start setting up, shaking their heads at each other.

Tenor moves to center to speak to audience as Alto stands near table looking at him)

Tenor: Thank you. Peace and harmony. And welcome to the third set. We, uh, kinda feel the need for a little catharsis right about now. So we're gonna lift the atmosphere with a composition of mine called, It'll Take Us All . . .

Others: Alll . . . Alll . . .

All: It'll take us alll, alll, alll.

(They back up, leaving Bassist down front center with the ball for his "solo")

Others: *(Whispered effect; with ending "all" extended in harmony)* It . . . will . . . take . . . us . . . all . . . all . . . allll. *(Repeat, softly)*

Bassist:

When I was a little boy,
In Tennessee,
I watched, in a meadow,
A butterfly,
And a bumblebee.
Each busy doing its thing
With sunlight music on their
Wings,
Each tending differently to the
Flowers,
Keeping in balance nature's
Powers.
And, ohhh, this vision I could
See,
Of the butterfly, the bumblebee
The meadow, the sky,
And me,
All three afloat in
This webbed-universe of
"We"—

Others: It'll take us allll!

Bassist:

Wee . . . Wee . . . Weee . . .
And ohh, the vibrating humm . . .

Pianist/Tenor: The humm . . .

Bassist:

Of the wings

Pianist/Tenor: The wings . . .

BASSIST: And the purring hearts
Of we three,
The butterfly, the
Bumblebee,
And me.
Vibrating on three connected
Strings,
Each purring heart,
Each sun-fed wing.
And I knew then
In that meadow
In Tennessee
That sustaining that purr,
That humm,
Would be the thing
For me . . .

PIANIST: Yesss . . . *(Whispered, extended)*

BASSIST: Yesss . . . *(Whispered, extended)*

(TENOR signals for them to soften, sweeten, continue the whispered "yesses")

ALL: Yessss . . . yessss . . . alll . . . alll . . . alll . . . yesss! . . . yesss! . . .

(Becomes a chanted mantra of peace, reflection. ALTO jumps to STAGE, "blowing")

ALTO: *(As shout to audience)* Kiss my ass! All you silly muthuh-fuckuhs!

(TENOR motions for OTHERS, to be cool, let him solo)

ALTO: *(Continuing)* Muthuh-fuckuhs—kiss my ass . . . You remember that riff? *(Scats it bee-bop fashion)* Shoo-bow-dooo! Uuuu-ba-doo-ba-doo-ba-doo-ba! Yeah! A Bird quote. Or was it Miles? One of 'em. One of 'em screamed it out in a moment of singular, solitary genius. Yeah, 'cause that's what all genius, all life, is: singular and solitary. Yeah, you come here: alone. You hustle through here: alone. And you carry yo' ass on away from here: alone! Love, joy, peace, happiness—all of that is a baby sucking a tit. Dig what I'm sayin'? Momentary gratification. Surceasement. Fulfillment of a need. Period . . .

PIANIST: *(Sense of Miles Davis's tune)* So what? So everybody has needs. Sooowhat?

OTHERS: Soo what . . .

ALTO: *(Blurting past her interruption, inhaling and exhaling deeply, audibly)* See that? *(Does it again)* That's all there is to the whole trip. Suckin' in and blowin' out air. And every person, every musician, must try to make something out of his puffs, his breathing. Make something identifying, memorable, lasting. And that's all any of us is really trying to do!

OTHERS: Sooo what?!

ALTO: So what, huh? So, Love, Marriage, Friendship, Brotherhood, Religion—are all just gluttonous needs, sucking and pullin' and feedin' on each other deep in the funky darkroom of the psyche where our true self-pictures are developed. Yeah, them stark black and white negatives we hide from the world . . .

OTHERS: Like, we hear you! Like she said! Soo what?!

ALTO: So some people get to blowin' dreams an' wishes. Harmony and rainbows an' shit. Get people applauding a cliché-flag-wavin' camouflage—so that they can be sure their real naked ass is still covered! Right, brother?! *(To TENOR)* Covered, 'cause the daddy of need is a masturbating faggot named Fear! Right—Uncle? . . .

(ALTO now moves on the TRUMPET as he takes out of his bag a white mask)

ALTO: *(Continuing)* Ain't that right, ol' ass-polishin', head-scratchin', shufflin'-hearted nigguh? Huh? . . . *(Puts on the mask and stands, fists on hips before the stunned TRUMPET)* Huh, *boy*?! Ain't that right, *boy*?!

(TRUMPET is caught in a moment of awful memory)

TRUMPET: *(Falteringly)* Uh . . . Well, uh, you see, uh . . . It was . . .

(He looks to PIANIST, who with scarf around head or shoulders, becomes TRUMPET's woman from the second blues set)

PIANIST: *(Shocked, almost tearfully)* What?!

ALTO: Yeah, boy! Speak up!

TRUMPET: *(Pleadingly)* That was a different time . . . Not like now . . . not like today . . .

DRUMMER: *(Angrily at ALTO)* Yeah, that was another time! Another life!

TRUMPET: *(Cowering, taking out handkerchief)* You couldn't . . . couldn't stand up to 'em, like you can today. You jus' . . . couldn't . . .

(PIANIST comes to him with tone and air of indignant incredulity)

PIANIST: Whaat?! . . . What?

TRUMPET: Not when you have kids!

(PIANIST turns away from him)

TRUMPET: *(Continuing)* We had kids. Was sharecroppin'. What else did I know? I wanted to play my horn. I mean guitar. I was playing guitar then. But we had kids. So, we was sharecroppin'. And we come to the store, me an' her, come to . . . to settle up for the year's work. And he . . . he said that *we* "owed" *him*.

PIANIST: *(Same pained incredulousness)* What?!

TRUMPET: That we owed him money.

BASSIST/DRUMMER/TENOR: What?!

ALTO: What I said, boy, was—you don't deserve no woman like that. A woman like that's 'spose to be wit' a man, boy. Hell, aroun' h'yere, you're no more'n a woman yourself. H'yere . . . *(Reaches into bag, pull out big dress, tosses it to TRUMPET)* Put on that dress.

PIANIST: What?!

TRUMPET: Sur?

ALTO: You hear me, boy. Now if you don't wanna go to jail for what you owe me, want seed for next year's crop, food for them kids of your'n, then you put on that dress an' let this gal see you for what you really are roun' h'yere . . . *(Turns to OTHERS as if to conspirators)* Heh, heh.

BASSIST/DRUMMER/TENOR: *(One after the other in bitter sarcasm)*

Heh, heh.
Heh, heh.
Heh, heh . . .

(With his woman watching him in disbelief, TRUMPET goes DOWN FRONT carrying the dress)

TRUMPET: I mean she knows what I am. And he's got all the power and the food. It's jus' another of his ugly jokes. So, I'll jus' . . . jus' . . . laugh along with him for a . . . a minute. Then we'll get our stuff, an' . . . an' . . .

(He puts dress on. His woman walks over to the white-masked ALTO, looks at him in resignation, then goes on ahead of him as he follows her, laughing softly)

TRUMPET: That's when she started . . . started . . .

(PIANIST turns back to embrace ALTO, begins lovemaking simulation)

TRUMPET: Naw, Mamie! Naw!! Not him, Mamie!! Please, Lawd! Not that man, Mamie!! Please!!

PIANIST: *(Turning on him bitterly)* You shoulda died before you let him do that to you! You shoulda died!

TRUMPET: Mamie!!

(ALTO laughs through it all)

PIANIST: *(Backing away as LIGHT FADES)* I'm gonna find me a man who'll die first. You hear me? I'm takin' the kids! You hear me! I'm takin' the kids . . .

(LIGHT OUT on her.

TRUMPET is alone in the center as ALTO laughs)

TRUMPET: I wanted to be like Louie. Louie Armstrong. Make my horn scream curses and laughter in dance time. Way up over their heads. Yeah. Make 'em think I was laughin' wit' 'em, while I'm snarlin' at 'em. Yeah, growlin'. You ever seen Louie's grin? Huh? Hell, that ain't no grin, that's him snarlin', showin' his teeth. Laughin', "Go to hell all you pale two-faced bastards!" Yeah, Lord! But I . . . I ain't no Louie Armstrong. Like Mamie said, I shoulda jus' . . . shoulda jus' . . .

(Doing these last lines, he reaches into his bag and pulls out a near life-sized mask of either: 1) Louis Armstrong, with his famous grin exaggerated into a fearsome, toothful scowl, with blood dripping from his lips, or 2) a mask of the TRUMPET *player himself, with a grin/snarl like Louie's, complete with the handkerchief and bleeding lips. Crouching behind this "voodoo" mask, he creeps over to a wall and slides down to floor, hidden behind the mask.*

ALTO *moves into light, laughing in the white mask. He takes it off and stands with it, laughing)*

ALTO: Truth! Miserable bastard! Truth!

*(*BASSIST *jumps out at him)*

BASSIST: Phony scavenger! The only truth for you is the part that stinks! The maggots! That's all, jus' the shit! Damned filthy hyena!

*(*ALTO *turns to him, throwing white mask away)*

ALTO: Oh, the wallflower wants to dance. Well, hallelujah! But you're forgettin' your role, sonny. *(They circle each other cautiously now)* You know who these people paid to see, to hear. The horns, junior. The horns carry the light, tell the stories. You supposed to be back there, yes-yes-yessin' an' uh-huhin'! Co-signin' and testifyin'—that's yo' part!

DRUMMER: Liar! Fool! Clown!

BASSIST: All you prima donna-ing, sublimating horn- suckers make me sick. Everyone of you! *(Glaring around at all the horns)* Posin' peacocks! Crowin' roosters! Standin' out here with your gold-plated extension rods. Let me see you cluck your tongues when your heart stops beating! Hear?! Yeah! I'm the heartbeat! *(Thumps chest)* You understand? I stop thumpin', you stop jumpin', baby! You dig it? You might book your little flights in your heads. But here's your runway! Here's your launching pad! Me! And don't you, any one of you, ever, ever, ever—never, forget that!

(He ends crouched in his intensity. After a beat, an awkward moment, he realizes the depth of the revelation, is embarrassed, tries to straighten, recompose himself. Even the TRUMPET *now stands, watching)*

ALTO: Uh-huh, the truth will out. Don't be 'shamed, baby. Let your ego show. 'Cause ego make the grass grow.

*(*DRUMMER *jumps out)*

DRUMMER: An' too damn much grows weeds! Time for you to go, mister. I'm gon' drum you right off the stand!

*(*ALTO *whips out daggerlike switchblade)*

ALTO: Naw, uh-uh. You might control their time, but tryin' to control mine you goin' too far. Drum all you want, but you better stay where you are . . .

(DRUMMER jumps to his bag, gets fighting stick. They circle each other as BASSIST moves out of their way)

DRUMMER: You gonna know the rhythm of wrath, my man! The rhythm of righteous indignation.

BASSIST: Machine gun rhythm!

DRUMMER: Atom bombs fallin'!

ALTO: Shit!

DRUMMER: Killing a snake with a stick!

ALTO: Shit.

BASSIST: Crack the head!

ALTO: Kiss my ass!

DRUMMER: Let the poison out!

ALTO: Go to hell! *(Backing away)*

BASSIST: Let it run!

DRUMMER: Let the venom run!

BASSIST: Let it soil the earth!

DRUMMER: Rather than spoil the man! You have run your course. Come to the hard rock in a bad place!

BASSIST: Machine gun rhythm!

DRUMMER: *(Lifting stick over head)* Atom bombs falling.

PIANIST: Stop it!!

TENOR: *(Coming to them)* Yeah, brother, don't let him take us there. Lift on away from him. Leave him there.

ALTO: You go to hell!

PIANIST: *(Covering ears)* No! . . .

TENOR: *(Touching DRUMMER's arm)* Hold it, brother. It's me he wants. Let him come with it . . .

(DRUMMER releases ALTO, who gets to feet as TENOR backs up)

ALTO: Yes, I want you, all right.

TENOR: I know. I know.

ALTO: Yeah . . .

(One UPSTAGE, one DOWN, they circle, removing coats, shirts, finally kneeling to remove shoes)

PIANIST: Please, don't. Please . . .

DRUMMER: And Cain talked to Abel . . .

TENOR: His brother . . .

OTHERS: And finding it impossible to be him . . .

TENOR: To have what was his . . .

OTHERS: He did set out to possess him . . .

ALTO: Or destroy him . . .

TENOR: My music, my spirit, is already in the wind. I've been heard, felt. How do you expect to catch the echo? Destroy memory?

ALTO: That echo, that memory, will be my preamble—*brother*. Your fall announces the new legend—me.

TENOR: No continuum? No natural extension? Only this old battle royal? This blood sacrifice?

ALTO: So it has been. So be it.

TENOR: Why do we have to come to this moment?

ALTO: Law of nature, the need to grow and dominate, take space, oxygen, sunlight.

TENOR: We have not yet evolved past that? You must stand in my space? Only one at a time. Not many? Not all?

ALTO: Damn all! Your reality, your way of being, your sound causes judgment and questions on mine. Conflicts. Shadows.

TENOR: Your judgments, conflicts, shadows? I only see contrasts. Colorings.

ALTO: Because you're looking down from the top.

TENOR: Then lift yourself, brother, take my hand.

ALTO: I don't trust no hand but mine. Blow, sonofabitch, blow!

(Stripped to waists and barefoot, they move to the center. BASSIST and DRUMMER bring to them each a new neck strap, as used for securing saxophones, but these are exaggerated, ceremonial in their red color, wide, roomy—almost like horses' bridles—with give enough for them to completely turn around inside the neck space. As DRUMMER and BASSIST step back . . .

The two clasp the ends of the neck straps together—putting them just outside arm's length from each other. BASSIST and DRUMMER bring the two daggers, each resting in a ceremonial bowl of "blood" [throughout the fight, the "cutting session," the daggers are redipped into the bowls, intermittently, so that the wounds will show])

DRUMMER/BASSIST: And Cain and Abel did meet in the field!

PIANIST: *(Sarcastically)* With the green-eyed monster presiding . . .

(The two square off, circling, choreographed through to end of fight)

OTHERS: Jealousy breeds Envy!

(Tenor shouts as Alto cuts him at his side)

Others: *(Countercircling the two)* Envy breeds Desire!

(Alto screams as Tenor cuts him on the arm. Daggers redipped in the blood)

Others: Desire breeds Passion!

(They both lunge, miss, circle)

Others: And passion demands! . . .

Tenor: Possession!

Alto: Destruction!

(He lunges, Tenor parries and now they strain against each other—each grasping the other's knife hand)

Tenor: You came to love, not to kill.

Alto: Yeah, I know. Hate is love. And piss is lemonade! Die, bastard!

(Suddenly Alto spins and cuts Tenor across his chest. Tenor shouts, slashes back. Blades are quickly rebathed)

Tenor: Hate is love clogged with fear.

Alto: When you have the power to grasp it, command it, it is simply another game of subjugation, another plateau of self-affirmation. And you will never get that from me! Never!

(They lunge and are again locked together, straining, grasping wrists)

Others: And the final word is—?

Tenor: Love!

Alto: Conquer!

(They repeat it once more, straining, turning)

Trumpet: Say, love conquers all!

Drummer: But not all the time!

Bassist: No, not all the time!

Pianist: The eagle and the snake!

Trumpet: One of 'em's got to break!

(Alto makes sudden move and knocks Tenor off balance, forces him to one knee, strains over him, his knife coming closer. Tenor strains to rise)

Bassist: And in the old days some of the tribes . . .

Drummer: Would kill a great enemy warrior-king . . .

Pianist: And eat his heart, his liver!

Bassist: So that his strength, his courage . . .

Drummer: Would be theirs!

(Tenor forces way back to his feet)

Tenor: What you want from me cannot be taken.

ALTO: You're nothing to me! A stone. A gate. A door.

TENOR: To a room full of distorted mirrors!

ALTO: Better than your echoes!

BASSIST/TRUMPET/PIANIST: Get it done!

ALL: *(Except TENOR and ALTO)* NOW!! . . . *(Clap hands.)*

(AS TENOR is getting upper hand, rendering ALTO helpless beneath him, bringing the knife to his throat)

DRUMMER: The eagle . . .

BASSIST: The snake . . .

PIANIST: You! . . .

TENOR: And I—I—I—Say it! . . . Let it go, brother! Say it, "You are my brother, and I Love you! I love you! . . ."

ALTO: Noooo! You are not my brother! Noo! I will not be naked again! I will not expose my heart! I will not give up the knife! Nooo!! . . .

(With the knife at his throat, the TENOR makes his decision; gets up, takes knife to group, to TRUMPET, who passes it on each one, ending with the PIANIST—all hesitating, making decision. PIANIST takes knife down front to cowering ALTO; she stands, then kneels and lays knife beside him)

PIANIST: Yes, you are my brother. And I love you . . .

(OTHERS all follow her, in turn, one after the other, repeating the same words with differing degrees of difficulty, sincerity, according to how each actor feels at that moment. Then they make semicircle around him, sing:)

ALL: *(Minus ALTO) (Sing:)*
IT WILL TAKE US ALLL! *(Repeat)*
IT WILL TAKE US. . . . *(PAUSE)*

(ALTO looks at them, gets to feet holding knife, sings with them on last sustained note of harmony.)

ALL: *(With ALTO)* ALLLL!

(It is a difficult thing for the ALTO to do, but he does it, caught in this moment of group harmony. At end of note, OTHERS smile at each other, move back to instruments. TENOR comes to audience as ALTO moves down left, shook)

TENOR: Thank you! . . . Thank you! . . . The piano! The bass! . . . Drummer! . . . The Trumpet! . . . Yours truly, the Tenor! . . . The Alto!

(He and the rest of the group extend their hands to him, indicating that he is to lead them off. He does. If he believes them, he leaves the dagger on stage, and joins others for group bow, indicating change of heart; if still uncertain, he carries it with him)

(BLACK)

What the Wine-Sellers Buy

CHARACTERS

Steve: 17 years old. Bright, aggressive.

Mrs. Carleton (Mrs. C): Steve's mother, late thirties.

Rico: "Old school" pimp/hustler

Joe: Steve's best friend

Mae: Steve's girl friend. Preferably dark. Very attractive.

Jim Aaron: Mrs. Carleton's friend. Hard worker, deacon in his church.

Melvin: Fast-talking young hustler, 19 or 20 years old.

Old Bob: Lecherous old man.

George: Philosophical hat shop owner. Marijuana smoker.

Mrs. Harris: Mae's embittered mother.

Marilyn: High school cheerleader, Mae's rival

Various male and female characters (these can be played by two men and two women, or doubled up with some of the characters listed above):

Man #1
Man #2
Girl #1
Girl #2
Boy 1
Boy 2
Hustler
Coach
White cop
Black cop
Candy, Rico's girl
Cab driver
Detective
Teammate
Various students, players, members of crowd

TIME

late 1950s–early 1960s

PLACE

Detroit/any other American inner city

ACT I

SCENE 1

SET

(STAGE RIGHT: Back steps, porch, and on UPPER LEVEL, small bedroom-bathroom sense. MAE/MRS. HARRIS's space. Coming RIGHT CENTER: Alley, CLEANER's SHOE SHOP, can be portable counter on wheels, with GEORGE's HAT SHOP sign above.

UP-CENTER, Carlton flat; CENTER, kitchen area, with rear door leading to hallway, rest of flat; LEFT, small living room, door left leading to hallway, front door, door rear, to kitchen, etc.; DOWN LEFT, three steps leading to "outside," DOWNSTAGE street level.

STAGE LEFT: Small raised area for RICO's hotel room, etc.

Entire DOWNSTAGE area for STREET/MILTON's PLACE/SCHOOL etc.

Lights come up with theme music, "Money, Money Money," by the O'Jays. Theme fades and is replaced by song, "Sex and Money," sung (if possible) by various members of the cast as the neighborhood population parades before us going about their particulr pursuits. Focus on TWO MEN (or as many as four if possible) leading the song, sung to the tune of the Clovers' Lovey-Dovey:

OOP-AU-WOOP/AU-OOO OOO WEE/
OOO OOO AU-WEE/WEEEE EEEEE/
SEX AND MONNN-NEEE
YESSS, SEX AND MONN-NEE
ALL OF THE TIME
SEX AND MONNN-NEEE
CAN'T GET 'EM OFFA' YO' MIND . . .

As this is being sung, STEVE dribbles basketball onto stage fron right, followed by MAE. He waves bye to her as she goes up back steps to her flat. He continues on through singers—waving and nodding to some—as the song continues:

DO IT/DO/
GOTTA GET TO IT,
SEX AND MONN-NEEE
TAKE YOU OUTTA' YO MIND!
SEX AND MONN-NEE
SHO' NOUGH/DRIVE YOU STONE BLIND! . . . *(Continues)*

The idea here being that the two subjects pervade the very air, the sciousness of everyone in the community, from street-walkers to housewives, with a couple notable exceptions (say, MRS. CARLTON, JIM AARON. That to be constantly confronted with these two suggestions—somehow joined—is a natural state for STEVE.

The basketball rolls near the two men down front; STEVE *hurries to retrieve it)*

STEVE: Hey, Slim, Tate, how y'all doin'? . . .

MAN #1: Hey, Youngblood . . . *(Points admonishing finger)* Sex: Gotta doit!

MAN #2: Yeah, Steve . . . *(Pointing)* . . . Money gotta get it!

STEVE: *(Pointing as* THEY *did)* Gotcha! Sex and money! Gotta get 'em!

MAN #1: Now you talkin' . . .

MAN #2: Goin' in the right direction! Jus' keep on walkin'!

STEVE: *(Waving)* Gotcha. Y'all be cool, now . . . *(To himself)* Gotta get some money that's for sure.

*(*HE *stops at steps to his flat; searching pocket for keys.* JOE *runs on)*

JOE: Steve! . . . Hey, man, wait up! I'm goin' your way . . . Hey, Steve, wait!

STEVE: Don't come near me, man! Just stay the hell away from me! . . . Some damned donuts! Don't be comin' in my house.

JOE: Aw, man, you know you wanted some too . . .

STEVE: Don't be comin' in my house, man! Get away from me.

*(*JOE *goes off, shaking head.*

BLACK.

Lights up on STEVE'S *house set. Left, the front room and hallway leading to the rest of the house. Right the kitchen where* RICO *sits at table trimming beard.* STEVE *is hanging coat on rack)*

STEVE: No basketball practice. No classes. No nothin' 'til I pay fifteen dollars an bring my mother to school. All for some damned donuts. Followin' that stupid-ass Joe, we sneaked out to get some donuts at lunchtime, an' comin' back in we dug Miss Copeland an' started runnin' and tripped over each other right into the damned display case. Thirty dollars. Fifteen apiece. For some donuts.

*(*STEVE *sits right chair in kitchen)*

RICO: That ain't no big problem, young fella. Lift yo' chin . . . when a sucker thinks he's got you down, that's when you show him yo' knife.

*(*STEVE *grunts sarcastically)*

RICO: *(Continued)* Naw, I'm serious, looka' here. I'll jus' gi' you fifteen bills advance on your tips for all the little runs you make for me to the shoe shop and the store and all . . .

STEVE: *(Rising)* You would, man!? . . . *(Going back down)* Aw, naw, that wouldn't do no good though. Naw. Thanks anyhow, man . . .

RICO: What you mean? Why not? . . .

STEVE: My mother's still got to go with me before I can get back in. And if I give her the fifteen dollars, and tell her where I got it, she'll—well, you know how she is about hustlers. My ol' man was a hustler, you know. And she's always on me about that stuff.

RICO: Oh?—That's right, you did tell me yo' ol' man was a hustler. But you didn't tell me what kind? . . .

STEVE: I don't know. Gambled mostly, I guess. I was just about three when he—died, got shot. So I don't really know what he was . . . *(Gets up and goes to counter to radio, looks for station)*

RICO: Shot, huh? . . . Gamblin'?

STEVE: Naw, him and two more cats robbed a bank. They got him at the car. Four times.

RICO: *(After beat)* You was just three, huh? Tough break for you and yo' ol' lady. But least you know he had heart. Wasn't robbin' no corner grocery stores . . .

(Goes into his room, off stage.

(STEVE can't find station HE wants, turns radio off. Stands at sink trying to figure out his dilemma. RICO returns buttoning up colorful expensive-looking shirt, carrying new shoes and shoe-shine rag. Tosses rag to STEVE who catches it)

RICO: Here—Dust me off, and I'll tell you what I'll do.

(RICO puts shoes on. STEVE kneels, RICO puts foot on STEVE's knee and STEVE shines shoe)

STEVE: What? . . .

RICO: Well, dig: You let yo' mama get a advance on her little salary, or take it outta' her lil' savings, or whatever, and go an' pay the fifteen an' get you back in school. Dig?

STEVE: Yeah . . . ? . . .

RICO: *(Changing foot)* Meanwhile I'm gone gi' you the fifteen now. And you tell her you done hooked some little weekend gig, and slide the fifteen back to her real quick. You know, five or six, at a time. And that'll ease the pressure on you . . .

STEVE: Yeah . . .

(RICO goes out.

STEVE gets half-gallon bottle of cheap dry wine from the refrig. Goes over and rinses out both glasses at sink. Pours RICO's glassful; then quickly downs one himself. Puts bottle back after putting RICO's glass on table. Whistling now, turns on radio to station where tenor-saxophonist is doing deep, medium tempo blues—maybe Sonny Rollins' "Blue Seven."

RICO comes back in. A tie hangs loose from his shoulders; HE carries a bottle of hand lotion and a can of Johnson's Baby Powder. HE drops two ten-dollar bills to table)

RICO: *(Continued)* There you go, big timer. There's yo' ol' lady's bread . . .

STEVE: *(Picking it up and pocketing it)* Cool, Rico, mello. This should make her give me a *little* space, anyhow.

RICO: *(Putting lotion on face, neck, hands)* Yeah, well, don't think you ain't gone earn it, cause I don't believe in spoilin' no good hustler, ya dig. Whoa, I got an idea.

STEVE: What?

RICO: Dig? They ever see yo' mama at that school? She ever been over there before? . . .

STEVE: Uh-Uh . . .

RICO: Cool, then. I'll jus' have onea' my girls go over wit' you. Say she's yo' ol' lady, an—

STEVE: *(Begins to shake his head, chuckling, laughing)* Uh-uh—Naw, man—uh-uh—Never mind. Thanks anyway, man, but nooooo—

RICO: Huh? What's so damned funny?—What you laughin' at? . . .

STEVE: Well, man, they—they all got them streaks dyed in their hair. And they wear all that stuff on their faces. And, most of 'em, man, the ones I've seen anyway, the way they talk, man. Like—Well. I jus' wouldn't want nobody sayin' that's my mama. That's all. I don't mean nothin'. But—you know . . .

RICO: *(After a beat)* You mean they look like ho's! Uh-huh. They damn sho' do. Definitely looks like 'ho's. 'Cause that's what they is . . .'ho's. Jus' like I'm a pimp. Definitely a pimp. Been one for a long time. And been *wantin' to be one* before *that*! . . . *(Rubbing lotion into hands as HE goes into wide-legged "pimp's stance")*

STEVE: Well, that's cool with me, man.

RICO: Damned right, I'm a pimp. Shit. That's Hastings Street out there. And you think it's somethin' now? Shoulda' seen it when I was comin' up. You couldna' stood it. Sheet. You think you and yo' old lady, po'? Sheet. Long as I been here I ain't never seen you go to bed on empty. But me an' my three brothers and fo' sisters? Hell, we used to try to hurry-up an' get to sleep, 'cause when one stomach start growlin' it remind all the others that they ain't ate shit, either . . . What you laughin' at? I ain't jokin' a bit. That's exactly how it was.

STEVE: Hey, Rico, man, I wasn't tryin' to put nobody down. I jus' said—Well, man, you know how it is . . .

RICO: Yeah, I know how it is. But do you? Sheet. Damned right. I wanted to be a pimp. Soon as I heard that's what they called 'em, you dig? Wasn't nothin' else to be 'cept onea' them dudes like my daddy. Carryin' his lunch in onea' them brown paper sacks. Been wearin' a factory badge so long the print of it's on his damned chest. Yeah, work nine days a week, ninety hours a day, and after he pay a few bills he lucky if he got enough left to get the lunches to go in them paper sacks—much less shoes for everybody and food for the damned house. Yeah, a damned mule. A fool. Ridiculous!—*(Sips wine)*—My daddy . . . wait a minute—let me show you somethin' . . .

(Exits to room leaving puzzled STEVE. Re-enters carrying sparkling new pair of shoes in one hand, in other, old, beat-up brogans)

RICO: *(Continued)* . . . See these raggedy motherhuggers? Well, I wore these my first year of high school, 'till I got tireda' people laughin' at my raggedy stomps, wit' the cardboard covering the holes, my funky socks showin', and quit school and started shining shoes. Now you see these? . . . *(Holding out new shoes)* One hundred and forty dollars! These is what pimps wear. Got 22 pair! Damn right, I'm a pimp. When they told me that's what they was, pimps, I said show me that do' 'cause that's the way I wanna go. Damn right. Put some of this powder on my back. You don' get me sweatin'. Gotta smell sweet for the bitches, you dig? . . .

STEVE: Rico, you somethin' else . . .

(As STEVE comes around table to take baby powder can from RICO, who leans hands on table with his shirt drawn up in anticipation, MRS.C. steps into view. EVERYONE freezes)

STEVE: *(Continued)* Ma, we was jus'—jus' talkin' . . .

MRS. C.: *(Pointing)* Get out there an' get those groceries off the back steps! Now—

STEVE: Ma, we was jus' talkin' . . .

MRS. C.: Now! I said! . . .

STEVE: Yes, mam. I'm goin'. Dog . . .

(Slides past her, out door.

SHE stands glaring at RICO, too enraged to speak. HE sprinkles powder on chest, rubs, picks up stuff and moves to door with a swagger)

RICO: Like he said, we was jus' talkin'. Nothin' serious—

MRS. C.: *(Nearly hisses)* You-leave-my-son-alone. You hear me?

(Knocks shoes off table.

THEY are standing close, eye to eye. One leering in a smile. The other glaring to warn a predator away from her nest. RICO slowly rubs powder onto his chest.)

RICO: You best be keepin' yo' hands off my shoes, Lady.

(If circumstances warrant it, following two "street scenes" may be cut)

(BLACK. Lights change. MAE is on street carrying her innocent schoolbooks. Music begins strange stop-start, slowed-down manner. FOUR OLDER MEN come on scene, approaching threatening from different directions, singing The Midnighters' "Sexy Ways," singing pointedly, threateningly)

ALL: *(Surrounding her, closing in, forcing her back)*

Do it baby
Get it baby
Do it baby
Get it baby
Just love your . . .
Sexy-ways!!

(SHE breaks past them; THEY hem her in, looking around as though for witnesses, singing in low menacing tones, "Do it baby. Get it baby," like panting hounds. MAE backs, then—just at the moment when rape seems inevitable—SHE gets enough-is-enough look on her face and breaks through them as THEY laugh.

As MAE comes past MEN, giving harassed look over her shoulder, a sharply dressed hustler type comes from stage left wings; eyes her)

HUSTLER: Hey, young fox. That's my hog parked over there. Come on, I'll float you where you want to go, young fox . . . And, dig it, if the car ain't smooth enough for you, you can sniff some of this an' sail on out like a pretty bubble, sweet thang . . .

(Taking out tin foil wrapped ball.

MAE steps on around him. HE starts to fall in with her, reaching for her arm. Sound of window opening; OLD WOMAN'S voice making them both look up)

VOICE: *(Offstage)* Leave that young girl alone. You devil. Jus' get an' leave her alone. And I mean it! . . .

HUSTLER: *(Looking up)* Ol' dishrag! Who the hell you think you talkin' to?! . . .

VOICE: *(Offstage)* I'm talkin' to you, an'—An', look, hyere come a squad car. I'm sho' gonna' put 'em on you . . . *(Calling out)* Hey!! Hey y'all!! Poo-leece!! Over this way!!

HUSTLER: *(Checking street)* Crazy ol' bitch . . . *(Suddenly tosses tin foil wrapped package into wings, hurries after it, giving nervous glance back over his shoulder)*

VOICE: *(Offstage)* . . . You better go! . . .

MAE: *(Waving up)* Thank you. *(Hugging schoolbooks, deciding to run off left)*

VOICE: *(Offstage)* Think nothin' of it, honey. Now you get on off these streets, you hear? Ain't no place for you . . .

MAE: *(Offstage)* Yes, mam!!

VOICE: *(Offstage)* I mean it!! Get on off these streets!

MAE: *(Offstage)* Yes, mam!!

VOICE: *(Offstage)* Go on! Hurry! Get on off these streets! Hurry!! . . .

MAE: *(Offstage)* Yes, mam!!

VOICE: *(Offstage)* All right, then! You better . . .

(BLACK.

"Sexy Ways," plays in dark)

SCENE 2

(Kitchen, perhaps an hour later. MRS. CARLTON slams refrig. door, angrily. STEVE looks up expectantly from his plate of spaghetti. SHE goes to sink to wash dishes.)

MRS. C: Gone tell that landlord one more time. Either that Rico gets outta here or I am. When white folk lived here all these rooms was part of one apartment. Now we are here and they split up the rooms and rent them separately. Boston strangler could move in one of these rooms with us and they wouldn't care as long as they paid the rent.

STEVE: The Boston Strangler. Rico. Aw, Mama, Rico don't hardly even be here. Jus' usin' this place for a front for his parole officer . . .

MRS. C.: *(Turning to look at him)* What you know about paroles and fronts? I told you to stop talkin' to him! I mean that now . . .

STEVE: *(Sighing)* I heard about paroles and fronts way before Rico moved here . . .

MRS. C: I bet you have. A whole lotta other things too, I bet . . . *(Drying dishes, back to him)* . . . About nothin', huh. Tryin' to raise a boy around here on these streets ain't no nothin'. *(Going on as though to herself)* . . . It's like there's some kind of fever out there. Yes. A fever to get . . .

STEVE: Mama—

MRS. C.: —that stuff in the movies. And the magazines, and the big-name stores. Uh-huh. Want it fast. Right now. Wait is a bad word. And work—work is for—for slaves! And fools. And—mules!—Uh-huh. Not me, Laura. They ain't gone run that trick on me. Workin' me till I'm bent over, never payin' me enough to get straightened-up, so I can be somethin'. Get somethin' for me. Naw, not me. 'Uh-uh. Naw, not for him. Not yo' daddy. He was goin' to outslick 'em. Just run up and snatch things from 'em. Take it. Uh-huh. I told him over and over. Just like I try to tell you.

You have to be patient, work, an' plan. But, naw, not him. He had to try to thieve from the thieves. Out dog the dogs! And, oh, God knows I loved him so. *(Slams something hard on sink)* I would hear his footsteps coming up the hall and jump up and stand there in the center of the floor just grinning all over. And Lord when they killed him I just wanted to die.

STEVE: *(Getting up, starting to her)* Mama? Come on, now . . . *(Stands helpless)*

MRS. C: *(Trying to gain control; wiping eyes)* He wasn't no snake, Steve. He wasn't no Rico. He wasn't made for no leftovers. But he wasn't really no bad man. He wasn't really bad, Steve.

STEVE: *(A beat)* Yeah, he was, Mama . . .

MRS. C: *(Looking up)* What? What you say? . . .

STEVE: *(Grinning)* He was bad—badd! Had to be nothin' but a bad cat to have a foxy chick like you. Ain't tellin' me nothin'! He was a baaad-dude!

MRS. C: Yes, and you jus' like him for the world. Wit' yo' sassy mouth!—

STEVE: Uh-huh. And gone be tougher than he ever was and get me a chick almost as foxy as you, lady.

MRS. C: Boy, hush . . .

(THEY smile at each other warmly. BLACK)

SCENE 3

(There are knocks at front door. MOTHER comes from room to answer. STEVE is in kitchen studying, goes out into hall, curious. SHE opens door for JIM AARON: Big-bodied, good natured, clean-living contractor, wearing nondescript dark suit.)

MRS. C: Good evening, deacon . . .

JIM: Jim . . .

MRS. C: *(Smiles)* Jim . . .

(STEVE comes into front room, clearing his throat)

MRS. C: *(Continued)* Uh, Steve, this is one of our deacons, Mr. Aaron.

JIM: *(Extending hand)* Jim . . .

MRS. C: And this is my ol' bad boy, Steve . . .

(THEY shake)

JIM: Looks all right to me. How you doin', son? Glad to meet you.

STEVE: All right. Glad to meet you.

MRS. C: All right. You behave while I'm gone now.

STEVE: Yes, mam. I don't get no kiss since Mr. Aaron's here, huh?

MRS. C: Shouldn't give you nothin' bad as you are . . . *(Offers cheek. THEY kiss)*

STEVE: *(Playing again)* All right. Y'all go 'head. But you bring her straight back from church, dig. I don't want no stuff out of you . . .

JIM: All right, sir, I'll bring her straight back.

MRS. C: Boy, can you shut yo' mouth for just a minute.

JIM: Glad to meet you, son. Think we'll get along jus' fine. Be seeing you.

STEVE: *(Waving as THEY start out)* Okay, Mr. Aaron. Later, ma.

MRS. C: Uh-huh. Remember what I said: Stay away from that—no-tellin'-what, back there? . . . *(As HE nods)* Don't know what I'm going to do with him . . .

JIM: Aw, he's all right. Don't have no salt, won't have no flavor.

MRS. C: Well, Lord knows, he's got salt—An' pepper too..

(THEY cross. Chuckling, STEVE goes back to kitchen table; takes up textbook again. RICO comes into kitchen smoking pot)

RICO: She gone, huh? . . . *(STEVE nods without looking up)* Give you a pretty rough time. About yo' ol' man an' everything, I mean.

STEVE: Wasn't too bad. Mama's all right.

RICO: Yeah, she's alright. Just wanna sell you on somea' that soft chickenshit, that's all.

STEVE: She's cool.

RICO: Yeah, naturally. She's yo' mama. All mamas is cool wit' they sons. Most of 'em anyhow. But they all got one bad habit. They always try to turn us into chickenshit punks. Uh-huh. They can't help it . . .

STEVE: Rico, man, I'm tryin' to . . .

RICO: Naw, they can't help it—thinkin' like mamas. They think: "What can I do keep my little black boy safe from those big bad white men? To make those white men like him? Oh, I know I'll make him a punk!" Yeah, they don't know that's what they thinkin', but that's what they thinkin'. 'Cause you dig, a punk accepts whatever is being handed down out there, wit' no questions. Least, not out loud. So, they don't cause no trouble. And that's all mamas care about: that you don't get into no trouble. Shit, trouble just the waves you make as you walk through the air. Get in trouble blowin' yo' nose, or, cuttin' yo' damn toenails. Yeah, mamas is cool. But, I don't know how you see it, big timer, but I'd rather be locked up somewhere wearin' stripes, than be a punk out here wearin' patches on my ass. Know what I mean?

STEVE: Yeah, Rico, man, you right. Okay? But I gotta get in this book right now, if you don't mind.

RICO: *(Gives hard look; softens it)* Naw, I don't mind, go 'head. Never can tell what you might find in a book. *(Going to sink for water)* . . . Somebody might've left ten, fifteen dollars in it. Never can tell . . . *(STEVE looks up at low blow)* Got in the habit reading myself when I was in the joint . . . But I'll tell you one thing you can't find in none of them books. *(STEVE looks)* . . . Guts!—Guts to be not only readin' about things. Thinkin' about things. But guts to be out doing things. Getting' things. That's what! Ain't in nonea' them damn books . . .

STEVE: *(A beat)* Maybe not, Rico. But my test ain't in guts tomorrow, it's in physics . . .

RICO: Test in guts come up everyday.

STEVE: Yeah, well, I don't have no problems with that—just with physics . . .

RICO: You sure? . . .

STEVE: Yeah, I'm sure. I'm not behind in guts—I'll pass all them tests. Just physics I'm worried about, you dig? . . . Not guts . . .

(After a beat or two, THEY call the tacit contest a draw, with false grins)

RICO: Yeah, you alright, Steve. Still my man. Go on wit' yo' physics . . . *(There are light knocks at front door. RICO starts for it, checking watch)* 'Bout time that heifer showed. Wastin' my damn time . . . *(Goes out and down hallway; opens door)* 'Bout time you . . .

(MAE stands there, uneasy, holding schoolbooks before her as though they were a shield. That defensive, defiant, near arrogance of a determined but unsure teenager showing; SHE has decided to come here so here SHE is, right or wrong, SHE won't be messed with—at least no one will know the effect but her)

MAE: Is Steve here? . . . I . . . He forgot somethin'—at school today.

RICO: *(Appraising her)* Steve?—Yeah, yeah, sugar, he here. Come on in—Steve? There's a lady here for you—*(Having heard her voice, STEVE is already on the way down the hall. Closing door behind her, indicating couch)* Have a seat, sugar . . .

MAE: *(Uneasy under his stare)* That's all right.

(STEVE enters)

STEVE: Mae? What you doin' here? . . .

(SHE looks away with exasperation and embarrassment for a beat)

RICO: Don't never ask no lady what she doin' here. Ask her what took her so *long to get here*, boy! . . .

STEVE: *(Wry)* Okay, Rico, man, all right . . . *(To MAE)* I was jus' wonderin' if anything was wrong. I mean you never came up before . . .

MAE: *(Quickly)* I need some help with our composition homework.

STEVE: *(Wondering)* Composition homework? . . .

(MAE looks away again)

RICO: Ain't nothin' wrong with your composition li'l girl. Not a thing.

STEVE: *(Still puzzled)* Well, I'll show you what I can, Mae. But you know I didn't even go to that class to—

MAE: *(Cutting him off)* Plus you forgot somethin' at school today . . . *(Pointed glance at RICO)*

STEVE: *(Still dumb)* Oh, yeah—?—Uh-huh. Well—uh—*(Looks at RICO)*

RICO: Well, y'all work it out. I'm getting' me another glass of water, then I'll be gone. *(Starting for kitchen)* Nice knowin' you, li'l girl . . .

STEVE: Oh, yeah. Rico, this is Mae. Mae—Rico.

(SHE nods. RICO appraises her again, nods approvingly)

RICO: Mae, huh? . . . Uh-huh. *(RICO goes down hall to kitchen; goes across to sink quickly to turn on water, returns to stand near door listening)*

STEVE: Forgot somethin'? . . .

(SHE sighs wearily at his slow pickup. Reaches into textbook, takes out and offers to him two folded dollar bills,exasperated with him and herself)

MAE: Here . . .

STEVE: *(Takes and separates the two)* . . . Fifteen dollars? . . .

(RICO perks up interest at kitchen door)

MAE: *(Shrugging, and putting on super cool to hide her embarrassment)* You *said* you needed it to get back in school. My father sent me some money today. So I'll loan it to you so you can get back in school tomorrow. And you can play in the game Friday . . .

STEVE: *(Touched)* Aw, oh yeah? . . . You gone loan it to me, huh? . . . *(Goes to her; takes her hand, giving money back, smiling his appreciation)* I already got the bread, Mae. It's cool now. But thanks anyway, hear? I really appreciate your wanting to help me, hear? I really dig that.

(Disgusted RICO goes over and shuts off water)

MAE: *(Flippant)* Oh, well, I'm glad you got it. Think nothin' of it. No big thing . . . *(Beat)* Guess I'll be goin' . . .

STEVE: *(Taking her hand)* Wait a minute. You don't have to leave right now . . .

(RICO comes out of kitchen, shaking his head)

RICO: Comin' through! . . . Comin' through! . . .

(STEVE and MAE put respectful distance between them. RICO enters, going to door)

RICO: I'm goin' on. If that—that broad come, tell her I got damn tired waitin' on her ass. Tell her to be where she's supposed to be wit' what she's supposed to have at four A.M. on the damned dot. Or I ain't gon' be responsible for what happens to her ass—*(Opens door)*

STEVE: Okay, Reec, see you later.

RICO: Uh-huh. You too, li'l girl.

MAE: *(Dryly)* Good-night.

RICO: *(To STEVE)* Uh-huh. Good girl there. Go through changes to bring you some money. Most of 'em jus' the opposite.

STEVE: *(Embarrassed)* Yeah, Mae's all right.

RICO: Now she won't try to make a punk out of you. Let you be a man. If you know how to be a man. How to get yourself somethin'.

STEVE: *(Uneasy along with MAE)* Yeah, Rico, okay, see you later.

RICO: Uh-huh. Y'all get into that—composition. And remember, the drugsto' ain't but two blocks up the street. *(Winks, chuckling. Goes out)*

MAE: What does that mean? The drugsto' ain't but—Ol' slimy somethin'.

STEVE: *(Staring pointedly)* Yeah, he's got a dirty mind. But it has been a long time, Mae . . . *(Advancing)*

MAE: *(Backing)* What? A week? . . .

STEVE: A week's a long time, baby . . . *(Embracing . . . kissing neck, ears)*

MAE: Naw, Steve, come on . . . Not here . . . . Your mother might come . . . That Rico might come back . . .

STEVE: *(Going over to dim lights)* Uh-uh. He ain't comin' back. And I got her schedule . . . Come on, Mae, baby . . .

MAE: *(Backing to door)* Steve . . .

STEVE: Come on baby, lay down . . .

MAE: Uh-uh. Saturday, Steve. After Melvin's party . . . I promise . . .

STEVE: Naw, sugar, now . . .

MAE: *(Backing out door, him following)* Saturday, Steve . . . Please . . .

STEVE: Now, Mae, please . . .

SCENE 4

(THEY are seen/heard as THEY move down to lower set. HE saying, "Now," SHE saying, "Saturday." HE saying, "Let me hold you a minute, baby." SHE saying, "No, Saturday after the party, I promise." BOTH pleading and cooing.

James Brown screams in the dark, and his "Hot Pants" comes up with the lights. MILTON stands down-center with card table raised above his head.

Brings it down to floor as others, including STEVE, *place chairs around it. Others rush to answer* JOE'S *call:*

JOE: All right! Line up, ladies! Let's see what you've got in the pot!

OLD BOB: *(Starting for dancers)* Come on, young girls. Let's do the thing-a-ma-jigg!

MELVIN: *(Pulling him back)* Dance, shit! You gon' play some cards! . . .

(Forces him into seat)

OLD BOB: Don't be pullin' on me, boy.

*(*MAE *tugs at* STEVE'S *arm to take him to dance floor)*

STEVE: I told you, Mae, I'm doin' some business, with Melvin, *(winks)* playin' cards. We can dance later . . .

*(*SHE *goes to sit with arms folded)*

JOE: Let's make some good strong line here! Hey, yeah, go, baby! Okay . . .

*(*BOYS *line up facing* GIRLS. *Lines go into rocking unison steps)*

JOE:Hit it y'all! Yeah! Again . . . Now when I say: Charge! I want you to come up on it and go nose to nose! All right: Charge!

*(*COUPLES *come up to each other and go through eskimo-like nose- and cheek-rubbing, still rocking to the music)*

JOE: Hooo! Fall back! Retreat! Retreat! Turn back, fore you get burned back!

*(*HE *calls more "charges"; each one more provocative than the last: chest to breast, to bootie to bootie, etc.*

Meanwhile at card table:)

MELVIN: You want a hit, Bob? Huh, you want a hit, ol' fool? (He is trying to sneak Steve a card under the table. It falls. Steve has to pretend he dropped a card to get it)

OLD BOB: I got yo' fool boy. Play!

JOE: Alright! Going down the middle now! Prancing down the road!

(A la Soul Train, couples rock their way down the center. Doorbell rings)

MELVIN: . . . Somebody, get that! Quick! Fore grannie come up here hollerin'! . . .

*(*JOE *moves through* DANCERS *to door.* MELVIN *deals)*

JOE: Guess who's here. Steve?

*(*RICO *steps in, dressed flamboyantly, a real showstopping outfit.* HE *is followed by* CANDY, *one of his girls, who carries a large grocery bag.* HE *is known to most of the kids who look up to him for his sharp car, clothes, reputation of being a big money ladies' man, etc.)*

RICO: Hey, everybody, how y'all doing? I've got just what you need to keep your party hardy—I got some popcorn—potato chips—balloons—Sorry

I thought that was yo' thing. Well, I got two jugs of wine in here. *(Greetings ring out as STEVE gets up and goes toward him. With JOE leading, BOYS rush to take bag, exclaiming approval)* And if somebody wanna go get it, there's a case of beer in the car downstairs . . . *(Holds up car keys. JOE takes them and with ANOTHER BOY starts out)* . . . The blue hog, parked right out front.

JOE: We know! . . .

MELVIN: And bring every damn bottle right back up here! . . . Thanks, Rico . . .

RICO: Nothin' to it. Go on with yo' party. Don't mean to break up nothin'. Jus' wanna' talk to my man, Steve, here. *(Putting an arm around his shoulder, leading him down center)* How you doin' my man? Remembered you said y'all was havin' this little thing here. Let's step over here a minute . . .

(THEY go down center. TWO YOUNG GIRLS are standing Down Left)

GIRL #1: . . . Fine clothes . . .

GIRL #2: Cadillac . . .

(THEY repeat. THEY move off slightly and watch RICO with fascination)

RICO: *(To STEVE)* Look, I'm gone be gone all night, dig? An' I might not get back over yo' house 'till three or four tomorrow afternoon sometime, see. But my man, George's gonna open his shop, his cleaners, special for me tomorrow, aroun' eleven.

STEVE: The cleaners? Tomorrow? Tomorrow's Sunday . . .

RICO: I'm hip. That's why he's got to do a special thing for me. So I can get my shit. My blue suit an' gray shoes. Especially the shoes. So, he jus' gon' be open that one hour, now, between eleven an' twelve, dig? So you got to be there right then. Best to hit it eleven on the nose. See? It's important now, I need that outfit. Understand? . . .

STEVE: Gotta have it, huh? *(Smiling)* Okay, I'll get it, man. Between eleven an' twelve. I'll be there . . .

RICO: Don't be fricking aroun' forgettin' now. I'm counting on you . . .

STEVE: I'll get it, man. You do me lots of favors.

RICO: Cool. Here's the ticket. It's all paid for . . . *(STEVE takes the ticket, nods)* All right, my man. And dig, I know you in arrears for fifteen, but you needin'? Want another five, ten? . . .

STEVE: Naw, I'm cool, Rico. *(Indicates card table)* Workin' on that twenty right now.

(JOE and OTHER BOY come back in with case of beer. Set it on floor. KIDS rush for it. JOE brings keys over to RICO)

JOE: And it's cold too, man. Thanks, Rico . . .

RICO: *(Taking keys)* Damn right it's cold. Gon' do somethin', do it right.

MELVIN: *(Coming back to table with beer)* You playin' or not, Steve?

STEVE: Yeah, I'm playin'. Deal. Gotta get back to my game, Reec. *(Winks)*

RICO: Go 'head. I'm pullin' up in a minute. *(As STEVE goes to table, RICO turns quickly to catch the TWO GIRLS watching him)* Hey, ladies. How you doin'? *(THEY both nod and say "Fine.")*—Umm-hum. *(Studies them)*—You two look like a team. Hello, Mae. How are you? . . .

MAE: *(Not looking at him)* Fine. How are you . . .

RICO: Fine. Fine. I'm fine too.

(Going to take upstage position where HE can watch card game and TWO YOUNG GIRLS.

MELVIN reaches over to snatch bill from in front of OLD BOB)

MELVIN: Busted again, ol' fool! . . .

OLD BOB: *(Obviously getting drunk now)* I told you don' snatch my money . . .

MELVIN: You busted ol' simple nigguh . . .

OLD BOB: Still, don't snatch my money . . . all right, I'm busted. Jus' gi' me my change . . .

MELVIN: What change? You bet the whole five, fool.

OLD BOB: Naw, I didn't either. Uh-uh. You jus' gi' me two dollars back. I bet three dollars. An' I know it . . .

MELVIN: You bet the whole five, fool.

STEVE: Give it back to him, man. He bet three. Ain't no sense in doin' him like that. We—you beatin' him anyway.

MELVIN: Yeah, and gone keep on beatin' him. Ain't giving' him shit! He bet five, and that's all it is to it! . . .

OLD BOB: Naw, I didn't. Hell I did. Bet three, didn't I, Steve . . .

STEVE: Yeah, man. Come on now, Mel . . . just take it easy, man.

MELVIN: *(Looks)* Steve! . . . *(Can't find words; explodes, throwing OLD BOB's change across table)* . . . Damn you an' him both! Forget it! I don't wanna play! . . . *(Pockets money, gets up)*

STEVE: *(Grabs his arm, takes him off to side)* Wait a minute, man, dig! . . . Come on . . .

MELVIN: Forget it! You gone come outta some chicken shit like that then later . . .

(STEVE tries to whisper some reason to him. RICO watches, sadly shaking head)

OLD BOB: *(Seeing MAE)* Hell, I don't care if you do quit. Rather be wit' my li'l dawlin' here, anyhow. Come on dance with me, you pretty li'l black thing you . . . *(Going to her)*—I'd rather gi' you my money, dawlin'. Yes, I would. Come upstairs wit' me right now an' I'll gi' you all my check! Yes, I will. Lord knows I will. *(Trying to hug her, as SHE backs off)* . . . Gi' you every penny in my pocket . . .

MAE: *(Backing off)* I don't wanna dance.

OLD BOB: *(Suddenly grabbing her tight)* Come on now. Jus' a little dance . . .

MAE: *(Getting desperate, angry as PEOPLE laugh)* I don't feel like dancin' . . .

STEVE: *(Turning from MELVIN)* Leave her alone, Bob . . .

OLD BOB: Jus' wanna hold you some . . . *(Holding on)*

MAE: Stop it, now! . . .

STEVE: *(Going to them)* Leave her alone, man!

OLD BOB: *(Releases her, backs off)* . . . Wasn't hurting her. Just' wanna—She jus' so pretty. Remind me of a gal I had once long long time ago. I give her all my money she jus' come upstairs with me. Swear I will . . .

(Laughter)

GIRL #1: Ha! . . . Go on, Mae, wit' you' bad self!—

GIRL #2: Watch out, Mae. He might drag you on up there with him onea these nights . . .

(OLD BOB moves away with arms stretched out innocently, a pathetic grin on his face. RICO watches with deep interest)

MELVIN: Ol' fool. Sheet, young girl like that send you straight to the hospital. Come on drink some wine that's yo' best bet . . . *(HE takes sheepish OLD BOB to table)*

STEVE: *(To MAE)* Wanna dance? . . .

(SHE nods. THEY move close to syrupy slow romantic quartet ballad)

GIRL #1: Aw, ain't they cute . . .

MELVIN: The jive-time hero . . .

STEVE: Yaw'l, go to hell . . .

(LIGHTS dim, a spot on STEVE and MAE, dancing down center.

A spot on RICO up, watching them)

RICO: Don't forget, Steve: Tomorrow at eleven!—*(STEVE nods, dancing)* And hold on to that girl: She's a winner! . . .

(STEVE looks back to check his meaning. MAE pulls him back into dance. LIGHTS become a soft glow around the two of them, RICO, nodding in spot, turning to go . . . STEVE and MAE dance to groovy music until LIGHTS go off on everyone else, then THEY dance STAGE LEFT for rendezvous . . .)

STEVE: The party's over Mae . . . we got a date remember . . .

MAE: Uh-huh, I remember.

("Hey, Girl" rising with darkness as STEVE and MAE dance DOWN RIGHT then sink to the floor in embrace)

SCENE 5

(Bell rings in the dark. Frame of counter set up at STAGE RIGHT *wings to represent cleaners/shoe shop.* GEORGE, *wearing hat, smoking pot, acting high, hands* STEVE *stuff in a stapled bag.)*

GEORGE: *(Quoting)*
As it is wine
that soiled my robe
of honor
Well, often I wonder
what the wine-sellers
buy,
one-half so precious as what
they sell.

STEVE: What? . . .

*(*GEORGE *laughs mysteriously.*

*(*RICO *and* TWO DETECTIVES, *one black, one white, appear* DOWN LEFT. *They crowd him; one collars him)*

WHITE COP: Where you been, boy? Huh? You tryin' to be cute or somethin'? Huh?

BLACK COP: Get it up, punk, 'fore we have to break something!

RICO: I got it! I got it! . . .

*(*HE *reaches to inside pocket; takes out envelope with money.* WHITE COP *takes money, counts it, then hands it to other detective, grabs* RICO's *collar again)*

WHITE COP: What's this? Some kinda' joke? You think we're playin' with you, boy? Huh? . . .

BLACK COP: May we oughta remind this nigguh how serious we are. Take him back up in the alley.

RICO: Hey, man!? All that ain't necessary! Dig it: Y'all done raised the price of the protection, but I can't raise the price of the goods! So it's gonna take a minute to get it together. That's all: a minute . . .

BLACK COP: Bullshit!

WHITE COP: How long, boy? Huh? . . .

RICO: Coupla days . . . Two days at best! Square business, I swear!

*(*WHITE COP *pulls* RICO *around to* BLACK COP, *who grabs his collar as* WHITE COP *snatches his hat off, crumples it, then jams it into his chest, to emphasize his words)*

WHITE COP: Two days, Rico! Two damn days. That's all! Understand?

BLACK COP: Yeah. And we betnot have to come lookin' for you, Nigguh!

RICO: You won't have to come lookin' for me, man, I'll be there. Square business . . . I swear! . . .

(BLACK COP releases him roughly. WHITE COP tosses him his hat)

WHITE COP: We like you, Rico-boy! That's why we're lettin' you have that setup on the north end.

BLACK COP: But you gon' have to pay up, nigguh, else it's gonna' be your "end." You dig? . . .

(THEY exit. RICO makes defiant gesture; straightens clothes, brushes hat, goes around to back of house. Fade . . .

In dark we hear:)

STEVE: *(Offstage)* Ten seconds to go—Northeastern has the ball—nine-eight-seven-six-five-four-three . . .

(LIGHTS up on him in kitchen, pretending dribble)

STEVE: *(Continues)* Carlton has the ball in the corner . . . He jumps! Shoots! Swish! It's good! The buzzer sounds! Northeastern wins! Tremendous finish right at the . . .

(RICO has come from back, unseen, to watch him)

STEVE: *(Seeing him now)* . . . buzzer.

RICO: If the coach knew how bad you is in the kitchen, you'd be captain.

STEVE: I did make a shot just like that Friday. Only the game wasn't so close, so it didn't make no difference.

RICO: Sho' didn't. They wasn't gone gi' you a dime for it noway.

STEVE: Naw, but I might get a scholarship.

RICO: Hell, yeah. If you wake up six or seven inches taller in the mornin'. Tell me that now the water boys got to be at least six-three so they can hold the cups up high enough.

STEVE: *(Goes to fridge for milk)* Don't have water boys no more. Student managers.

RICO: Whatever you call 'em, they got to be tall.

STEVE: *(Getting plate from the cupboard)* Yeah, a lotta people called for you yesterday.

RICO: *(Interested)* Oh, yeah?—Who were they? How many?

STEVE: About four while I was here. They didn't leave no name.

RICO: Yeah, been keepin' me plenty busy . . . *(As STEVE puts silverware and plate on table, HE studies him carefully)* As a matter of fact, thinkin' about opening a joint on the north end. *(Takes out a gansterr and lights up)*

STEVE: Yeah? A after-hours place? A gamblin' joint? . . .

RICO: Naw. We gone be dealin' in—hot stuff. Yeah, hot clothes. Got me some hip boosters now, stealin' like mad dogs. Gone open a sto'—

STEVE: Cool. Well, you know my size, Reec.

RICO: *(Smoking)* Uh-huh. I was thinking maybe I'll let you make you a little change—run a few errands.

STEVE: *(Hesitant)* Well—maybe . . .

RICO: All you—got to do—is pick up a few things from here *(Sniff)*—an' drop 'em over there—that's all—make yourself a little bread.

STEVE: I don't know, man, with my mother thinkin' like she do. I'll have to think about it a minute.

RICO: Yeah, uh-huh. Your mother, huh? You know I hate to say it, but I think you developing a heart murmur at a very young age. Uh-huh. Heart trouble and yella livuh . . .

STEVE: *(Getting up and moving around table)* Damn you, Rico! Shit! I ain't developing nothin'. I just said I gotta think about it that's all! Aw, later for you, man. I ain't got to be chickenshit just because I don't wanna get all boxed up in your shit! Later on for you . . .

RICO: Don't be getting' all hot and hard with me, Sonnyboy. I ain't the one trying to turn you into a punk. Check *your*self out. Yeah, yourself and yo' mama, them the ones trying to bend you over, not me.

STEVE: You jus' leave me alone, Rico. Get up off me and leave me alone, man . . .

(Gathers up books and starts for the door.

As HE passes, RICO blocks his way, reaches out and grabs him by shoulders)

RICO: Listen, young jitterbug—

STEVE: *(Furious)* Freeze, Rico! . . .

(HE drops books to floor, starts a punch. THEY begin to scuffle. RICO smiling. STEVE furious. RICO wards a few punches; holds scuffle to one of wrestling. HE is stronger and more experienced than STEVE—but not as dominant as HE might have thought. Struggle ends with STEVE being pressed down on table, one arm being twisted up behind him)

RICO: *(Breathing hard)* You gone quit tryin' to punch me out? If I let you go? Huh?—Huh?—

STEVE: Let me go, man. Let me go—

RICO: *(Forcing arm higher)* You gone swing on me? Huh—Huh?—

STEVE: Naw!!—Naw!!—*(RICO lets him go, steps back near doorway. STEVE, humiliated, rubs arm, wrist)* Silly-ass-mothuh—

RICO: Hey, little buddy, dig, I wasn't tryin' to front you off. I jus' wanted to make sure you'd hear me for a minute . . .

STEVE: I ain't hearin' shit from you no mo'. You jus' get the hell away from me. And stay the hell away from me! . . .

(Bends for his books.

RICO follows him)

RICO: You shamed'a yo' daddy too? Like yo' mama?

STEVE: What?! Ain't nobody said nothin' 'bout my father. I jus' want you to get up.

RICO: Look, man. What I got to do? Kiss yo' feet? Turn into a fag or somethin'? Huh? Can't you dig what's happenin'? Like you don't have no father, and I don't have no son, you dig? So, like I want to—uh—adopt you! Yeah, adopt you, and lay it out, turn you on to it all, jus' like if you was mine. You dig what I'm sayin'? Is that all right? Or you think, like yo' mama, that a hustler ain't good enough to be yo' ol' man? Adopted, or otherwise? . . .

STEVE: *(RICO has reached a vulnerable spot)* I wasn't sayin' all that, man. I—I jus' don't want nobody messin' over me. Twistin' my arm and carryin' on . . .

RICO: *(Kingfish grin)* Say, man, sometimes I get to thinkin' like you really my son, you dig. Get to thinkin' you need a spankin' now an' then, you know? . . . *(Grins as STEVE looks)*

STEVE: I don't need no damn spankins . . .

RICO: Cool. From now on we'll sit down an' discuss our little miunderstandin's like two dudes should. Right? . . . Shake . . . *(STEVE hesitates; then THEY shake. RICO takes another joint from pocket)* . . . Wanna smoke the peace pipe?

STEVE: *(Shaking head)* Know I don't mess with that.

(There are hard knocks at front door. More)

RICO: Why not? Who the hell is that?!

(More knocks)

STEVE: I'll get it . . . *(Going down hall as more knocks)* I'm comin'! I'm comin'!

(As STEVE goes to door, RICO goes quickly off to room; returns checking pistol, sliding it into back of his waistband. STEVE opens door. CAB DRIVER in cap stands there)

CAB DRIVER: You Steve? . . . Your mother's downstairs in my cab, sick. Can't leave the cab alone in this neighborhood.

STEVE: Mama? Sick? . . .

CAB DRIVER: Picked her up at her doctor's.

STEVE: Doctor's? . . .

(Rushes out, downstairs.

Gun in back pocket, RICO comes out, goes to look downstairs as CAB DRIVER goes after STEVE)

RICO: She in bad shape? . . .

CAB DRIVER: *(Offstage)* Don't look too good to me.

(RICO watches them go)

STEVE: Come help me with her, Rico.

MRS. C.: *(Offstage wearily, labored tone)* I'm all right. Don't need no help from him . . . *(RICO goes offstage. Footsteps. Then the THREE enter. MRS. C. stands erect in their grasp but her eyes closed from the climb)* I'm all right . . . *(Curtly to RICO, removing her elbow from his grasp)* . . . Thank you . . . I can make it by myself now . . .

(RICO steps away from her. THEY enter the house)

STEVE: Thanks man . . . Come on, Mama, go to bed. You'll be all right . . . *(Leading her off left to room STEVE gives RICO apologetic gesture as HE goes on into hallway, into room. STEVE helps MOTHER take off coat)* What happened, Ma? What you doin' at the doctor's? Thought you was at work? . . .

MRS. C.: Was . . . I passed out . . . Jus' passed right out—

STEVE: What? . . . What's wrong? . . . What'd the doctor say? . . .

MRS. C.: Blood pressure . . . high blood pressure . . .

STEVE: What? How long've you had it, Ma?

MRS. C.: I felt it coming on from time to time, but Lord, today it was like a bunch of rabbits racing around, jumping up and down in my chest. Lord . . .

(Sits on couch as STEVE takes her coat)

STEVE: So you went to Doctor Bennett's, huh? Well, didn't he give you no pills or nothin'? . . .

MRS. C.: *(Getting them from her purse)* Oh, yes, I'm supposed to take two of these pills. And he gave me a prescription to fill. But he said it would cost twelve dollars. Get me some water. *(As HE starts out)* But when I called the job they said the checks wouldn't be ready until tomorrow. So, I guess the prescription will just have to wait until then . . .

(STEVE goes into kitchen; followed in by RICO)

RICO: Checks won't be ready till tomorrow afternoon? Ain't that a bitch? Sonofabitches. Don't care if she die . . .

(STEVE runs glass of water at the sink. RICO peels a twenty off from thick roll of bills)

RICO: *(Continues)* Damn tomorrow. Get your mother's medicine, now! We care! . . . Go 'head . . .

(He gives the stunned, grateful Steve the money. Steve smatches jacket from chair)

Steve: Thanks, Reec, man . . .

(He rushes to front room; gives mother water)

Steve: Here, Mama. Take your pill. Give me that prescription . . .

(Takes her purse and get prescription)

Mrs. C.: Steve? . . . How you . . . ? Told you it cost twelve dollars. Where you gon' get . . . ?

Steve: *(Running out)* Don't worry about it, Mama! Be right back! . . .

(Mrs. C. goes into hallway to look after Steve. Turns and sees Rico smiling at her. He goes into his room.)

Scene 6

(Before dawn that next morning. Entire flat is dark. Steve suddenly sits up on his couch bed in front room. He is disturbed, pained; begins to pace. Goes into kitchen. Rico comes to his door.

Steve fills glass with water, drinks, leans over sink—absolutely defeated. Rico comes quietly in behind him, bluish light coming with him. He is again smoking pot, offers it to Steve)

Rico: Want some for your nerves? *(Startled, Steve almost jumps; shakes no)* She's pretty bad, huh? . . . *(Sucking smoke)* Uhhh. So—quiet as it's kept, they really just fired her, right? . . .

Steve: Yeah, laid her off, an' now she's in there cryin' . . . Aw, man, the world ain't shit! You know that, Rico? It ain't worth a damn!

Rico: *(After beat)* So what you gon' do about it? . . .

Steve: I don't know, man. I don't know . . .

Rico: You don't know? . . . Yo' mama's in there sufferin'. Done damned near worked herself to death with them greys for yo' lil' ass. An' you don't know what you gone do about it? . . .

Steve: *(Turning in pain to "window" down front)* What can I do, man? I'm goin' to school, can't hardly find nothin' part-time—

Rico: School? . . . Part time? . . . You wanna know what you can do? Huh? You can quit talkin' yo' part-time little boy shit. And start being a man full time. Quit ridin' yo' mama in the ground. What I'm talkin 'bout, hell, you could go on an' finish school if it's that important to you—or to her.

Steve: *(Going over to table)* Huh? . . . You mean that place you gone open? Those hot clothes? That job—Yeah, I'll take it, man. I'll take it.

RICO: *(A beat)* Oh, you'll take it, now, huh? . . .

STEVE: Damn right.

RICO: *(Moving, smoking)* Well, like, the joint ain't open yet, Steve. *(STEVE slumps heavily)* Anyway. That would still be little-boy shit—runnin' errands. So you take the job, what you get? A little chicken scratch? Fifty, sixty dollars. So what you don' do with it? Pay the rent on this joint maybe. Buy some half-ass meals?

STEVE: It would least be a start.

RICO: A start at being a petty-ass nothin' all you' life. A start at keepin' yo' mama right here where she's been all her life. Wouldn't you like to move her outta this joint into something big and nice and pretty, like she deserve? . . .

STEVE: You know damned well I would, man. But how?

RICO: I ain't talking about you being no flunky. I want it like a father would want it for his son—with you movin' up getting' ready to be a full partner.

STEVE: Partner Rico?! Where!?

RICO: You show me you ready to deal, to maneuver, and you'll be my partner in everything, all of it. Make more money than yo' mama ever seen. Dress her in silk. Sail her around the damned world on her own private ship—jus' to give her a rest. An' that ain't no bullshit. I could do it for her right now. But she yo' mama, I want you to do it. An' you can—All you got to do is show me how you can handle things, startin' with that little girla yours—Mae . . .

STEVE: *(Thrown for a curve, lost, puzzled)* Mae? . . . What you mean? . . . What can I do with Mae? . . .

RICO: What you think you can do with Mae?

(STEVE stares up at him, realizing)

STEVE: You mean—hustle Mae. Pimp? . . . Mae?? . . . Aw, man, you . . . *(Gets up, moves)* . . . Mae?? Mae ain't nothin' like that. She's just a—a—nice little . . .

RICO: Jus' a nice young girl, right? Too nice for that, right? To work with what she's got to get somethin' for you 'n' her. Too nice for that. But not too nice to be workin' herself to death for them greys. Like yo' mama . . .

STEVE: *(Turning away)* Stop saying that, Rico!

RICO: Uh-huh. Not too nice to end up all bent over and broke down for a dollar an hour, right? All her pretty gone. All her fine gone. All her strength gone. Just a old broken-down tool for some ol' grey farmers.

STEVE: Stop sayin' that, Rico!

RICO: Why? It's the truth. And you too nice too, ain't you? Too nice to take hold of that young girl and make something for yourself outta her. Too nice to hustle *her*. But not too *nice to pimp off yo' own mama!*

(STEVE first is stunned to silence; then reacts with both indignant rage and a sense of guilt)

STEVE: What the hell you say? You jive mothuh! I'll . . .

(HE swings at RICO. RICO slips the punch and gets him down over couch with his arm twisted)

RICO: You heard me! Pimpin' off her! She's workin' herself to death to buy yo' clothes, get yo' lunch money, and carfare an' all the while you jus' sit back an' wait for her to bring it to you. Yeah, pimpin', nigguh! Pimpin'! That's what you doin', pimpin' yo' own mama!

(HE releases STEVE. STEVE slumps at table, crushed by a powerful, new, degrading concept of his life)

STEVE: *(Without conviction)* Naw, man, naw . . . You jus'—jus' talkin' a bunch of filthy shit . . .

RICO: Talkin', life. Facts. Look, Steve. *(Helping him into chair)* You my man, Steve. But you jus' been livin' a bunch of jive-ass bullshit. I want you to start to look at things like they are. Like a man 's'pose to. An' then move an' grab things like a man . . . *(Putting an arm around his shoulder)* Looka here, Steve, that young broad 'a yours, has got somethin', man. A light in her eyes that burns tricks right down to where they hide their cookies. An' you the one turns that light off an' on. Gets that heat movin' . . .

STEVE: *(Starting off)* Mae?? . . .

RICO: Yeah, Mae. Fine li'l black ho. Listen to me. That ol' suckhuh wanted to give her all his money to go upstairs with him? Make her take him up on it. Hustle him. Get that money! . . .

STEVE: Mae? . . . ?? . . .

RICO: Yeah, Mae. Get her up there with that ol' chump, an' that jus' be the start for both of you. 'Cause when you show me you can deal, hustle, turn that l'il broad over, I'll show you how to turn yo' whole world over. Have the best damned doctors in the city beggin' to treat your momma.

STEVE: Mae? Man, Mae wouldn't go for nothin' like that . . .

RICO: Not till you tell her to. Make her do it. Only two kinds of people in this world: Those standin' 'roun' tremblin' waitin' to be told when and how to move—and those wit guts enough to jump in and tell 'em when and how. And that's you and her, Steve: Her waitin', you tellin' . . .

STEVE: But she wouldn't go for nothin' like . . . uh-uh . . .

RICO: 'Cause she scared. And that's the first thing you got to do: Stop her being scared of things she ain't tried before . . . *(Takes out and lights new stick)* Jus' like this—She probably scared of this. But this won't hurt her. It'll help her. You oughta get her to try it. But how you gone get her to stop being scared of things when you scared of every damned thing yourself? . . . Be a man, stop being scared. Here. Take it . . .

(STEVE hesitates more from habit than anything else; then takes it almost absently)

STEVE: *(Smoking)* Mae? . . .

RICO: Yeah, Mae. Suck it in, partner. Smoke up. You gone start being a man, right now . . .

(STEVE takes a draw, chokes; chuckling, RICO slaps him on back; motions for him to try again. HE does)

STEVE: *(Smoking)* Mae? . . .

RICO: Yeah, Mae . . . An' she's jus' the beginning, Steve. Jus' the beginning . . .

STEVE: *(Wondering now rather than questioning)* Mae . . .

(RICO nods. LIGHT narrows in on their faces, there in the dawn in the kitchen)

RICO: Mae . . .

(BLACK)

ACT II

SCENE 1

(TWO MEN, seen at opening as street types, now wear business suits and carry briefcases. Talking as THEY wait for bus along with STUDENTS carrying books)

MAN #1: Sex and money, definitely. Definitely.

MAN #2: Absolutely. Money Sex. Sex. Money.

MAN #1: Certainly Certainly. Always. Always. All the time. *(Sound of bus stopping offstage. Men lead students off)*

(STUDENTS sing as chorus:)

SEX AND MONN-NEE! . . .

CAN'T GET 'EM OFFA' OUR MINDSS!! . . .

(SCHOOL BELL rings. STUDENTS are on the street. STEVE ignores MAE. SCHOOL BELL rings again. ALL exit except STEVE and MAE. RICO is in MRS. CARLTON'S house.)

MAE: Something wrong? Or you just not speakin' today? *(No answer from STEVE)*—Your mother all right?

(STEVE stares at MAE as RICO talks as though STEVE were in RICO'S "room" with him)

RICO: Start with lunch money . . . Make her understand that that's all that's important, all you need, money. Money. Just money . . .

STEVE: *(To MAE)* Yeah, she's all right. And, yeah, there's somethin' wrong. I need some help. Some money. You got some money? *(Taken aback, MAE shakes her head no. Turns away from MAE)* . . . Naw? Then you can't help me then, can you? Guess we ain't got nothin' to talk about—

RICO: Get somethin' out of her, every time. Get her use to givin' to you . . .

STEVE: *(Whirling back at MAE)* You got lunch money?! Huh!

MAE: *(Struck by his intensity)* Yeah—I got lunch money . . .

STEVE: For *both* of us?

MAE: *(SHE nods, goes into her wallet, hands him dollar)* Yeah . . . You wanna borrow it?

STEVE: Naw, I want you to *give* it to me!

(SHE holds it out to him, watches his face curiously. HE takes it and turns away)

RICO: Yeah, heh, then you reward her. You know, like you train a puppy? . . .

STEVE: *(HE turns back to MAE)* Thanks, Mae . . . Thanks, baby . . . *(STEVE kisses MAE on the cheek . . . SCHOOL BELL rings and THEY exit)*

RICO: Yeah, you can use that place over there anytime you want. That is if you gon' be taking care of business. If you jus' gon be freakin' you can pay like any other chump . . . You suppose to be coppin' her mind! Not her body. You already got that! You want her mind! Her mind! . . .

(LIGHTS come up on RICO'S PLACE. STEVE and MAE are embraced on the bed)

MAE: What you talkin' about, Steve? I don't know what you talkin' about? . . .

STEVE: You don't huh? . . . Well I'll tell you what I'm talkin' about! You say you crazy about me! Loove me! Is my woman, right?! . . . *(SHE nods)* Well, prove it, baby. Prove it!

MAE: *(A beat as SHE can no longer duck the meaning)* Prove it how, Steve?

(STEVE turns away, turns back, gesturing futilely, opens mouth, and it is RICO again who speaks)

RICO/STEVE: I'll tell you how. That old Bob, up to Melvin's place? That old fool always wantin' to give you his check to go upstairs with him? Well, let him. Go with him. Take all his checks.

(MAE backs and slumps into chair, staring)

STEVE: *(Without RICO)* . . . Yeah, baby, see, we'll take that money and use it to make something for us, Mae. Build something. Understand, baby? We got to use everything we got to get everything we want . . .

MAE: Steve?

RICO/STEVE: . . . All we got is our youth! Our strength! My head an' your fine young body! That's all we po' ass nigguhs got. An' we got to put 'em togethuh, baby, an' make us somethin'! Get us somethin'! So we don't have to be po' ass nigguhs no mo' . . .

MAE: *(Looking at him with wonder, amazement)* Steve? . . . You serious? . . . You mean you really think I would? . . . Would? . . .

STEVE: *(Turning away)* You damn right, I'm serious . . . Don't look at me like that. Yeah, I mean it. Look, you wanna know what's happenin'? I'll tell you what's happenin'. I'm standing around watching my mother die! That's what's happenin'!

MAE: Die? Aw Steve, please, don't be saying that to—

STEVE: Aw Steve, my ass! Don't give me no: Aw Steve! I said die! Damn dead die! They been grindin' the life outta my mother. An' I jus' been standin' roun' watchin' it! Woulda' still been watchin' it without seeing it, if Rico hadn't pulled my coat to myself!

MAE: Yeah, Rico. That's who's got you talkin' like this. That damned Rico . . .

STEVE: Yeah, uh-huh, that's right. I been listenin' to him, all right. And watchin' him too. And you know what I see? Huh? I see that Rico ain't dyin'. Uh-huh. Rico's really livin', baby. Oh, he's just growin' right on up like a damn tree . . . But my mother now, she jus' keeps getting' dimmer by the minute. One day I'm gon' look up and I won't even be able to see her, she'll be done just faded right on out . . . It's like Rico said: They've traded her some pennies for her life. Some pennies, Mae, that's all my mother and your mother's life was worth to them greys—jus' some pennies. *(MAE watches, trying to fathom how this can be him saying these things. Going to her)* Understand, Mae? Me an' you can get together an' set them down an' give them something for all that time—understand? Me and you, Mae, we can do it right now . . .

MAE: *(Gets up)* The bes' thing I can do for my mother is—stay away from nigguhs like—like Rico—an' you!

(STEVE looks up, but MAE is going off. Rushes to grab her by arm)

STEVE: You gotta listen to me, Mae . . .

MAE: Let me go, Steve! . . . Let me . . .

STEVE: Listen! You want to be a—a—nice girl, right? A nice, neat, nigguh, huh? Think them greys gon' gi' you somethin' for being nice, huh? . . . *(Flings her arm down)* . . . Yeah, my mother is nice. An' yo' mother. An' probably yo' father is too . . .

MAE: You don't know nothin' about him! I don't need you tellin' me nothin' about him . . .

STEVE: Yeah . . . Uh-huh. But not me. I'm gon' do it like my ol' man, an' either be a man with everything I need. Or be nothin' at all needin' nothin' at all. All the way dead, or all the way alive.

MAE: *(Backing off)* Well, you go right ahead. Jus'—jus' keep that junk away from me. That's all. Jus' leave me outta it . . .

STEVE: Mae, you don't understand. Look, it's not about . . . about jus'—that. We won't be into that but a minute. You see, Rico's gonna have this joint with hot clothes, and after I—me an' you—get into something . . .

MAE: *(Nearly shouting)* I don't care what Rico's got! You hear!! . . . Tell you what he ain't got—me. He's got you. But not me. You remember that, hear?

STEVE: Aw, Rico don't have me. What you talkin' about? You don't understand what the deal is. Maybe I put it to you wrong. Jus' sit down a minute, an' let me . . .

MAE: Oh, I know what the deal is. You the one don't understand, 'cause if you did you couldn't never—never—Rico! Huh. Yeah, I know what he thinks. Ever since I was a little more than a baby, ol' dogs like him an' that Bob been shakin' their heads over me, givin' me that look—that look that make me feel like somethin's crawlin' on me. Even way back then. Noddin' and grinnin', tellin' my daddy, "Better watch that one, Jim, she gon' be a killer." Yeah, I use to go to the mirror to try to see what they saw. They said it was in my eyes. But I didn't see nothin' there. Figured out that it wasn't in my face at all, funny-lookin' as it was. So, it had to be from the neck on down, yeah, they even made me self-conscious about how I walked. Made me stiffen up and move real careful . . . Uh-huh, I know what they thought, think, when they look at me, "A ho'! A tramp!" Jus' 'cause I'm a funny-lookin' little black girl with nothin' but a body. Well, that's all right, I don't give a damn what they think, 'cause I know better. You the only one ever could put a hand on me and lead me out of the way. But I thought you could see me better than they could, Steve. I don't know how you . . . How you . . . *(A teariness threatening)* . . . But, then that's all right, too, you know. 'Cause I'm not gone let you make them right about me either. Uh-uh. Not gone let you put that on me, either . . . Uh-uh. You—you can jus'—jus' kiss my butt! An' go to hell with the rest of 'em! *(Shouting)* Jus' go to hell with the rest of 'em! *(Running out)* Hear?! Go to hell, nigguh! *(Sobbing quality in the shouting. STEVE runs to wings after her)*

STEVE: Damn right . . . Damn right . . . Like my daddy . . . *(On "daddy" HE nearly screams it out like a lost little boy calling for his dead father. Then gathers himself and resumes macho attitude)* Hell, yeah, Like my old man.

(He looks around as if suddenly frightened, bewildered. Runs over right where Rico meets him. Steve goes through gestures, pantomimes of explaining as Rico puts an arm around him and leads him off right)

Scene 2

(Dim lights as Boys and girls come from wings singing and clap-stepping to tune of Percy Mayfields, "Bad Bad Whiskey")

Girls:

BAD BAD NORTHEASTERN
(HEY, HEY! CLAP CLAP)
(Repeat line)
MADE SOUTHEASTERN
LOSE THEIR HAPPY HOME
(Repeat "Bad Bad . . ." from above.

Banner announcing Northeastern's victorious score over Southwestern is hung up rear center. Victory dance begins to chant. Varsity Players, Steve among them, come in wearing jackets, cheers greet them. Girls from cheer team—Mae not participating—lead Crowd into hip-paced rhythm cheer)

Girls:

THE BIG N.E.
(HEY, HEY, HEY, HEY
CLAP, CLAP, CLAP, CLAP)
GOT THE FOLKS WHO SCO'S
THE MOST! *(FOUR QUICK CLAPS)*
THE BIG N.E. *(FOUR HEYS, FOUR CLAPS)*
GOT A TEAM
THAT'S AWFUL MEAN! *(HEYS, CLAPS)*
THE BIG N.E.
GOT THE BADDEST TEAM
YOU'VE EVUHH SEEN! *(HEYS, CLAPS)*
THE BIG N.E., THE BIG N.E., THE BIG N.E.

(The crowd cheers, slaps palms. Party begins, dancing to "Sexy Ways." Mae stays off to side as Steve glances over at her from time to time. Joe comes to Steve)

Joe: *(Over music)* How many you hit tonight, my man?

Steve: Took it easy on 'em tonight, only copped ten or twelve . . .

Teammate: Sho' did take it easy. Almost went to sleep a couple times . . .

STEVE: *(Moving away)* Yeah, well, we won. What do you want? Blood? —Hell, I'm gettin' tired of this silly shit, anyhow.

TEAMMATE: Bet not let the coach hear you say that!

STEVE: I ain't got no paychecks with his name on 'em! Might be doing me a favor if he did put me off!

(STEVE goes over right and makes point of—for MAE watching—flirting and dancing provocatively with MARILYN, one of the girls seen earlier at MEL'S party. TEAMMATE and JOE exchange shrugs about his new attitude.

Dancing and music going full-tilt when TWO BOYS come out carrying punch-bowl, walking as though THEY were pallbearers. Music is turned down as singing starts to rhythm of BOYS' wedding strides.)

ALL: HERE COMES THE PUNCH

(Repeat) . . . HERE COMES THE PUU-UNCH!

TWO BOYS: STRAIT FROM A TEA-TOOTLER'S
LUNCH! . . .

(Laughter, as the TWO set it down, saying)

BOY #1: Compliments of the coach . . .

BOY #2: And Miss Copeland . . .

JOE: *(Holding hands up)* All right . . . One . . . *(ALL look left)* Two! . . . *(Look right)* . . . Three! . . . *(Look around)* Hit it! . . .

(EVERYONE who has one rushes to the punch with their bottles and spikes it up real strong. Cheers, protests. Dancing starts again, this time to a slow grind piece. COACH—big-bellied, Irish type, comes from the wings. HE moves across the floor waving his arms above his head like some conception of a celebrity—throughout his spiel HE is obviously working his way to and out of the door)

COACH: All right guys! Way to go out there! All right; let's hear it now!! *(Calling out)* THE MORE REBOUNDS WE GET!!?? . . .

PLAYERS: *(All but STEVE)* THE MORE CHANCES WE GET TO SHOOT!! . . .

COACH: THE MORE CHANCES WE GET TO SHOOT!!?? . . .

PLAYERS: *(Minus STEVE)* THE MORE CHANCES WE HAVE TO SCO'!!

COACH: THE MORE CHANCES WE HAVE TO SCORE!!?? . . .

PLAYERS: *(Minus STEVE)*THE MORE CHANCES WE HAVE TO WIN!!

COACH: *(Waving his fist)* Win! Win! Win! . . .'At's the way! 'At's the spirit! . . . *(Looking at his watch, reaching for the door)* All right, guys! All right! Way to go! . . . *(Waves. Is gone)*

STEVE: *(Moving down front)* Yeah, and the more we win, the more chances he's got to get a better job, and get on away from the colored N.E.! . . .

(Laughs, slaps palms with some agreeing with him. JOE grabs GIRL, down front.

HE goes to record player, puts on something like, say, Count Basie's "April in Paris") Hey, Steve! Here's yo' number. Get yo partner, and do yo' thing! . . . *(Indicates MAE, who turns away)*

(STEVE looks at MAE, then turns to MARILYN, takes her to floor)

STEVE: Had to get a new partner, man. My ol' one can't follow me no mo' . . .

(MAE whirls around angrily to watch)

JOE: Oops, excuse me—I didn't know!

(MAE fumes as CROWD laughs; watches a moment as STEVE executes fancy ballroom type steps)

MAE: Forget you! Don't wanna follow you no mo' either!! . . .

(Runs off left. Laughter, that increases when after a few more steps, STEVE excuses himself from angry MARILYN and runs after MAE)

MARILYN: *(Indignant)* Forget you is right! Ol' jive square time, square ass nigguh!

(Laughter. ANOTHER BOY comes up to offer his reassurances. EVERYONE chuckling, love-whispering, begins to drift off in COUPLES stage left.

LIGHTS dim)

SCENE 3

(Sound of bus stopping, opening and closing door. MAE comes out from stage right, hurrying, head in air. STEVE comes running after her.)

STEVE: Hey, Mae, wait! Wait a minute now . . . *(SHE keeps on, HE catches up, tries to put an arm around her. SHE pushes him off, keeps going)* Come on, Mae Harris, I'm sorry. Damn, why you have to sit beside that ol' woman on the bus? Have her lookin' at me like that?

MAE: 'Cause I wanted to sit beside her. Jus' like you wanted to go with Marilyn . . .

STEVE: Aw, Mae, I'm sorry about what I said back there. You know Marilyn ain't nothin' to me.

MAE: Oh? I thought you were going to get her to help you with your—your plan.

STEVE: Aw, I was jus'—jus' tryin' to bug you a little . . . *(Reaches for her. SHE moves away)*

MAE: *(Obviously false)* You didn't bug me . . .

STEVE: *(Smiles, puts an arm around her)* And Mae? . . . I'm—I'm sorry about that—that other thing too . . .

(SHE looks at him. Sounds of passing cars, their radios throwing pieces of music, their lights sliding past)

MAE: No, you ain't. You were serious. I don't even want to talk about it . . . *(Moves away)*

STEVE: *(Stopping her)* Naw, Mae, listen. I—I jus' went kinda wild, you know. I mean, when I saw what was happening with my mother. And then Rico told me about his setup, I . . .

MAE: Yeah. Rico. Rico, yo' slimy teacher. I don't wanna hear about Rico . . . *(Starting again up right)*

STEVE: Look, I got plans don't have nothin' to do with Rico. Like, look, we gon' get this truck, see? . . .

MAE: A what? . . .

STEVE: *(Fast)* A truck, baby. One of those little trucks like they sell popcorn and ice cream on? Well, ours will sell everything. We'll start with records and jewelry and stuff. You know, makeup and deodorant, like that. Junk that everybody needs but don't like to be makin' no special trips out for. Well, we'll bring it right to their houses. Right out in the street with the loud speaker blasting out the latest jams. Yeah, start with stuff like that. But soon, we'll be bringin' 'em everything. Probably even handle some of Rico's hot clothes for a while. But then we'll be strictly legit, Mae, I swear . . .

MAE: *(Amazed)* Trucks? . . .

STEVE: Yeah, Lady, a whole fleet, whole navy of 'em . . .

MAE: *(With wonder)* Trucks, Steve? . . .

STEVE: Yeah, lady, a whole bunch of 'em, all over the city. Yeah—the S & M mobile markets. You dig? S. & M., Steve and Mae . . .

MAE: Uh-huh. Yeah. That's a good idea, Steve . . .

STEVE: Damn right it is. Shit, I ain't no dummy. Gi' me a minute an' I'll figure all this shit out. Hell, we can have our mothers workin' with us. Helpin' us get the stuff together, you dig? See, they can't really help us much no more. But we can help them. All we gotta do is get started. Get some money to get started with . . .

MAE: *(A beat)* Yeah, some money, huh. And how *we* gonna get it, huh, Steve? . . .

(Moves quickly past him toward two block platforms up right, one small, one large.

STEVE goes to her and hugs her from behind. Sits on lower platform as if on steps, forcing her to sit on his lap)

STEVE: Look, Mae, I said I was sorry about that. Let me talk to you? . . .

MAE: About what? . . .

STEVE: About us, Mae. You still don't understand. Like I told you I don't wanna be jus' a pimp. Swear I don't. But I know that whatever I do, whatever I be, I want you to be there too, Mae. As my woman. In my corner. But, Mae, baby, look: I can't call myself yo' man if I'm gon' stand aroun' an' watch them wear you down into the groun' like they doin' my mama. Uh-uh, Mae, I couldn't stand that happenin' to you. I'd rather not be aroun' to see it . . .

MAE: Steve, it don't have to be that way with us.

STEVE: The only way it'll be different is if we take it an' make it different. The only way! And the only way I can see to do that now, is Rico's way! That's the only way.

MAE: But, why, Steve? We can work!

STEVE: Work where! What kinda jobs can we get, right now. Right now, 'cause I'm not talkin' about no five or six years. I can't be waitin' 'cause somebody might die or somethin' . . .

MAE: Aw, Steve.

STEVE: Let's look at it. Now, you can be a waitress, right. And I guess I can go on out to the factory, huh? Shit.

MAE: But it don't have to be the factory. When we finish school . . .

STEVE: *(Forcing her off his lap, getting up)* Finish school! I told you Mae, I don't have time for all those games! . . .

MAE: But Steve we have to. You can't do anything if you don't have a diploma . . .

STEVE: *(Looks at her wearily)* A diploma—games! Games! Jus' like Rico said . . .

MAE: Rico . . .

STEVE: Yeah, Rico! Rico got a whole lotta sense, baby. He got his diploma right out here where you're gonna have to come no matter how many times you graduate! . . . Diploma. Yeah, know what Rico says? . . .

MAE: No. And I don't give a damn, either.

STEVE: You should. He said it's like that game, Monopoly, you know. Like when you go to school and get that—that diploma. It's like you passed "Go" and they give you the two hundred dollars to get in the game with. That is if you've learned something they can use. They give you the two hundred every other week or so, and say, "All right, boy: Go!" . . .

RICO: *(Appears on top level, smoking boo, putting in cuff links, or . . .)* And you set-out bookety-bookety wit' yo' little diploma in one hand and yo' two hundred in play money in the other! Bookety-bookety-bookety! An' every damn where you step! Everything you need! Or want! Or think you want! They own it! They sellin' it! An' you jus' buyin' and rentin' beggin' on a humble . . .

STEVE: An' it's all you can do to get back around the board an' end up with carfare. All you livin' for is to get back aroun' there to pay day . . .

RICO: . . . Get so they don't even give you the money no mo', 'cause *you* owe *them*. They giv' you *credit* for it! Food stamps! Shit like that! . . .

STEVE: . . . Hell, Mae, you ain't playin' in the game! The game's being played on you! The players own the game! The game don't own them! They sellin' not rentin'! . . .

RICO: *(As HE goes off)* The only real players in the game's the one's got the money to own and the goods to sell . . . *(Crosses)*

STEVE: . . . That's what I'm gonna be, Mae, a player! Not some monkey in a trick cape. A player . . .

MAE: *(A beat)* And what're you gonna own and sell, Steve, huh? . . . *(As HE stands stumped, SHE turns away and goes up onto lower platform. HE recovers and rushes to her)*

STEVE: Listen Mae . . . *(Turns her around)* If I can find any other way than Rico's to get that first lump of bread to put down on something I can own, something I can sell, well, then I'll do it that way. And have you with me all the way . . . (She starts to speak, touching his face. He cuts her off) But if I can't find no other way, fast enough, good enough, then I'm gonna have to do it his way, an . . . naw, now, listen . . . in the first hard, dirty part, I won't bother you with none of it. None of it! So, I'll have to do it with . . . with somebody else . . .

MAE: Steve . . .

STEVE: I know, baby. I know how you feel when you see me with somebody like Marilyn. But when you do jus' remember this: It's for you too, baby. Understand? 'Cause as soon as I get over that hump and get it going, get it together? Then *I'm* going to come to you an' say: "Here it is, Mae, baby, our thing." We can go do it now, baby, jus' me an' you, Mae, me an' you. 'Cause it won't be no good unless it's that way. Ain't no other way it can be, but you an' me havin' it together. Nothin' else.

MAE: *(Uncertain)* But . . . But, you don't understand, Steve; if you get it like that I won't want it . . .

STEVE: *(Putting a finger on her lips)* Don't say that, Mae. You'll have to take it, baby—it'll be all I got . . .

MAE: *(After a beat, hugs him)* Steve . . .

(On upper platform, MRS. HARRIS, *large, sloppy-appearing woman, appears in spot)*

MRS. HARRIS: Mae!? . . . That you down there!? . . . Mae!! You hear me girl!! You better answer me!! . . . Mae Mae . . . *(Dark.* STEVE *exits with wry look)* How come y'all had to stand out there an' talk?! What you sayin' that you can't say in the house?! . . . *(*MAE*, silent)* . . . What kinda basketball game last this long anyhow? . . .

*(*MAE *moves to upper level)*

MAE: Mama, I told you we had a victory dance . . .

MRS. HARRIS: Where? Downstairs in the hallway? . . . Victory dance. Jus' getting' fas' that's all. Ready to start rippin' an' runnin'—If you haven't already started . . .

*(*THEY *hold each other's eyes)*

MRS. HARRIS: *(Continued)* . . . Jus' keep on, an' I'll send you to Cleveland to yo' daddy. Let him worry about you. I got enough to worry about with those other two in there.

(Starts to cross through curtains)

MAE: Mama, maybe that's a good idea . . .

MRS. HARRIS *(Stops)* What?—

MAE: Go stay wit daddy for a while.

MRS. HARRIS *(Advancing)* Girl, I'll slap you through that do' . . .

MAE: *(Backing)* I don't mean to go stay or nothin' like that, Mama. I mean jus' to get away for a little while . . .

MRS. HARRIS: Away from what, huh? Away from me, huh? You think you can do more runnin' up there with him, huh? . . .

MAE: Aw, Mama, ain't nobody thinkin' about no runnin' . . .

MRS.HARRIS: Well what you want to get away from? Can't be tryin' to duck no work. 'Cause you don' hardly do a damned thing aroun' here no mo'! . . .

MAE: Mama, I help you as much as I can, and you know it . . .

MRS. HARRIS: You mean you used to. 'Fore you got all wrapped up with cheering for that Steve! . . .

MAE: *(Turns away in exasperation)* Aw . . .

MRS. HARRIS: Here I am working myself to death to keep you and yo' sisters in school with decent clothes and something in yo' bellies. And now that you getting' big enough to just about be some help to me, you want to run off to him. Yes, I guess you his daughter all right. I ought to jus' knock you down . . . He didn't want none of you before, don't know why you think he want you now . . . *(Starts into curtains)* I was jus' talkin' mean about sendin' you anyhow, honey. I wouldn't do that to no chile a mine. Even if she do think she's grown . . . *(Crosses offstage)* Come on in here an' clean up the kids' room. And get that kitchen, too. I'm tired . . .

MAE: *(Goes over to curtain smoldering; turns, sits down on edge of platform and dials phone. Imaginary if necessary)* Operator? . . . Wanna make a collect call to Cleveland, Ohio . . . Area code, 216, number, 721–9354. Jack Harris . . . Tell him it's his daughter from Detroit . . . Huh? Oh—Mae. Mae Harris . . . Daddy? Hi . . . Fine. Oh, she's . . . all right. Her usual self . . . You havin' a party? Oh. That's nice . . . Oh, nothin' I jus' felt like talkin' to you . . . Well, Daddy, I was thinkin' about—about comin' to see you. Maybe during the holiday. Jus' for two, three days, maybe . . . Huh? . . . Oh, when you goin'? . . . Chicago, huh? I've never been to Chicago . . . No, it's all right. I was jus' thinkin' about it. Jus' wanted to do somethin' different, I guess—What do I want for Christmas?—Nothin' . . . I don't know . . . Yes, I know what I want. I want a truck. *(Smiling)* Yes, a truck. No, a real truck, daddy! A pickup truck. With a loudspeaker on it. And a sign saying—saying—S & M . . . *(SHE may be near tears)*

MRS. HARRIS: *(Offstage)* Mae, if you don't get off that phone! I'm gonna come out there an' beat you to death! . . .

(MAE looks back, freezes as LIGHT goes out.

BLACK.

LIGHTS up on stage right area, where counter, shine stand representing cleaners/shoe store again appears, with GEORGE behind the counter. Bell rings as STEVE enters. GEORGE hesitates handing STEVE the stapled closed shoe bag)

GEORGE: *(Slow-dripping, drug-high talk)* Yeah, baby, you know there's an African proverb, goes: By the time a fool learns the game, the players have . . . dispersed!

(Laughs as HE hands STEVE the bag.

BLACK)

(LIGHTS up on RICO, CANDY, and TWO DETECTIVES)

BLACK COP: *(To CANDY.)* Go turn a trick, baby. We got business with your man, here . . .

RICO: Stay right there, Candy.

WHITE COP: Like we told you, boy: The price of living is going up.

RICO: Yeah, and so am I . . . *(RICO snaps his fingers at CANDY)* Give me that card, baby. *(CANDY reaches into bra and pulls out a business card; hands it to RICO. RICO pretends to read it)* Yeah, Lt. O. A. Patrick. The First Precinct. *(COPS glance at each other. RICO hands the card to the WHITE COP)* Yeah, good ol' Lt. Pat. He says for you two to give him a call and he'll straighten everything out! Yeah, come to find out! *He* runs the North end. But then he runs a whole lotta folks, don't he, now? *(The Cops stand stumped and glowering as Rico and Candy exchange grins)* Yeah, I don' worked my way to the top-drawer—so I don't have to deal with you two Heckle-and-Jeckle muthuh-fuckuhs no mo' . . . *(Black Cop starts for Rico, reaching for gun. Rico reaches for his. White Cop restrains Black Cop.)*

White Cop: You're gonna be sorry about this, boy . . .

Rico: Naw I ain't, chump. I got me some real protection now. *(To Candy)* Go 'head, baby, do like I told you, I'm going in an' change. I'll see you later. *(Candy exits as Rico starts up steps)*

Black Cop: We'll see you later too, nigguh.

Rico: Maybe. But you gotta call the lieutenant first. *(Rico grins, points at the card.*

Black)

Scene 4

(Day.

Steve comes into kitchen where Rico waits in shirtsleeves; hands him stapled-up bag from shoe shop/cleaners. Rico nods, hands him a bill)

Rico: *(Going off into room)* So it went off like I said last night, huh? She's on her way? Coming? . . .

Steve: Yeah, I think so. Yeah, she's comin' . . .

(Fiddles around a moment as offstage Rico tears open bag, opens drawers. Rico comes back in wearing suit coat, carrying a whisk broom, and shoeshine paraphernalia. Hands them to Steve, who begins brushing him off)

Rico: Told you it'd be easy, didn't I?

Steve: Yeah. And you know why? . . .

Rico: Damn right. 'Cause a master was tellin' you how, that's why.

Steve: Yeah, I know. But, naw, it was because I believed it myself man. *(Rico chuckles)* Naw, for real, I believed it man. I meant it.

(Steve goes to one knee, draping a rag over his other thigh. Rico puts the foot to be shined on his thigh)

Rico: You gotta believe it while you sayin' it. Else how *she* gon' believe it. Yeah, jus' like all them dumb humpin' bunnies waitin' for that chicken farm to come through. They believe it too.

Steve: What? Waitin' on what? . . .

Rico: Ain't you never heard of the 'ho's chicken farm? . . .

STEVE: Naw, man, uh-uh. *(Chuckling)*

RICO: Well, it's a ol' joke we still play on them dumb bitches. The young ones anyhow. Dig, here's how it go: You wanna know what I'm breaking my ass out here hustlin' for? . . .

Uh-huh, daddy. Uh-huh. Uh-huh . . .

A chick-ken farm! That's what? A mothuh-huggin' chicken farm! . . .

A what'who, daddy? . . .

A chicken farm, that's right. Sound funny to you, don't it? Yeah, well, jus' goes to show you how nigguhs could be livin' on a diamond field an' make a parkin' lot out of it. Think a minute, silly . . .

All right, daddy. I'm thinkin' . . .

Now how many times a week you think the nigguhs in this block have chicken? Least once. Probably twice. Maybe three times. Right?

That's right, daddy, 'cause I know like Sue Ann an' them they . . .

Yeah, yeah, now you multiply that times all the neighborhoods in the city, the state, the fuckin' country! Now. An' how much is chicken a pound? Now is that some money, honey? Or ain't it, huh? . . .

Oooo, daddy, yeah! That's a whole lotta mon . . . Listen, listen: it ain't the chickens . . . it's the eggs. *(Slaps laughing-STEVE's palm)* I'm talkin' 'bout a chicken farm with ten, twenty, thirty thousand chickens! I done already make the down payment! Now do you know how many eggs one of them boss bitch-hens can lay a day! Five, six, dozen eggs a goddamn day! Hear me?! A damn day! . . .

(STEVE is laughing under all the rest)

Oooo, daddy, that's a whole lotta' . . .

Yeah! An' how much for a dozen eggs nowadays? Huh? Well, multiply that by five or six, times, twenty or thirty thousand a whole damn day! Huh?! How much money is that, huh? Can you count it?

Ooo, daddy, that's a whole lotta lay-innnn . . .

STEVE: *(Laughing in disbelief)* Aw, man, come on . . .

RICO: Dig, dizzy, this is the sound of money—cock-a-doodle-do! *(He and STEVE laughing)*

STEVE: An' they go for that shit?

RICO: Jus' like Mae went for them trucks . . .

STEVE: But I wasn't jus' shammin' man. I meant it. I really did . . .

RICO: Oh nigguh, meant it my ass. Just as fulla shit as you can be *(Laughs)*

STEVE: Aw, how you know man? Jus' 'cause you fulla shit and don't believe in nothin' you think everybody gotta be like you . . .

(A heavy pause as STEVE wishes HE hadn't said it. RICO grabs him by chin)

RICO: That's right, young punk: jus' like me. You jus' like me. Jus' like I was when I started. Wantin' and needin' a whole lotta things, and doin' whatever I had to to get 'em. Jus' like you . . . *(STEVE pulls his face free after a moment. RICO laughs, puts other foot on him to be shined. Takes couple marijuana cigarettes from pocket, offers one to STEVE who hesitates, then takes it. Chuckling, sniffing the cigarettes)* Like my man George at the cleaners say, " . . . wonder what the wine-seller buys one-half so precious as what he sells."

(Laughs, starts to light it.

BOTH tense at sound of voices, keys at door. Hear MRS. C.. RICO decides to go on into his room, taking shine equipment, etc., with him. STEVE stands sliding boo into his pocket

MRS. C. enters with JIM AARON. SHE leads him to kitchen)

MRS. C.: *(After moment showing uneasiness between her and STEVE)* I'll be ready in a minute, Jim. Steve'll show you where the coffee is.

(Cross right to room)

JIM: *(Pulling out chair)* Guess we'd better sit down. If that's one of those female getting ready minutes, no tellin' how long it'll last . . . *(As STEVE stands silent, indicates pot on stove)* Any coffee in there? . . .

(STEVE nods, turns on fire)

STEVE: Guess Mama made it this morning. Guess it's still cool . . .

JIM: Hope she's not doin' too much with her blood pressure like it is.

STEVE: *(Bitterly)* Especially since they've put her back on her ol' job.

JIM: Job's too much on her. We got everybody at the church lookin' out to find her somethin' else. Might be able to get her a li'l position right there at the church . . .

STEVE: *(Cold)* You all didn't have to find her nothing. I'm gettin' a—job. I'll take care of her. We don't need you all takin' up no collection.

JIM: *(Hesitates)* Helpin' a friend find a job ain't takin' up no collection, Steve. And sure you'll help her, but we want you to finish school first.

STEVE: What "we" you into, man? Huh? What, "we"? . . .

JIM: *(Moving to cut fire off under pot)* Well, your mother an' me . . . An' everybody aroun' the church . . .

STEVE: *(Indignant)* Everybody around' the church?! What y'all do? Sit up an' discuss me an' my mother at the—the Good Samaritan board meetings? . . .

JIM: Now why you wanna put yo' butt up on yo' shoulders? Somebody give it a good boot an' it's subject to displace yo' head . . . Keep the cups and saucers up here? . . . *(Moves to cupboard. STEVE looks, taken aback)* I wish

I was in a position to hire her myself. But there ain't much for women in my line of business. Not till you get big enough for a office staff.

STEVE: *(Wry)* What line of business is that?

JIM: *(Getting coffee)* I'm a general contractor.

STEVE: *(Sarcasm)* Oh, yeah. That sounds real hip: General contractor.

JIM: Uh-huh. Do all right too. Least, when it's warm. Most summers that is. This summer wasn't too good. Winter time, like now, there's hardly nothin'. You have to sort of gather up what you can while the sun in shinin'. Then live through the winter on what you gathered. Sort of go into hibernation like the ol' bear.

(RICO comes to doorway, wearing overcoat)

RICO: Yeah, ants, and squirrels, and chipmunks make it like that too. Groundhogs—all them kinda little things have to pull up an' hide when it gets rough and cold out there.

(A moment of STEVE watching the TWO, JIM AARON glaring, RICO grinning slyly)

JIM: I wonder what snakes do when it gets cold? . . . I know rats just make a hole an' come on in the house and eat off other people . . . Sometimes they make a meal off of somebody's baby . . . *(Looks at STEVE)*

(RICO loses his grin, makes a motion toward his back pocket. JIM AARON lowers cup, tenses to throw it. STEVE watching, apprehensive. RICO freezes, smiles, decides to let it go)

RICO: Have to watch myself. I almost went back to jail just then. About nothin'.

JIM: You almost went to the hospital . . .

RICO: *(A beat, grins)* Uh-uh, jail. Hospitals are for squirrels, and chipmunks, and groundhogs—Steve? I'm splittn'. I put my phone outside the door. Take my messages for me. Give you a li'l someun' when I get back.

STEVE: Okay, Reec. Take it easy, man.

RICO: *(Looking at JIM AARON)* Don't worry, I will. Guess I'll be seein' you aroun', my man . . .

JIM: Yeah, you sho' will.

(RICO goes out far left. JIM AARON passes moment with STEVE, then sits)

JIM: I can certainly see why your mother is worried.

STEVE: Worried about what?

JIM: About your attitude here lately. Says you're changing. Don't care about the things you usta. Not about school. Or even about that basketball no more. And she thinks she knows where this new attitude is comin' from: that two-legged alligator just left here.

STEVE: *(Moving to lean at sink)* Uh-huh. She's worried so she put you on the case, huh. So what you suppose' to do?

JIM: Don't know. Depends on what you tell me.

STEVE: Don't depend on nothin'. Cause I don't have nothin' to tell you, man. Why should I? . . .

JIM: Well, I'm gon' tell you somethin'.

STEVE: You mean you gon' be talkin'. You ain't gon' be tellin' me nothin' . . .

JIM: Maybe not. But listen, Steve: A man who trades his woman to get his bread is got silk sheets but no bed.

STEVE: You hear that in church. Sounds real nice. Real cute. But it don't have nothin' to do wit' me.

JIM: I hope you're right. I hope it's got nothin' to do with you because if you read the book and just really look at things like they are, you'll see that every woman you hold up as yours is like a carry-on of the first one that was yours. That woman is there now . . .

STEVE: Man, what kinda—stuff—are you talkin' about?! I don't wanna hear all this *mess*!

JIM: Well, you oughta hear about it. Because when you look back at that first woman of yours, you see—along with your father—where your life came from. And when you look at whatever woman you choose to be with now, you lookin' at where your next life, your children, might be comin' from. And that ain't nothin' to be tradin'. The tree of life? The reflection of you an' your life? No. Uh-uh, no tradin' . . . *(STEVE can only stare at JIM)* . . . I'm tellin' you, Steve, you wanna know what a man is. Don't look at his suit, his bank account. Uh-uh, look at his woman. Whatever he is will be right there in her and vice versa. If she's a 'ho then he is too.

STEVE: Uh—man, look—I don't know what your thing on women is, but I don't know why you bringin' it to me . . .

JIM: I'm bringin' it to you, 'cause I want you to look at it. See it's like—like your woman is like—like—

STEVE: Man, what is this?! Nobody wanna hear what you think somebody's woman is? Damn . . .

JIM: Damn me if you want to, but I'm going to tell you anyhow. You know what she's like, your woman? She's like, what you call it when you got a kind of material but it ain't good enough, finished enough by itself, and you have to put another material with it? What they call it? . . .

STEVE: *I don't know!* . . .

JIM: . . . Supplement! Yeah, that's what a woman is: a man's supplement. What he needs to finish himself. And whether he knows it or not, he chooses her according to what he thinks he's supposed to be. Like one might need salt, another green vegetables, another fruit . . . Know what I'm tryin' to say? . . . What he needs to feel finished is right there in her. His finisher. His shellac. His polish. See? . . . If he's trading her, his other half, for a car or a suit, then he's got to be a whore, see? And a man like that who'd trade all that for some thing—Well, he ain't hardly worth patterning yourself after, following nowhere, now is he? . . .

STEVE: *(Moving around angrily)* Nobody's talkin' about patterning themselves after nobody. Don't take Rico to tell me that she's working herself down just so we can keep on livin' in a hole like this? Don't take Rico to make me see that the only way we gon' get out of this is if I do somethin', 'cause I'm the only man named Carlton aroun' here. Dig? So I'm gon' do somethin' . . .

(Unseen, MRS. C. has come from her room; stops, listening)

JIM: I'm jus' tryin' to make sure you do right by yourself. And by her. She's too good a woman to be worried like this.

STEVE: How come the people doing right, being good, always got to wait till summer time to live huh? . . . Got to crawl in a hole with some can goods for the winter.

JIM: You didn't listen to me at all, did you? . . .

STEVE: Yeah, man, I heard you. Real clear. His supplement. His reflection. Right? Uh-huh. And she's my first woman, right? Well, look at her, man: They made her a slave, mule, a workhorse! So what that make me, huh? What that make Mr. Supplement?!

JIM: *(Rising)* Your mother won't—won't allow me to help her right now. Not until we . . .

STEVE: Aw, yeah, tell me anything. Uh-huh. If she's a 'ho', he's a 'ho', right? Well, I'll tell you one thing they pay 'ho's a lot better than they do horses . . . *(MRS. C. comes angrily into kitchen, trying to get around table to strike STEVE. JIM AARON grabs her)* Mama, I didn't . . .

MRS. C.: Jus' shut yo' filthy mouth, you hear?! Shut up an' show some respect! . . .

JIM: Come on now, Laura. Jus' young. Going through a tough time. Come on, honey, now. Don't . . .

MRS. C.: You make me ashamed! Sick to my soul! You hear me?! I don't even know you. You ain't my son . . .

STEVE: Mama . . .

MRS. C.: . . . No. Not no more, my son wouldn't' talk like that . . .

JIM: *(Leading her out)* Come on, Laura, 'fore you say somethin' you'll be sorry for. Come on . . . He doesn't know what he's saying.

MRS. C.: Jus' not my Steve, no more . . . What am I gonna do with him, Jim? What can I do? . . . Lord, help me, please . . .

(THEY cross)

STEVE: *(Whirls and leans on table)* Lawd, help me! Lawd, help me! . . . *(Runs into hallway, shouts:)* I am yo' son, Mama! Yeah! And *I'm* gonna be the Lord aroun' here! I'm gonna do the helpin'! Hear?! Me! Steve! Your son! Yeah! . . .

(Turns, goes back into kitchen; snatches up coat from chair; lights boo, smoking it as HE goes out the way RICO went.

BLACK

Music: "Sexy Ways" playing in dark over bare stage. Then STEVE bursts from stage left, pulling on shirt, coat. MAE falling to knees trying to hold on to his waist, wearing only slip)

STEVE: Chicken-shit bitch! Get the hell away from me then! . . .

MAE: *(Crying)* Please don't leave me, Steve, please! If you go I don't have nobody! Nobody! . . .

STEVE: *(Repeating with emphasis)* Chick-en-shit! Phony-ass little red-ridin' hood! Yeah, don't want me to leave you. Want me to stay in yo' corner! But you won't do nothin' to be in my corner! Won't help me do shit! Phony ass! *(Makes sound of spitting)*

MAE: *(Incredulous, pitiful)* Steve, please . . . ?? . . .

STEVE: Don't call my name, phony ass! You gon' be jus' like the rest of these nigguhs sittin' aroun' beggin' tryin' to get somethin' for nothin'! Well, I'm gon' leave you here wit' what you get for nothin' . . . Nothin'! . . . *(HE starts out. SHE rushes to hug him from behind)*

MAE: Steve, please, please . . . Don't leave me . . . Don't . . .

STEVE: *(Bending to grip her elbows)* Think about those trucks, baby! Think about all we can do! For ourselves! For our folks! . . .

MAE: *(Crying, shaking head)* Steve, stop, stop, please . . .

STEVE: *(Shaking her)* Naw. Naw, I ain't gon' stop 'till I get it! *(As SHE cries)* . . . You love me?! Wanna be with me!? Help me get somethin'? Be somethin'!?

MAE: *(Nodding, crying)* Yes—yes—yes—

STEVE: Then cut this chickenshit an' go with that ol' suckuh! Hear?!—Understan'!?

(SHE slumps head almost to knees; nodding and shaking no intermittently)

MAE: Steve, help me—I can't—I jus' can't—I—

(Breaks up tearfully.

HE stands with her at his feet; weakens, bends to her)

STEVE: Mae?—Listen, baby, listen. Shh, stop cryin'. Listen: Remember I told you I would try to think of some other way? *(Lifts her chin, wipes her eyes)* . . . Well, I think I've got an idea. Just wanted to see if you had the guts. If you were really in my corner see? Understand? . . .

MAE: What idea, Steve? . . . Whatta you . . . Whatta you mean? . . .

STEVE: *(Moves away)* All right, so you tell the ol' fool, yeah, it'll cost him twenty-five—thirty dollars. Thirty dollars, tell him. Then you go on up with him. But before anything can really happen me and Joe busts in on y'all. Dig? An' I'm all mad, see, gon' kill the ol' suckuh, an' you too. But then, I decide to get even by takin' the old dude's money. Take every penny he's got. Dig?—You won't have to do nothin' wit' him. See? . . . Nothin'.

MAE: You mean, rob him? . . .

STEVE: Naw, baby, not rob him. Jus' make him pay. Hell, look what he's doin'. Tryin' to entice young girls . . . *(Grins. After beat, SHE grins too)* Like that idea better? . . .

(Gets on floor with her. SHE nods, then hugs herself as a tremor passes through her)

STEVE *(Continued)* . . . Damn, baby, quit trembling like that. Here. Here's somethin' for your nerves . . . *(Takes marijuana from shirt pocket, lights it)*

MAE: Uh-uh. You know I don't fool with that . . .

STEVE: Uhn. Remember now—guts. If we gon' be somethin' new and different from our folks, then we gotta have the guts to try new an' different things, right? . . . *(SHE nods vaguely, uneasily. Tries it, gags. HE laughs, coaxes her to try again)* . . . Draw it in deep, baby. Jus' let it go deep an' relax you—Go 'head . . . Get deeper . . . Deeper . . . We gon' have everything baby. Fine foxy pad. And one for your mother . . . And one for mine . . . *(Kissing her neck, etc., as LIGHTS fade to blue-red glow)* Where they can jus' lay back and not worry about a damned thing . . .

MAE: *(Puffing, caught up)* . . . And we could send my sisters to college . . .

STEVE: . . . Yeah, baby, you could go yourself. If you still want to. Lotsa time. I mean, after we get started.

MAE: You sure, Steve? . . . I mean, you really think we can have all that . . .

STEVE: Sure, baby, we gon' have it all . . . Right now. Right now . . . Right now.

(Laying marijuana aside as HE moves to cover her . . . RICO comes to watch them, speaking)

RICO: Right now. Make her do it now. What you wanna do? *(Cunning, casual, conversational)* Turn her out *twice*? *Tell* her you an' Joe gon' save her. But don't do shiit! . . . Like a chick's either pregnant or she ain't dig? Ain't no halfway. When you turn somebody out, turn 'em all the way out. Dig? . . . *(Grins with double meaning)* Yeah . . . All the way . . . Say, Steve, you wanna try some cocaine? Huh? . . . Why not? . . .

(BLACK)

ACT III

SCENE 1

TIME

One week later

SET

(STEVE'S flat, kitchen area.

STEVE and JOE talk in conspiratorial whispers. JOE, almost squealing with anxiety and delight. Wearing only his undershirt, STEVE brushes his shoes; his sportcoat and shirt rest across back of chair)

JOE: *(Offering his palm)* We-gon'-start-pimp-in'-to-nite! . . . Sheeeet!

STEVE: *(Tapping his palm)* I'm gon' start . . .

JOE: An' baby, my debut won't be far behind. That sudden wind you hear rushin' up behind you, will be me an' Frances, baby. Anything my boy can do—I can do!

STEVE: Yeah. The first thing you got to do man, is go get ready and get back here so we can go. I'm steady getting' ready, and you steady standin' round talkin'. Know we've got to both be there, so Mae'll feel cool about us comin' up to stop the ol' chump.

JOE: *(Starting out)* Yeah, yeah, right, right, cool, cool! But that's one thing that worries me . . .

STEVE: What, man? What worries you? . . .

JOE: Well, like when we don't come up, you know, like after a certain length of time, you dig? Like, suppose she starts to holler or throw the ol' dude off or somethin'? You know?

STEVE: *(Puts the shoe brush down, and turning his back so that* JOE *can't see, takes a pill out of the breast pocket of his sportcoat)* Don't worry. I—I got something for that . . .

RICO: *(In memory. Steps from stage left wings looking toward audience, offering pill)* . . . Like she'll already be high if you give her the boo. So, jus' before she goes up, give her this . . . Jus' a—a—sedative. Yeah, like that. Just relax her, you dig? . . . Yeah, she be so relaxed she'll, like, think she dreamed it all you dig? Won't know what went down until you tell her. Yeah. You dig? . . . But it won't hurt her—won't hurt her . . . won't hurt her . . . won't hurt her . . .

*(*RICO *backs off stage, repeating that it won't hurt her)*

STEVE: *(Turning to* JOE*)* . . . See, I've told her, she's got to let the cat be in the bed with her, see. Otherwise us breakin' in won't mean nothing. See? So I figure once they get that far the old dude will force her the rest of the way. 'Cause, like, she can't holler too loud, and have everybody downstairs knowing she's in bed with the old cat. Understand? . . .

JOE: *(Admiringly)* Yeahh . . . Say, man, you sound just like a hustler, a pimp. Yeahh, man, it's jus' like Rico is standin' there runnin' it to me. Damn. You really got all that shit down ain't you?

STEVE: *(A beat)* What you mean? . . . *(Then angrily)* . . . Why don't you quit runnin' your damn mouth and go 'head so we can get this shit over with? . . . *(Turning his back)*

JOE: *(Startled)* Huh, man? . . . What's wrong? . . .

*(*LIGHTS *out.*

LIGHTS *up on stage left platform where* MAE*, in bathroom, is finishing up stick of pot, spraying deodorant, raising window to cover smell.* MRS. HARRIS *appears outside bathroom door)*

MRS. HARRIS: How long you gone be blockin' that bathroom? . . .

MAE: *(Putting out joint, slipping it into her purse)* Jus' a minute . . . Tryin' to get this—this window open . . . *(As* MOTHER *snorts and folds arms,* MAE *finishes motions, simulates opening door and steps out)* Hi, Mama . . .

*(*MOTHER *leans inside and sniffs air . . .)*

MRS. HARRIS: Can't tell which got the most perfume on, you or the bathroom . . . umh-huh, you think sprayin' all that stuff 'roun keep me from knowin' you done started smokin' that mess, don't you? . . .

*(*MAE *turns guiltily to stare at her)*

MAE: Huh?

MRS. HARRIS: Huh, nothin'. I know you smokin' cigarettes, now. I been smellin' 'em aroun' here. Ain't gon' try to stop you; won't do no good. If you don't smoke 'em in here, you'll smoke 'em out there. You wanna be a fool an' burn out yo' lungs, go right ahead. Done all I could to teach you rights from wrong, can't do no more . . .

MAE: *(Back to her; still avoiding a meeting of eyes)* Yes, Mam . . . *(Smiling slightly in her "high")*

MRS. HARRIS: You so fast now, I don't even try to keep up with you. Got too much to do. Got the others in there to look after—all by myself—can't be worryin' myself 'bout yo' foolishness . . .

MAE: *(Back to her)* Yes, mam . . . *(Ironic smile)*

MRS. HARRIS: Uh-huh. Jus' like now: All dressed up to go to another one a' them parties, ain't you? . . . *(MAE nods)* . . . Well all right, go right ahead. But I'll tell you this, Miss Fast: Onea' these times you gon' come draggin' it in here all time a' the morning and you gon' find that door locked, and it's gon *stay* locked! . . .

MAE: *(Quietly)* Why don't you whip me, Mama? . . .

MRS. HARRIS: What you say, girl? You tryin' to get smart?

MAE: *(Turning to face her, but backing off, pained)* No, Mama. *(Voice rising)* It's too late now. Wouldn't make no difference. But sometimes I used to wish you would whip me. Know why? Because when you really think about it, when you stopped whipping me, you stopped touching me. Dig? Jus . . . Jus—took yo' hands away and let me go . . .

MRS. HARRIS: Girl? What're you talkin' about? . . .

MAE: I'm talkin' about whippin' ain't the only way to touch somebody, Mama. Naw, uh-uh, and hollerin' and cussin' ain't talkin' to nobody. And it's too late now, 'cause I can't feel you! I can't hear you! . . .

MRS. HARRIS: Girl, shut your mouth an' sit down there!

MAE: No, Mama, uh-uh. I got somewhere to go. An' I'll be back when I get back! . . . And you can do whatever you gon' do, 'cause, quiet as it's kept, you *been* done closed the door on me—a long time go. Ever since then I haven't had nowhere to go. Daddy didn't want me either. I realize that too, now. But Steve wants me, understand? He wants me. So I got someplace to go, and something to do. And I'm goin' there an' doing it. And me and Steve'll buy our own damned doors! . . . *(Starting to cross)*

MRS. HARRIS: *(Struck)* Mae? . . . Mae, baby?

MAE: *(Hesitates)* Don't call me baby, Mama. I ain't no baby no more. But you still got two in there . . . Better crack yo' door a little so they can get in . . .

(Rushes out.

MOTHER moves toward exit, stunned, pained)

MRS. HARRIS: Mae? . . . I want you, baby. Mama, wants you . . . *(Rushes to exit as a door slams)* Mae?! . . . MAE!! . . .

(BLACK.

LIGHTS UP on STEVE in kitchen fully dressed now, except for sport coat; sitting at table impatiently waiting for JOE. MRS. CARLTON comes out of room and crosses front room to kitchen. STEVE looks startled, gets up guilty. STEVE crosses to bed, puts wine in coat, crosses to table, sits.

MRS. CARLETON enters, stands at sink)

MRS. C.: Steve? . . .

STEVE: Mama, don't start preaching again, okay? . . .

MRS. C.: I'm not gonna preach. It's just . . . just . . . Now I think Jim was right when he said he thinks you listen to Rico because . . .

STEVE: Ah, here we go again! Later for what Jim thinks! . . .

MRS. C.: *(Raising voice)* . . . listen to Rico because he's a hustler and your father was a hustler, so you think maybe he's something like your father was . . .

STEVE: *(Pause)* You sayin' that, I ain't . . .

MRS. C.: Umm-hmmmm. Well just in case Jim's right, and you thinkin' yo' daddy was some kind of pimp, I'm gonna tell you somethin' that happened with me an' him. I want you to sit down, please, and listen to this . . .

STEVE: *(Dry)* I'll stand up, okay? . . .

MRS. C.: All right, then. Now, when I was about three, four months pregnant with you, he, your daddy, went to jail. Some friends of his broke in some warehouse an' took some fur coats. Somebody told the police he was in on it. So they come to the house an' took him. He told me he didn't do it. And I believed him. For one thing we didn't have a penny, and if he hadda' been in on takin' a whole truckload of fur coats, he certainly would've had some money. Least enough for a lawyer. But there I was four months pregnant and them talkin' about lockin' him away for *four or five* years?!! I couldn't stand it. Was about to go out of my mind! . . .

STEVE: So what happened? . . .

MRS. C.: Well, when I went to see him he mentioned this lawyer who he jus' knew could get him off on a case like that; had all kind of connections with the judges and all. But he was a real shyster and had to have his money right-off. And we jus' didn't have it. So I jus' kept cryin' an' cryin' and he kept tellin' me not to worry he would figure out somethin', and pretty soon it was time to go. I was waitin' for the elevator, still cryin' an' everything, and this other woman who had come to see her man too—and looked like neither jail or nothin' else was new to her—asked what was wrong. Boo-hooin' like a baby I told her our troubles. And she mentioned this same lawyer. Looked me up an' down an' told me I was jus' the kind of sweet lookin' little colored gal didn't have to worry about no money with him. All I'd have to do was lay up on that couch of his an' . . . an' sign some paper sayin' I'd pay him later, an' he'd get my man off. Oh, yes, he was a sure 'nough hound for young fresh-lookin' black gals—was known for it . . . So . . . So I decided that's what I would do . . .

STEVE: *(Sits down heavily)* What??? . . .

(A moment as THEY *look at each other)*

MRS. C.: . . . Uhm-hmh. Yes, thought about it all night. And the next mornin' I went out an' called that lawyer and made a appointment with him.

STEVE: I don't think I wanna no more of this, Mamma . . .

MRS. C.: And when I tole yo' daddy I had a appointment with that lawyer, he put his hands palms down on that table an' jus' looked at me. An' I knew that woman was right; everybody in the world knew about that lawyer. If that screen hadn't been between us I know I woulda' got hit. Then he told me in that real quiet way he had when he really got hot with me, said: "So you gon' help 'em get me, huhm Laura? Gon' let 'em lock me up in here and use you to beat me huh? Well you and that lawyer can both jus' wipe off an' keep on walkin the hell on out of my sight." . . . I felt like two cents. Told him I was jus' tryin' to keep him. Do whatever to get him out of there. I thought his eyes was gon' hit me by theyselves the way they was lookin'. He told me to shut up an' listen. Then he started tellin' me. Tellin' me his life was like a big card-game with him gamblin' it everyday—stealin' an' snatchin' things off the table from 'em—bettin' his life that they couldn't make him be what they wanted him to be, "a dumb mule pullin' their plows, Laura. Like my folks in Alabama!" That was the game. Him against that. And he told me that I was the only thing he had that wasn't in the game. That he wouldn't put up on the table to bet. "You mine. They ain't in it. Don't have nothin' to do with it. Understand me, woman? You mine!" Oh, yes, get him goin' an' yo' daddy could sure talk hard an' sweet. Told me that if I did that with that lawyer, he would've lost me in the game too. And I could jus' kiss it and forget it, 'cause he'd have to find something else to be all his, that wasn't in the game, something they couldn't take away from him. Yes, I'll remember 'til I die: "Stay outta this shit, Laura, you the only clean place I got!" . . . I couldn't do nothin' but nod my head, thank him, and love him jus' that much more . . . *(Sighs)* . . . Yes, now that was what yo' daddy was really like. Now you tell me if that sounds like some Rico? . . .

(Steve stares, then gets up and comes down front pulling on sport coat)

Steve: Naw, it don't sound like Rico . . . Rico woulda' had that lawyer in his pocket . . .

Mrs. C.: *(Lowering head)* Oh' my Lord, help me . . .

(Covers face.

Black)

Scene 2

(Lights up on Steve pacing in the kitchen a few moments after the last scene. Knocks at the front door. Mrs. Carlton enters from hallway, opens front door; Jim Aaron enters.

Steve stays in kitchen, obviously avoiding Aaron)

Mrs. Carlton: *(Giving him kiss on cheek)* Hello, Jim . . . be ready in a minute . . .

(Holds his hand a moment, then shakes head, and goes off, obviously depressed.

Jim Aaron hesitates, then goes to kitchen)

Jim Aaron: How you doin' this evenin', Steve? *(Steve nods, grunts)* Your mother looks kinda' upset . . .

Steve: *(Turning back to him)* She always looks upset—That's cause she don't have no money.

Jim Aaron: Now, it's not that. She needs to know she did a good job being a mother. She was jus' a young girl all alone with everybody shakin' they heads over her, saying, "I told you so," when your father got killed. And that's all she's been tryin' to do ever since: Prove she was a good woman, an' a good mother.

Steve: When she gets dressed, y'all leavin', right? Well, I hope she hurries up—'Cause listenin' to you is a drag.

Jim Aaron: *(After beat)* I think me an' yo' mother are too late. I can already see the worms—in a minute the alley's gon' be 'bout the only place fit for you.

Steve: Don't let it worry you, man, hear?

Jim Aaron: *(Rising, starting out)* If you weren't hers, I sure wouldn't. 'Cause I can see now that being a man is too hard for you. Easier to be one of these street animals, rippin' an' snatchin' an' runnin' wil'. That's all you'll be: jus' a wil' dog loose in the streets . . . I better wait in the kitchen 'fore I forget whose little boy you are.

(As Jim Aaron goes into hallway, Rico comes in front door. Jim Aaron decides to go back into kitchen and wait for him. Rico enters kitchen, looks from Steve to Jim Aaron)

Rico: *(After hesitating)* Uh—You fixin' to go on with your—party? *(Steve nods. Rico tosses claim ticket to table along with a bill)* Stop by the shoe shop on your way, pick those up. Take 'em wit' you. I'll come by there an' get 'em later on. If you leave, bring 'em here; put 'em outside my door. You can keep the change . . .

(Steve nods, reaches for ticket and money. Jim Aaron snatches them from table)

Jim Aaron: Find yourself some other errand boy!

Steve: Say, man, that's for me! Come on now.

Jim Aaron: Naw, it's his. Let him come get it.

Rico: *(Reaching for back pocket, coming forward)* Say, man, look, don't be fuckin' wit' my stuff—my shoes, man. My money—*(Jim Aaron and Rico struggle, Jim Aaron comes up with Rico's gun)* Listen, man . . .

Jim Aaron: Naw, you listen . . . You a gamblin' man, ain't you. Well, Rico, let's take a gamble on grabbin' this gun. Winner takes this young fool here. *(He puts gun down on table; stands with hand raised)*

Steve: *(Starting forward)* Say, man, why don't you cut this junk out? . . .

Jim Aaron: *(A moment of assessment)* How about it, Rico. Loser stay way from this boy? . . .

Steve: Man, you can't tell me who to stay way from!

Jim Aaron: How about it, Rico? . . .

Rico: *(Lowering hand, backing off)* Told you once, you ain't worth me doin' a jail bit for . . . *(Moving to door)* But I got some nigguhs kill God for a quarter. And you done got to be a nuisance. Better grow some more eyes, nigguh. You gone need 'em . . .

(Crosses right to room.

Contemptuously, Jim Aaron tosses money and ticket to table)

Jim Aaron: His guts in his back pocket. His respect parked out on the street. Now what is that, huh? . . .

Steve: Leave me alone. All yall . . . leave me alone.

(Steve takes coat from chair and walks out of front door.

Mrs. C. comes out of room. Jim Aaron goes to her.

Circle of light dims, narrows, disappears.

Black

Steve sits on steps, gets paper cup of wine from two Winos; pays them for it. They leave. He begins soliloquy)

STEVE: *(To audience)* They say—woman—is life, yeah, and money—is life . . . And wine is—life—Yeah, woman, money and wine. Uh-huh. So I'm drinking life, so I can get ready to sell life, so I can get me some life. Dig? Yeah, it all goes round in a circle, dig. Shit'll make you *dizzy*. Make you *sick*. Yeah, see? I'm feeling weird about it, see—'cause like Mae don't really know what's happening, see, and like my ol' lady say, my ol' man wasn't even into that and, so, I feel funny 'bout it. But I know what I got to do. *(HE takes out pills)* Got to give Mae this shit whatever it is, yeah, see, it's like—what they call it—preventitive medicine, yea, prevent her from knowin' what's she's doin' and gettin' sick about it—yeah, like I'm getting' sick about it, yea—but I got to do it 'cause that punk-ass Aaron, he don't know shit!! He ain't nobody's daddy!! Don't know shit!! Naw—Don't *know* nothin'! Ain't *got* nothin'!! And think somebody gon' be like his dumb ass!! Naw—uh-huh. I know what I gotta do!! Damn right, damn right—Yeah, know what I got to do! But if it just wasn't Mae!! Why Rico want it to be *Mae*—huh? Why? Mae—If it was Marilyn or—or Helen—or—Naw, man, wouldn't make any difference—Still be woman—life—money—life. Still be trading life to get life, and drinking life to get ready to sell me some life. See? Shit goes round in—circles. Shit, makes you—dizzy—Shit makes you— *(Runs to wings to throw up)*

(LIGHTS UP on LOWER LEVEL: Party going on at MELVIN'S. "MONEY HONEY" blasting away with strobe effects distorting the three or four dancing COUPLES.

STEVE enters. MAE is dancing with OLD BOB, keeping him at distance. SHE and STEVE exchange looks. STEVE goes down front where MELVIN stands sipping wine)

STEVE: What's happenin', Mel?

MEL: Nothin'. I just now decided to start chargin' these nigguhs to dance at my house. A dollar to come in . . . Make me some money off these nigguhs . . .

STEVE: *(Looking at MAN and OLD BOB)* Yeah, gotta' get that money.

MEL: Yes, money honey.

(Slaps STEVE's palm, moves away as MAE breaks away from OLD BOB, playfully dances over to rest hands on STEVE's shoulders)

MAE: *(Chuckling, still high)* Money, honey . . . You want some money, honey?

STEVE: You damned right. And right now that's all I want.

MAE: He's already asked me to go upstairs with him!

STEVE: Well . . . What you say? . . .

MAE: *(Smirking, jaded air; self-ridiculing bravado)* Like you told me to tell him: "Ain't nothin' no ol' man can do for me baby. But gi' me some mun-ney!" Hey, now, ran it down jus' like my man tol me . . . *(Chuckles highly)*

STEVE: So? . . .

MAE: He offered me ten dollars . . .

STEVE: Shiit. He's got to come better than that. Ten dollars . . . shiit.

MAE: *(Stops)* Well how much am I worth? Steve, huh? How much am I worth?

(THEY freeze, staring.

LIGHTS DOWN. LIGHTS UP on UPPER LEVEL: RICO at front door with JOE, handing him the money and the ticket)

RICO: Yeah, you pick these up for me, an' run 'em on back. You can have the change an' I'll gi' you another five when you get back.

JOE: I don't know, Rico, we got this deal tonight. Maybe I should check wit' Steve first . . .

RICO: Check, shit! I know 'bout yo' deal. Hell, I set it up. You got time. I tell you, he jus' left. Get this stuff first an' make yourself some money. Go 'head now an' rush on back here . . .

(Pushes him out door. Goes into kitchen to wait; sniffs cocaine . . . BLACK.

LIGHTS UP on LOWER LEVEL: STEVE and MAE have started dancing during JOE and RICO scene; dancing to slow, romantic, slow song, Chi-Lite's "Oh, Girl" or the Dominoes' "Don't Leave Me This Way." THEY are in yellow spot, all else in red-blue. THEY simply walk circle in rhythm to talk. OLD BOB watches in back sneakily)

STEVE: *(Dancing)* Tell him forty dollars! Yeah . . . *(Looks away)* An' if he won't go for that you can come down to thirty-five. Thirty. Twenty-five. But no lower than that!

MAE: No lower than that, huh . . .

STEVE: Naw . . . Where'd he go anyway? *(Looking around for OLD BOB, who's gone)*

MAE: Went to get me some more wine.

STEVE: Wine? Thought you didn't drink? . . .

MAE: I don't. But what the hell. You know. I do all kinds of things. Now.

(THEY freeze, staring. LIGHTS DOWN.

LIGHTS UP on AREA STAGE RIGHT, where shoe shine stand and counter represent shop. GEORGE is behind counter, his back to wings. MAN in trench coat sits on shine stand reading newspaper. JOE comes into scene, running. Bell rings as HE enters)

JOE: Hey, George! Come to get Rico's stuff, man! Here's the ticket—*(Hands it to him. GEORGE hesitates, looking to MAN in trench coat; shaking his head no, not this one)* Come on, man. I gotta' go.

GEORGE: Uh huh, no go, little Joe. Now, I told Rico, I'm a junkie, half-ass poet and a snake, but beneath some levels even my soul won't take.

JOE: What man?

GEORGE: I told Rico it was no-go. I would slide this shit on the kid just one more time and now here you come peeping in the realm of the blind.

JOE: What the hell you talking about George?

GEORGE: *(Glancing around counter, pulls shoe box from under counter)* Here! Dig this shit fast. Then tell Rico to kiss yo ass!

JOE: Huh?

(BLACK)

MAE: Well, here he is.

STEVE: *(Pause; then forcing himself to plunge in hard)* Well, what you standin' here for!! Go on! . . . An' dance a little closer this time. Let him have a sample—then run yo' price on him.

MAE: *(Hurt, hardly able to keep face straight)* You mean your price. I don't have no idea what to charge for this.

(STEVE watches her go over to BOB, take the cup of wine, begin slow grind with him.

MELVIN comes to STEVE with cups of wine, just as MAE, after first getting nod from STEVE, begins talking to OLD BOB about money—not heard)

OLD BOB: *(Across the floor)* What! No, lil' dawlin', now, listen . . .

(Cups her face in his hands, tries to kiss her. SHE pulls back looking at STEVE)

GIRL #1: *(Dancing)* Better leave that ol' fool alone, Mae. 'Fore he be done slobbered all over you!

GIRL #2: *(Dancing)* Or somethin!! . . .

(THEY laugh, slap palms. MAE looks to STEVE, who turns away, sipping wine)

MELVIN: *(Unaware)* Ol' fool still tryin' to buy your Mae out from under you, huh? . . .

STEVE: *(Pausing to see how much MELVIN knows; decides HE's ignorant)* Yeah . . . What you think about that kinda' stuff, man?

MELVIN: What a ol' fool an' a young broad? Hell, what I wanna' think about it for? I ain't old! An' I ain't no broad!

STEVE: Naw, whoring. Pimpin'. Stuff like that!!

MELVIN: Huh? I don't know, man. Chick feel like getting' into that I can dig her thing, you know . . . but a chick really have to be dizzy to work for a pimp, if you ask me.

STEVE: Why?

MELVIN: Well, dig it, man, like—lessen they tryin' to buy off cancer, or the damn plague or somethin'—don't nobody sell nothin' they really want!

Dig! Don't be loanin' it to no strangers! Understand? And ain't about to *rent* it out! . . .

(Raises his hand high to slap STEVE'S *palm.* STEVE *hesitates long beat, then gives his palm.* MELVIN *slaps down on it.*

BLACK.

LIGHTS UP *on* STAGE RIGHT. MAN *in trench coat is putting handcuffs on George)*

JOE: You mean Rico had Steve carrying dope, George?

GEORGE: Naw, this here is some brand new popsicles. Get the hell outta here, you dumb son of a bitch!

DETECTIVE: Yeah, you can go. But tell your buddy, Steve, we're gonna want you both for witnesses . . .

JOE: Huh? . . .

DETECTIVE: Tell him his buddy Rico was all set to wire him up and turn him loose on the rest of you dummies . . .

GEORGE: Start 'em young and run 'em long. Tell Steve the next time a snake give him a apple he oughta' check it for poison.

JOE: Huh?

GEORGE: Huh, my ass: Get the hell on!! . . .

*(*JOE *starts in one direction)*

JOE: Mama!! . . . *(Stops, goes in opposite direction)* . . . Steve! Steve! . . . Steve! . . .

*(*LIGHTS UP *on party scene.* STEVE *watching* MAE *and* OLD BOB *dance, turning away as the scene, lights, music, whirls around him.* MRS. C. *appears down right in spot of light)*

MRS. C.: . . . Stay outta' this shit, Laura. You're the only clean place I got . . . Does that sound like some Rico? . . . Like some Rico? . . .

*(*SHE *backs off.*

Holding a bottle now, STEVE *pours and drinks more wine. Music, dancing, lights, roll on.* JIM AARON *comes into same spot as* MRS. C.*)*

JIM AARON: . . . I can already see the worms startin' . . . Alley's gonna be 'bout the only place fit for you . . . Only place fit for you . . .

(Backs off as light fades.

Remembering, STEVE *drinks more wine.* MAE *comes over as song ends.* OLD BOB *lurking in back)*

MAE: *(Swaggering attitude)* I think he's ready to go for—*our* price. Maybe jus' a little more samplin', huh? Tell me all that hip shit again—I mean all the reasons why I've got to do this? *(A beat)* . . . Nevermind. I smoked that stuff before I came like you told me. But I think I need some more. It's wearin' off . . .

STEVE: I got these pills.

(Staring at her HE reaches to pocket, takes out two pills, has one in each hand, holds them vaguely. SHE turns away)

MAE: Don't worry, my man. I'm gon' get him for you this time . . . *(Starts off. Stops)* Steve? . . . You're sure this is what you want? . . .

STEVE: Damn right . . .

As SHE returns to OLD BOB, STEVE pockets the pill. Downing the wine. There is immediately swirling, strobe effect, speed up of music, dancing, etc. HE touches head, staggers . . . LIGHTS OUT.

LIGHT on JOE running across stage as if on street, pausing, holding aching sides)

JOE: *(Gasping)* Steve . . . Steve, man . . . Wait . . . Wait . . .

(HE runs on off slowly.

BLACK. LIGHTS UP on party Lights, music, dancing, going fast, Fast, FAST—Laughter everywhere. EVERYONE dancing and laughing but STEVE . . . who is trying to keep from staggering.

IN a spot, MRS. C. AND JIM AARON dance)

MRS. C.: *(Sing-song)*
Sound like some Rico?
Sound like some Rico?
Sound like some Rico?

JIM AARON:
Wild dog loose in the streets!
Wild dog loose in the streets!
Wild dog loose in the streets!

(Strobe-effect. MAE dancing with laughing OLD BOB, spot on them)

MAE: *(Laughing)*
Hey everybody: Free samples!
Free samples!
Free samples!

(SHE and OLD BOB laugh. STEVE staggers around in vague circle, wondering; takes other pill out, looks at it, touching his head, trying to shake clarity into it. SPOT on dancing MELVIN)

MELVIN: *(With other dancers)*
Sell it!
Sell it!
Sell it!

(ALL, MELVIN, MRS. C., JIM AARON, MAE begin to shout and laugh their things at him at once. Then it goes into slow/strobe motion with people moving their

mouths but no sound coming . . . FREEZE. LIGHTS OUT ON EVERYONE *but* MAE *and* OLD BOB*)*

OLD BOB: All right, Lil' dawlin'. I'll pay it. Let's go. Right now . . .

*(*HE *takes her hand, starts for door.* SHE *hesitates looking back at* STEVE. FREEZE. BLACK . . .

JOE *runs across stage, shouting:)*

JOE: Steeve!! . . .

(On off.

LIGHTS UP, MAE *follows* OLD BOB *to door—dancing continuing—picking up her coat from chair as* SHE *goes. Puts it on.* EVERYONE *laughing, dancing, to* "MONEY MONEY MONEY". SHE *pauses as* OLD BOB *goes out, her back to* STEVE . SHE *waits. A spot on her and on* STEVE, *dim elsewhere, as slow motion again, sounds cease)*

MAE: *(Her back to him)* Now, tell me again, Steve? . . . I have to go with *him*, to be with *you*, right? *(Turns to look at him)*

STEVE: *(Motions angrily, pointing for her to follow* OLD BOB; SHE *does.* HE *turns to front)* Damn right . . . Damn right . . .

*(*HE *starts to take the pill, stops, looking at it strangely. Strobe effect is back as* HE *staggers. Then everything is strangely slow—*"MONEY MONEY MONEY" *at too slow speed: . . .* RICO *comes out grinning, coming to him, taunting him with a finger, flicking at his shirt, his chin)*

RICO: If you gonna' turn somebody out, suckuh—turn 'em all way out . . . Yeah, all the way . . . *(Laughs as* STEVE *tries to back away, stumbling)* . . . Yeah, want some cocaine, baby? Huh, suckuh, want some cocaine!? HUH!? WANT SOME COCAINE, SUCKUH?! HUH!?! . . . *(*STEVE *moves away, mouth open as if shouting "No!" Shaking head.* RICO *follows shouting right into his ear now, offering him more pills)* . . . GIVE HER ONE OF THESE!! GO' HEAD GIVE HER ONE OF THESE! GO 'HEAD TAKE 'EM!! GIVE 'EM TO HER!! . . .

STEVE: *(Flings pill at him)* No!! . . . Noo!! . . .

*(*MELVIN *and* OTHERS *are aware now that something is happening with him; music stops;* ALL *stare at him.* LIGHTS NORMAL. HE *is crouched, sinking)*

STEVE: *(Desperate shout)* MAEE!!?? . . . MAEE?!! . . . HELP ME, MAE!! . . . MAEE!! . . . MAE! . . .

*(*HE *starts for door, can't make it.* PEOPLE *moving out of his way.* MELVIN *starts to him, but stops short)*

MELVIN: Steve? Steve, man? What's the matter, man?

STEVE: Maeee . . . Maee, naw, naw! The wine-sellers, the wine-sellers.

(Sinks to knees, OTHERS *making loose circle before him. Everything stops. Then* MAE *bursts back through door)*

MAE: Steve!?! . . . Steve!?! . . . What happened?! What happened?!

MELVIN: *(Picking it from floor)* Fucking wit' these damned pills . . .

(SHE goes to STEVE on her knees with him on floor)

MAE: Steve . . . Steve, baby? What's wrong? . . .

STEVE: Mae . . . Mae . . . *(Embraces; breaks it trying to clear head and meanings)* The wine-sellers, Mae . . . The wine-sellers, see? . . . See. If I sell you, what I'm gon' buy, baby, huh? . . . If I sell you what am I gonna buy?

MAE: *(Grateful, relieved)* Oh, Steve, Steve, baby . . .

STEVE: Yeah, Yeah, the damn wine-sellers . . . damn wine-sellers . . . *(Rising, almost falling)*

MAE: Come on, baby, sit down a minute. Rest . . .

STEVE: Naw, Mae, I wanna walk. Get some air. Walk with me, Mae. Walk with me . . .

MAE: I'll walk with you, Steve. Anywhere, anywhere . . .

(THEY leave party area, her supporting him)

STEVE: Rico tried to mess me up, baby, mess us both up.

MAE: I know, Steve, I know. I told you . . .

STEVE: Pills . . . cocaine . . . But he's right about a lotta things, I mean, they ain't gon' give you no air. You're gonna' have to take it. But Rico, he got tricked, baby, he made a bad trade . . .

MAE: What, Steve?

STEVE: See, to try to get in their game, Rico had to trade everything for money. See, all the things that keeps you alive, like loving a woman, or having a friend. Everything like that. He had to trade all that, see?

MAE: I think so, yeah.

(RICO steps out from alley, with travel bag. HE and STEVE stare eye to eye)

STEVE: And when you trade all that, it's like trading away your insides. Like trading yourself. Like being dead. Yeah, a ghost, wearing those clothes and driving that car. A ghost baby, a shadow. See what I mean? (Sees RICO)

MAE: Yeah, uh-huh.

STEVE: Yeah. Ol' Rico got faked out. Yeah, he's cool about a lotta things but we ain't going his way, Mae. Uh-uh, it cost too much. It cost so much . . . *(RICO shrugs, looks right, goes off hurriedly left)*

MAE: Yeah, Steve, yeah.

(RICO exits)

STEVE: And we ain't tradin'. Dig? We ain't tradin' . . .

MAE: Naw, we ain't tradin' . . .

STEVE: Naw, an' we gon' have something too. Dig? We gon' have somethin'.

MAE: We already got somethin', Steve. We already got somethin' . . .
(THEY embrace)

STEVE: *(Softly)* Damn right, damn right . . .

JOE: *(Running to them from right, grabbing STEVE)* Steeve!!!! Man, Rico ain't shit. . . . *(Sits)* You got to help me explain this shit to my mama! . . . (BLACKOUT)

Books in the African American Life Series

Coleman Young and Detroit Politics: From Social Activist to Power Broker, by Wilbur Rich, 1988

Great Black Russian: A Novel on the Life and Times of Alexander Pushkin, by John Oliver Killens, 1989

Indignant Heart: A Black Worker's Journal, by Charles Denby, 1989 (reprint)

The Spook Who Sat by the Door, by Sam Greenlee, 1989 (reprint)

Roots of African American Drama: An Anthology of Early Plays, 1858–1938, edited by Leo Hamalian and James V. Hatch, 1990

Walls: Essays, 1985–1990, by Kenneth McClane, 1991

Voices of the Self: A Study of Language Competence, by Keith Gilyard, 1991

Say Amen, Brother! Old-Time Negro Preaching: A Study in American Frustration, by William H. Pipes, 1991 (reprint)

The Politics of Black Empowerment: The Transformation of Black Activism in Urban America, by James Jennings, 1992

Pan Africanism in the African Diaspora: An Analysis of Modern Afrocentric Political Movements, by Ronald Walters, 1993

Three Plays: The Broken Calabash, Parables for a Season, and The Reign of Wazobia, by Tess Akaeke Onwueme, 1993

Untold Tales, Unsung Heroes: An Oral History of Detroit's African American Community, 1918–1967, by Elaine Latzman Moon, Detroit Urban League, Inc., 1994

Discarded Legacy: Politics and Poetics in the Life of Frances E.W. Harper, 1825–1911, by Melba Joyce Boyd, 1994

African American Women Speak Out on Anita Hill–Clarence Thomas, edited by Geneva Smitherman, 1995

Lost Plays of the Harlem Renaissance, 1920–1940, edited by James V. Hatch and Leo Hamalian, 1996

Let's Flip the Script: An African American Discourse on Language, Literature, and Learning, by Keith Gilyard, 1996

A History of the African American People: The History, Traditions, and Culture of African Americans, edited by James Oliver Horton and Lois E. Horton, 1997 (reprint)

Tell It to Women: An Epic Drama for Women, by Osonye Tess Onwueme, 1997

Ed Bullins: A Literary Biography, by Samuel Hay, 1997

Walkin' over Medicine, by Loudelle F. Snow, 1998 (reprint)

Negroes with Guns, by Robert F. Williams, 1998 (reprint)

A Study of Walter Rodney's Intellectual and Political Thought, by Rupert Lewis, 1998

Ideology and Change: The Transformation of the Caribbean Left, by Perry Mars, 1998

"Winds Can Wake up the Dead": An Eric Walrond Reader, edited by Louis Parascandola, 1998

Race & Ideology: Language, Symbolism, and Popular Culture, edited by Arthur Spears, 1999

Without Hatreds or Fears: Jorge Artel and the Struggle for Black Literary Expression in Colombia, by Laurence E. Prescott, 2000

African Americans, Labor, and Society: Organizing for a New Agenda, edited by Patrick L. Mason, 2001

The Concept of Self: A Study of Black Identity and Self-Esteem, by Richard L. Allen, 2001

What the Wine-Sellers Buy *Plus Three: Four Plays by Ron Milner*, 2001